Lady Mary Wortley Montagu

and the

Eighteenth-Century Familiar Letter

Lady Mary Wortley Montagu

AND THE

Eighteenth-Century Familiar Letter

CYNTHIA LOWENTHAL

THE UNIVERSITY OF GEORGIA PRESS
ATHENS & LONDON

© 1994 by the University of Georgia Press
Athens, Georgia 30602
All rights reserved
Designed by Louise OFarrell
Set in 11 ½/13 Garamond #3
by Tseng Information Systems, Inc.
Printed and bound by Thomson-Shore, Inc.
The paper in this book meets the guidelines for permanence
and durability of the Committee on Production Guidelines
for Book Longevity of the Council on Library Resources.

Printed in the United States of America

98 97 96 95 94   c   5 4 3 2 1

Library of Congress Cataloging in Publication Data
Lowenthal, Cynthia.
Lady Mary Wortley Montagu and the eighteenth-century
familiar letter / Cynthia Lowenthal.
p.   cm.
Includes bibliographical references (p.) and index.
ISBN 0-8203-1545-1 (alk. paper)
1. Montagu, Mary Wortley, Lady, 1689–1762—Correspondence.
2. Diplomats' wives—Great Britain—Correspondence.
3. Authors, English—18th century—Correspondence.
4. English letters—History and criticism.   I. Title
DA501.M7L68   1994
826'.5—dc20   92-41757

British Library Cataloging in Publication Data available

For my parents,

Richard Edward Lowenthal

and Jeanne Parker Lowenthal

Contents

Acknowledgments

It is my pleasure to acknowledge both my scholarly and my personal debts to those who have contributed to the writing of this book.

Years of extraordinary commitment by the late Robert Halsband resulted in a beautiful three-volume edition of Lady Mary's collected letters; his work quite literally made my study possible. I am grateful both to him and to Isobel Grundy for making Lady Mary's works available to modern readers. I wish to thank Patricia Meyer Spacks and Bruce Redford for being two of the first modern scholars to recognize Lady Mary as an important voice in eighteenth-century literary culture and then to write with insight and clarity about her work.

I am grateful to the American Society of Eighteenth-Century Studies, in conjunction with the Newberry Library and the William Andrews Clark Memorial Library, for grants that allowed me to read many of the eighteenth-century texts Lady Mary herself read. I am grateful also to the editors of *Eighteenth-Century Life* and to the Johns Hopkins University Press for allowing me to reprint, in chapter three, part of an article that originally appeared in that journal. I thank Tulane University's Committee on Research for three summer grants that helped to support this research. And I thank Karen Orchard, of the University of Georgia Press, for her many kindnesses.

I wish to express my deepest debt of scholarly gratitude to Susan Staves, who not only introduced me to the wealth of eighteenth-century women writers but also provided me with a new framework for understanding the complexities and the power of eighteenth-century literature. I have benefited immensely from her continuing encouragement and support, and it is my pleasure to thank her.

Many friends, colleagues, and teachers have been generous with their time and energies in reading parts of this manuscript, in providing rigorous and helpful criticism, and in discussing with enthusiasm the joys of studying eighteenth-century literature. I offer my thanks to Janice Broder, Lennard Davis, Lee Heller, Benjamin Hoover, Robert Markley, Michael McKeon, Robert Maccubbin, David Morrill, and Rose Zimbardo. I extend heartfelt thanks to Janice Carlisle for her always gracious support. And very special thanks go to Molly Rothenberg and Maaja Stewart, who read many drafts of this manuscript with more enthusiasm than I could have wished for; their insightful comments, strong encouragement, and cheerful criticism made my task not only easier but much more enjoyable. I am deeply grateful to both.

Finally, I would like to thank my family for being patient with my peripatetic, sometimes eccentric, but I hope always interesting choices. My thanks and love go to my parents, to Lynn, Ken, Parker, and Elizabeth, and to Richard, Kim, Katie, and Meagan.

Introduction

In July 1725, at the midpoint in her life, Lady Mary Wortley Montagu pens a letter to her sister, the Countess of Mar; writing philosophically of the balance necessary to create a happy life, she describes the desired equilibrium in a metaphor drawn from embroidery, one of the female "accomplishments": "I work like an angel, I receive visits upon Idle days, and shade my Life as I do my Tent stitch, that is, make as easy Transitions as I can from Busyness to Pleasure. The one would be too flaring and gaudy without some dark Shades of 'tother, and if I work'd all together in the grave Colours, you know 'twould be quite Dismal." [1] This same combination of light and dark, of contraries woven into the fabric of an artifact, could just as easily describe the more public "accomplishment" for which Lady Mary is justly celebrated: a lifelong correspondence filled with energy, sophistication, and intelligence. It is the artistic power of her "textual tapestry"—itself displaying the same colorful "Transitions" between business and pleasure, the gaudy and the grave—that secures her correspondence a place in the larger world of literary culture.

Her commitment to producing a body of work worthy of inclusion in a canon of eighteenth-century literature deepened after she first read the correspondence of Mme de Sévigné, the writer who set the standards for epistolary excellence in the minds of many eighteenth-century readers. Admired by Chesterfield, Gray, and Burney for the ease and naturalness of her style, she was worshiped by one of England's best letter writers, Horace Walpole. Calling her "ma sainte" and "that divine woman,"

Walpole appreciates her ability to communicate with "the warmth of a dramatic writer, not with the chilling impartiality of an historian." [2] After reading a rare 1725 edition of Mme de Sévigné's collected letters, Lady Mary speculates to her sister about the future value of her own literary productions: "I assert without the least vanity that [my letters] will be full as entertaining 40 years hence. I advise you therefore to put none of 'em to the use of Wast paper" (June 1726; 2:66).

These remarks point not only to Lady Mary's understanding that a tradition of female epistolary excellence was there to be cultivated but, more emphatically, to her intention to play a central role in it. As part of that program, she does *not* join in the celebration of de Sévigné's artistry:

> Well turn'd periods or smooth lines are not the perfection either of Prose or verse; they may serve to adorn, but can never stand in the Place of good Sense. Copiousness of words, however rang'd, is allwaies false Eloquence, thô it will ever impose on some sort of understandings. How many readers and admirers has Madame de Sevigny, who only gives us, in a lively manner and fashionable Phrases, mean sentiments, vulgar Prejudices, and endless repetitions! Sometimes the tittle tattle of a fine Lady, sometimes that of an old Nurse, allwaies tittle tattle. (20 July [1754]; 3:62)

As an attack on the lack of substance in de Sévigné's letters, Lady Mary juxtaposes the appreciative adjectives that celebrate excellence in both plain and formal style—"smooth" and "lively"—with the serious objections that only "mean sentiments," "vulgar Prejudices," and "tittle tattle" inform the whole. De Sévigné's letters reflect only "false Eloquence," she argues, because the Frenchwoman lacks the one element essential to the best familiar letters—good sense. Thus Lady Mary sets up, within the female letter-writing tradition, a new rivalry based on the importance of substance over style. By claiming superiority in the former, Lady Mary represents her predecessor as the last of the old epistolary guard while she casts herself as the head of the new.

Her remarks also emphasize one of the central conflicts of an aristocratic woman's letter writing: she must find a way to exploit a supposedly "private" epistolary discourse so that it does not violate her class and gender imperatives while it simultaneously creates a stature for her within the "public" realm. Edmund Curll, after commissioning the translation of de Sévigné's letters in 1727, published extracts under the title *Court Secrets: or, The Lady's Chronicle Historical and Gallant . . . Extracted from the Letters of Madame de Sévigné, Which Have Been Suppressed at Paris*. The preface to his edition praises the easy naturalness of her style but also expresses a similar complaint about "tittle tattle" by locating the problem specifically in the private and the domestic: "The Letters of Madame *de Sévigné,* tho' written in a careless Style, yet are so natural, so easy and entertaining, that few Epistolary Performances can be compared to them, in those several Respects. They likewise contain many curious Particulars, never before Published; . . . But then it must be acknowledged, that they contain a multiplicity of private Domestic Occurences altogether useless to every reader."[3]

The letter, because it occupies an indeterminate status between public and private, necessarily contains elements of these "useless" domestic concerns while also allowing a woman writer to cultivate and capitalize on her literary skills without transgressing the boundaries of her class and gender. In the eighteenth century, the letter, as an ostensibly private document, was a sanctioned, legitimate vehicle for women: Lady Mary used it as a domestic tool to arrange household goods to be transported to a new residence or to ask her sister to buy some French lace. As such, it was a simple instrument by which the daily routines of life were accomplished. It could also disseminate "tittle tattle," a discourse that actually performed quite a meaningful emotional function on those occasions when Lady Mary expressed her affection to her daughter and granddaughters; thus the letter acted as a conduit for displaying—and making permanent—declarations of affection. Eighteenth-century seductions, with their demands and covert manipulations, often proceeded through the letter, a "messenger" that could perform a dual function: it could act as a bridge, connecting the writer to the beloved, or it could be constructed as a barrier, a wall of silence and refusal. In equally substantive ways, the letter allowed friends to share their "news" as a way of maintaining their community, cementing their solidarity, and subtly redefining their values. Lady Mary narrated the events of her social world, authorizing and rejecting social custom, in letters that circulated "publicly" among her acquaintances. Letters such as these opened even larger spaces for a more literary treatment of experience, containing within their very form a space for the exploitation of the "high" modes, the established and public genres, while allowing a writer to downplay their importance through an insistence on the insignificance of the "private" epistle. Precedence for the published intermingling of the public and private had been set by early periodicals that often included readers' letters, especially those purportedly written by women. In *Women and Print Culture,* Kathryn Shevelow argues that women's letters "virtually defined the private" and that "the publication of women's letters, presented in a literary context that encompassed and revealed a private world of experience, asserted the legitimacy of the translation of the private into the public, manifested as the transfer of women's experience into writing and the assumption of women's authority to tell their own stories."[4]

In the context of this public and private division and of a changing set of eighteenth-century class and gender codes, Lady Mary's letters are particularly important for modern readers, for she views eighteenth-century English society from the inside and from the upper ranks. From this privileged and female point of view, she produces a lifetime of correspondence, spanning the years 1708 to 1762, which provides for modern readers a glimpse of the difficulties encountered by a sensitive, intelligent, and gifted woman writer living through and expressing her reactions to the events of the first half of the eighteenth century. Her letters chart the social, political, and ideological changes she observes and shed light on the tensions inherent in the competing demands of public and private life as well as on her own discomfort about the problems of authorship and authority for a woman and an aristocrat living in the early decades of the eighteenth century; her dual status as a "noblewoman" illuminates the conditions of power for each state as well as the pressures brought to bear from "above and below."

Such conditions also make the self-in-conflict strikingly apparent. The letters reveal the degree to which she herself creates and is constrained by such cultural codes, for her own life is a paradigm for the clash of class and gender imperatives.[5] As the daughter of a duke, she spent her youth in the company of aristocrats. Surrounded by the trappings of status, she enjoyed winters in London before retiring to the family country house at Thoresby in Nottinghamshire. Yet even though her father delighted in her beauty, he denied her any systematic education because of her womanhood.[6] Forced to educate herself by drawing on her father's magnificent library, she studied literature and languages throughout her life and reportedly learned to some degree French, Italian, Spanish, Turkish, and Greek. She became so proficient in Latin that she translated Epictetus's *Enchiridion* and, in an ambitious move for a young and untutored woman, sent it to Bishop Gilbert Burnet for his comments. Her early life was thus shaped by privilege and her self-generated intellectual accomplishments.

The dynastic ambitions of Lady Mary's father played a powerful role in shaping her life. Lord Dorchester's desire to create wealthy futures for all his children was most apparent in the marriage contracts he devised for them. He went so far as to contract a completely mercenary marriage for Lady Mary's brother—one that required a parliamentary bill that made her brother's nonaristocratic intended the sole heiress to a significant fortune, even though, as an illegitimate daughter, she replaced the legitimate heirs. So dejected by the match her father had contracted for her, with the son of a wealthy Irish peer, Lady Mary insisted she would rather remain single forever than marry Clotworthy Skeffington. Her father was eager for the alliance, in part because he was aware that Lady Mary had been engaged in serious correspondence with Edward Wortley (later Montagu).

Eleven years her senior, a student of the classics, and a member of Parliament, Wortley was not born to status, even though he had real possibilities for future advancement both in government and through his family connections. His staunch Whig sensibilities, however, would not allow him to accede, during negotiations, to Lord Dorchester's demand that the estate be settled, through the marriage contract, on the firstborn son. Lady Mary chose to elope, in 1712, with this man who would never be ennobled but who would become one of the richest men in England (reportedly leaving at his death £800,000 in ready money and £17,000 annually in land).[7] The Wortleys lived in London or in their country house in Twickenham, where Lady Mary enjoyed the friendship of Pope and Gay, and with them authored parts of "The Town Eclogues." Even though she surrendered the security of a marriage contract and ensured an estrangement from her father by eloping, she was rewarded, four years later, with an extraordinary opportunity to travel to Turkey when Wortley was made ambassador there. Lady Mary and her infant son journeyed with him on an odyssey that would open to her, because of her status and gender, a world denied to the common male traveler: entertained by both men and women of Turkish rank, she visited a mosque, dined with a sultana, and explored the women's baths. There she composed the remarkable Turkish Embassy Letters, a correspondence that treats a wholly new subject—the manners and customs of Turkish women. Following the dictates of her class and gender, she saw to it that the collection was published—her aristocratic privilege—but she made certain publication occurred after her death, the only acceptable recourse for an aristocratic woman.

Upon her return to England, she began to build a series of brilliant satirical letters about the follies of the English aristocracy, a correspondence she sent primarily to her sister, the Countess of Mar. Lady Mary wrote in an effort to raise her sister's spirits: Lord Mar's Jacobite sympathies had caused him and his family to be exiled to France, and her sister suffered from a severe and recurring melancholy. Lady Mary attempted to amuse her sister by pointing to the absurdity of their aristocratic social circle, paying special attention to the sexual scandals of aristocratic women. Later, her periodical *The Nonsense of Common-sense* (published anonymously December 1737–March 1738) became a personal vehicle for expressions of her Whig sensibilities and for support of her friend Sir Robert Walpole.

Even though she was making a name for herself as a wit and covertly exploring her role as a "lady of letters," her private life was less than satisfying. Her marriage was without real interest for both parties: Wortley cared mainly for his business, and, as Patricia Meyer Spacks has pointed out, "his wealth and his avarice became part of eighteenth-century mythology."[8] Elizabeth Montagu, a cousin of his by marriage, wrote that, in an attempt not to be cheated, he kept records of the exact number of trees in the forests he owned, and she described him as cold and detached, even "anxious and odious." Her children were also a source of concern. In 1736 Lady Mary's daughter fell in love with a poor Scot, John Stuart, the Earl of Bute and nephew of the Duke of Argyll and of Lord Islay; against her parents' advice (but finally with their grudging permission) they married. The family fears about Stuart were never realized, however, because he rapidly proved himself an able politician, ultimately taking the position of prime minister to George III. In contrast, Lady Mary's son was a source of deep sorrow. His "careers" were always eccentric: trading all his life on the illustrious family name, he was forced to flee to Holland and elsewhere on the Continent in order to escape debtor's prison (Wortley refused to cover his exorbitant bills); he studied law and Asian languages and, after a short-lived interest in Catholicism, converted permanently to Islam. After a brief stint as a soldier—during which he fought, behaved himself admirably, and was captured and released in England's war with France—he returned to his profligate ways. At the age of twenty-one, he married a woman much older and, Halsband claims, "of very low degree"; seventeen years later, he burst back on the London scene, wearing shoes with diamond buckles and traveling in the company of Elizabeth Ashe, a woman Halsband also describes as "a lady of bad reputation who moved about in good society." He was subsequently bigamously married to her by an unfrocked parson. He proved so incorrigible that, later in her life, Lady Mary agreed to meet with him only if he traveled to her incognito. When Wortley died, he left the bulk of his estate to their daughter, while at her death Lady Mary left her son "one guinea," affirming that Wortley had provided adequately for their wayward son.

A turning point in Lady Mary's private life occurred when she became infatuated with a young Italian writer, Francesco Algarotti, who would be one powerful reason for her abandoning England for the Continent in 1739. She was, at the time, without family responsibilities: Wortley tended to his businesses, her sister had returned to the Mar family's care, her daughter was happily married in Scotland, and her son was tucked away in Holland. Two years after her departure, however, when she was forced to acknowledge that her hopes for a life with Algarotti were illusory, she did not return to England, where life held little promise of personal or intellectual pleasure; instead, she chose to spend the next twenty-two years in self-imposed exile on the Continent, roaming the Italian countryside and residing for part of the time in Venice, Avignon, and then Brescia. In her later years, she returned to Venice, where she kept a country house in Padua.

During this time, she began one of her most important correspondences. Writing faithfully for over twenty years to her daughter, Lady Mary sent literary criticism, advice on the granddaughters' education, descriptions of her retired life, and "novelistic" treatments of events in the Italian countryside. During these same years, she cultivated the friendship of the exiled Sir James and Lady Frances Steuart, quarreled with the British Resident John Murray, and corresponded with friends until Wortley's death in 1761. Making her way back to England shortly afterward, she died of breast cancer in 1762, less than a year after returning home.

Lady Mary's letters play an especially important part in the modern recovery of eighteenth-century women writers because she does not fit comfortably into the categories often set up to describe the lives of these women. Most modern claims about women's history began, understandably, to be generated through examinations of mid- to late-eighteenth-century writers. The feminist recuperation of a female domestic space—an appreciation of the didactic tracts and courtesy books that create Mary Poovey's "proper lady" or an embracing of the Wollstonecraftian maternal influence—has led quite naturally to Felicity Nussbaum's groundbreaking *The Autobiographical Subject,* a study that treats "the formulation of a gendered bourgeois subjectivity." Nussbaum's arguments about what constitutes such autobiographical writing rest on the claim that the autobiographical "subject" is an "ideological construct that is recruited into place within specific historical formations rather than always present as an eternal truth. . . . 'Autobiography' then comes to depict the special position that the 'self' exists and that it can be represented in text."[9] Lady Mary's letters, while without a controlled and sustained thread of coherent narrative weaving the events of her life together, nevertheless still contain an equally textual "I" that is also "recruited into place" by specific historical circumstances; but it is precisely the difference in circumstances that separates her work from that of the midcentury autobiographers.

While modern attention to the mid- and late-century women writers is an essential part of an accurate rewriting of women's culture, such scholarship often assumes a middle-class perspective that only peripherally acknowledges that aristocratic women felt a burden of personal and social responsibility different from their bourgeois counterparts and that their attempts to create identity vary significantly from middle-class strategies. An examination of Lady Mary's life (1689–1762) and letters (1708–62) reveals those differences separating her from bourgeois, domestic, late-eighteenth-century women writers. Her sensibilities were composed of an odd mixture of "old" and "new" social and literary influences that impinged epistemologically and ontologically upon her reactions to experience. She was enamored of seventeenth-century romances and the even more fantastic classical, Ovidian narratives of transformation. Yet in harking back to these older models and by writing in the form of the familiar letter, she is different from seventeenth-century women writers—a difference that results not just from the scandals and charges of prostitution suffered, and exploited, by that "first" woman writer, Aphra Behn, but also from the very public status of the 1690s playwrights such as Delariviere Manley (whose *Ata-*

lantis Lady Mary eagerly read), Catherine Trotter, and Mary Pix. Yet she had to control a status more public and thus more potentially threatening than either the aristocratic Countess of Winchilsea or the virtuous Katherine Philips.

Simultaneously, Lady Mary was influenced by the psychological and the political theories of seventeenth-century philosophers, particularly Locke, and she advocated the same Whig sensibilities articulated in *The Spectator* by her friends Richard Steele and Joseph Addison. Married to a man unstinting in his support of Whig economic practices and enjoying a friendly relationship with the Whig Prime Minister Robert Walpole, she composed letters that reveal the negotiations she conducted between the pull of older literary traditions, and their "aristocratic" values, and the attractions of a new Whig system shaping the changing social and economic climate.

The most powerful distinction between Lady Mary's letters and bourgeois autobiography, however, is perhaps a *result* of Whig influences: the change Nussbaum perceives in the memoirists' "new emphasis on the published self as property in a money economy." [10] Lady Mary's status as an aristocratic woman prohibited her from entering into such an economy, even though she recognized and responded to the published accounts of female "subjectivities": she avidly read the midcentury novelists and memoirists and found them powerfully attractive but ideologically threatening to her status as an aristocrat and a woman. Her own confusion not simply about a woman writer's proper place but also about an aristocratic woman writer's place is so central in her correspondence that it often informs both the substance and the metaphorical structure of her discourse.

Moreover, questions about the maintenance of social, moral, and political integrity in a world no longer looking to aristocrats for the answers—in fact, in a world that demanded members of this class justify their status and defend their right to govern—were sources of concern for her. Her letters reveal that, in a world where all women were beginning to be told that it was improper for them to engage in public participation, an aristocratic woman had to confront the fact that her very aristocracy was in great measure dependent upon public view. Kathryn Shevelow's work is useful here, too, for she suggests that, as forums for the transmission of cultural values, the early periodicals began to refine their representations of femininity into "the systematic naturalization of a normative, domestic figure," a domestic "ideal"; while women might be represented as readers, writing subjects, and textual figures, the periodicals tended from the beginning "towards an overdetermination of one feminine figure: the domestic woman, constructed in a relation of difference to man, a difference of kind rather than degree." [11] Lady Mary's reaction to this conflict is most apparent in her anxiety about remaining outside the money economy while simultaneously insisting on her right to a public visibility, a self contained in the same textual apparatus, but one without a social stigma.

Yet her identity was indeed publicly available, if only in "limited editions"—that is, in letters circulated among her correspondents and their social circles. Such "public" visibility created a particular kind of public identity, one she could not be charged with creating in order to achieve "the Vanity of public Applause," as she called it (10 October 1753; 3:39). Her resistance to the midcentury novelists' attempts to re-order, even to reconceive, experience and consciousness reveals the most important way that she differs from them: Lady Mary relies on an older model of experience drawn from the theater. The supposedly transparent and unmediated consciousness available in prose fiction does not, for her, reveal reality, because it does not fit into her definition of the "subject": one who acts in the world, not one objectified within a domestic discourse. Instead, performance—the visible, gestural, mannered behavior presented to others—shapes and fashions a fluid identity. The letters collectively reveal her lifelong performance of a series of identities, a constantly evolving presentation of a dramatic and emerging "self," a theatrical recreation of experience, and a specifically fashioned form of conscious artistry. In this, she represents what Shevelow calls the persistence of a "rationalist feminist" writing inherited from the seventeenth century, one that presented "other, oppositional representations of women's experience" and that "contested the shifting norms of patriarchal constructions of women even when constrained by their own difficulties in establishing conceptual distance from them." [12]

Thus at stake in a study of Lady Mary's letters is a new understanding of the way an intelligent, learned, sensitive, and often opinionated aristocratic woman renegotiates the issues of public and private, attempts to define the meaning and production of a female subjectivity, and describes the tensions of the rapidly changing society of the early eighteenth century. Her public, aristocratic status in the early decades is important for modern readers because her letters shed light on these still contested scholarly questions. They reflect epistemological upheavals, changing social codes, and cultural pressures in a discourse that insists that truth can be communicated in the fiction of literary style, but only through an aristocratic theatricality of performance, textually represented.

The series of performative selves Lady Mary creates throughout her lifelong correspondence—the identities configured through varying styles and embodying varying emotions—is the subject of the investigation that follows. The first chapter examines the nature of epistolary discourse. Itself a material and ephemeral "document," the letter occupies an indeterminate status signaling both presence and absence, and thus the best writers exploit the fact that letter writing is predicated on this dynamic of exchange. Scholarly evaluation of epistolary discourse too often emphasizes either the "thematic" (biographical) content or the "formalist" (stylistic) characteristics of a given correspondence. A comprehensive aesthetic for the letter must account for the dynamic of epistolary exchange, the process of associational logic that creates the style of the best eighteenth-century letters, and the means by which a writer communicates emotion through the performance of an epistolary "self."

Lady Mary's correspondence with the men in her life forms a paradigm for performance, and the second chapter examines her struggle, as a woman, to fashion a textual subjectivity and to create an appropriate epistolary voice that allows her to express her passions while maintaining some measure of female autonomy. These "courtship" letters grow out of conflicts occasioned by the men in her life—Edward Wortley Montagu, Alexander Pope, and Francesco Algarotti. In these relationships, Lady Mary learns to exploit the power of epistolary discourse through recourse to literary heroines as substitutes for self-presentation and as models for the particular kind of subjectivity she fashions. Literary heroines provide guides to "love" as she composes strategies of seduction and resistance to generate and respond to her own and to male desires.

The third chapter treats Lady Mary as cultural relativist. Drawing on her extraordinary opportunity to visit Turkey and to report on the lives of aristocratic Turkish women, she creates letters that reflect on the deficiencies of life for gentlewomen in England as she celebrates, by making visible, "hidden" elements of Turkish manners and customs, especially the sensuous and exotic character of aristocratic Turkish women. While not guilty of the imperialist "othering" found in earlier travelers' reports, Lady Mary still brings her own interpretive strategy to Turkey: in this exotic land, the natural always metamorphoses into the aesthetic, and such transformations result in her perceiving Turkish women through the empowering but distorted fictional veil of romance.

The fourth chapter traces her continued role as cultural commentator, but this time as she details the follies of the English aristocracy, especially the sexual scandals of women. Focusing almost exclusively on transgressions, Lady Mary both celebrates and laments the violations of social "decorums." She attempts, unsuccessfully, to differentiate among sexual, political, and religious "categories" of transgressions, only to discover that for aristocrats each realm shapes and informs the other. These letters most clearly emphasize the theatricality, wit, and even farce found in the comedy of manners, but they also contain her greatest anxiety about aristocratic women on display, an anxiety that remains constant until she begins her life on the Continent.

In retirement, her concerns about the problems inherent in the status of the "gentlewoman" are developed through a faithful correspondence with her daughter, letters that also offer advice about the education of Lady Mary's granddaughters. While living in the Italian countryside, Lady Mary spends an inordinate amount of time reading English novels, and she sends literary criticism that serves, beyond its attempt to create an aesthetic for this "new" genre, as her means of codifying a standard of female behavior that rejects novelistic representations—the bourgeois models of women as properly situated only in the domestic—as well as the old license of public ostentation. Her solution to the "problem" of being a gentlewoman is the one she herself chose: an aristocratic and, for most young women, altogether impractical ideal of Horatian retirement. In retreat, Lady Mary insists, a gentlewoman may cultivate both her mind and her body as she remains visible in the public arena, celebrated for the part she plays in her community, while simultaneously warding off censure and generating personal pleasure through a systematic education that results in a vigorous female autonomy.

The final chapter isolates two contradictory self-performances from late in Lady Mary's life. From Italy, she sends to her daughter descriptions of herself as the energetic, productive, aristocratic patroness of her community; she celebrates the autonomy she advocates for her granddaughters in letters overly idealized and particularly "fictionalized" in their noncritical evaluation of her satisfaction. A few years later, she begins a correspondence with Sir James and Lady Frances Steuart that reveals the much darker, more troubling role she plays in the English community abroad. She expresses her vulnerabilities, her fears, and her anxiety about "authorship" to two equally exiled English citizens, emphasizing the pains of being older, alienated, and alone. Yet her always ironic sensibilities—concerning both her isolation from her family and her role as "Lady Bountiful" in the Italian community—suffuse her performances with the dignity befitting an older, often wiser, and even occasionally humble Lady Mary.

She chooses, as the vehicle for expressing her joys and concerns, the familiar letter—a form whose elasticity and indeterminacy allow her to create such a textual identity, but one that can be modified serially and performed alternatively, an identity that can be as indeterminate, sequential, and multiplicitous as the form itself. The letter's shifting status sheds light on the ways Lady Mary alternates between actor and spectator as she creates an authority in authorship, without being charged with a too visible display of herself in an unsanctioned arena and, more important, without the constraints of locating herself in a stable but static identity.

Chapter One

Epistolary Performances

In a comment about epistolary excellence and a perceived schism between style and substance, Lady Mary makes a joke, in a letter to her
friend Lady Pomfret, that contrasts the stylistic quality of a letter with
its physical properties:

> I saw Mrs. Bridgeman the other day, who is much pleased with a letter
> she has had the honour to receive from your ladyship: she broke out,
> *"Really Lady Pomfret writes finely!"* I very readily joined in her opinion; she
> continued, *"Oh, so neat, no interlineations, and such proper distances!"* This
> manner of praising your style made me reflect on the necessity of atten-
> tion to trifles, if one would please in general, a rule terribly neglected by
> me formerly; yet it is certain that some men are as much struck with the
> careless twist of a tippet, as others are by a pair of fine eyes. (January
> 1739; 2:133)

Lady Mary creates a multilayered metaphor about the aesthetics of letter writing that begins with a reference to Mrs. Bridgeman's failure to
distinguish between a tidy manuscript and a lively turn of phrase, a
contrast between superficial readers and those who can see beyond the
externals. But she then compares such "naive" letter readers to certain
male interpreters of the semiotic codes of female beauty who fail to

distinguish between "trifles"—"the careless twist of a tippet"—and the female beauty found in "a pair of fine eyes." Thus their inability to perceive the deeper qualities of female beauty relegates them to the same category of "naive" readers.

This anecdote also contains within it many of the issues one must account for in defining an aesthetic for the best eighteenth-century familiar letters. First of all, Lady Mary's remark acknowledges the material properties of the letter, in this case, an attention to the "trifles" and rules of decorum in letter presentation. Moreover, the anecdote reveals Lady Mary's pleasure in making fun of such conventions, an ease and a humor that point to an intimate and affectionate epistolary relationship with Lady Pomfret. Such affection both drives and shapes the content of a given correspondence, and thus any aesthetic of letter writing must account for that dependence. However, such biographical questions (for instance, the nature of Lady Mary's relationship with both Lady Pomfret and Mrs. Bridgeman), while important, must be viewed in light of the literary and stylistic character of a given letter, the formal structures a writer uses to express that affection. Most important, all these elements—the dynamics of a letter exchange between epistolary partners who must communicate their emotions in various literary styles—serve as the means a letter writer employs to create an epistolary performance of the "self."

I

The anecdote above serves first of all as a reminder that the letter is a material *object,* the product of both mental and physical activity. The importance of the physicality of a letter should not be overlooked, for the result of the effort is an object the recipient can touch, carry in a pocket, take out and read again. It may provide psychological comfort or intellectual challenge in its very physical qualities because, as a handwritten document, it is suffused with the imprint of the writer: the penmanship itself—scrawls, exclamations, and underlinings—reveals emotions and, as Lady Mary ironically acknowledges, displays character. Writing by candlelight strains the eyes, just as secreting oneself in a closet and scribbling for hours takes its toll on the body. Lady Mary also understands that the physical property of a letter has a changing value for the recipient, as she wryly admits to her daughter: "I tattle on, and forget you're in Town and consequently I ought to shorten my Letters, knowing very well that the same Letter that would be read thrice over in the Country will be cramm'd into the pocket before 'tis halfe gone through when people are in a Hurry to go to the Court or Play House" (1 January 1755; 3:79). Letters were, however, such valued commodities that writers often made copies of the documents, and, as a matter of courtesy, heirs to an estate would return to the writer the collected letters; when Lord Hervey's son sealed up and returned Lady Mary's letters, politely remarking that he had read none of them, she thanked him by assuring him that the letters displayed a long and steady friendship.[1]

The very materiality of the letter, however, performs a complex function. When one considers the ephemeral nature of the physical status of any letter, it is almost remarkable that eighteenth-century letters could be preserved. Yet for all the document's essential vulnerability, Lady Mary could rely, when in London, on the city's half-penny post for relatively efficient delivery.[2] Always aware of the difficulties, she often incorporates self-reflexive references to the mechanics of exchange: in a closing remark to Frances Hewett, she writes, "The post bell rings; my next shall be longer, with some account of your fair family" (8 March 1712; 1:119). Delivery outside of London was more difficult. Early in the century, the mail traveled along only half a dozen outlying routes into the heart of the system in London. There the letter would be stamped with the day and the month before being sent out again with the post boys on the same limited series of roads fanning out of the city like spokes on a wheel. When Lady Mary resided at Thoresby in Nottinghamshire, she addressed a letter to her friend Philippa Mundy, in Leicester, this way: "To Mrs Phillippa Mundy at Osbaston / near Leicester / Leicestershire by way of London" (4 May 1711; 1:107). Because there were no by-posts between these two midland towns, a letter had to travel south to London before it could be sent north again.[3] Lady Mary also uses the tenuousness of the system to apologize in advance for a lack of regular correspondence with Wortley's sister, Anne: "For the future, if you do not receive letters very constantly from me, imagine the post-boy killed—imagine the mail burnt—or some other strange accident; you can imagine nothing so impossible as that I forget you, my dear Mrs. Wortley" (8 August 1709; 1:6).

The material properties and technologies of letter writing also inform and actively shape its content. In 1710, when Lady Mary and Wortley began their secret courtship, the problems of letter delivery become a recurring theme in their discourse. When both resided in London, Wortley could count on mail being safely directed to him, although he often suggested that she send letters through his friend Richard Steele or Goodwin the bookseller. Lady Mary was in a more difficult position. Her correspondence, monitored by the family, was used against her as evidence of her affections, and thus she writes, "An Answer cannot be directed to me. 2 penny post Letters would give Occasion for Enquiry. Direct to Lady Margaret Creichton at the Earl of Loudoun's in the Pall Mall, near St. James" (10 February 1711; 1:74). When both resided in the country, living about thirty miles apart, sending a letter through the post was unnecessarily cumbersome: the delayed delivery frustrated any attempt at real dialogue, and the fact that the expense was tallied according to the distance a letter traveled made the procedure unnecessarily expensive.

A more serious threat posed by the letter's material status was the danger that it would be incorrectly delivered into the wrong hands, and consequently Lady Mary and Wortley had to rely on the old system of finding a personal messenger whose discretion they could trust. This recourse, however, always provoked so much anxiety that it affected not only the substance of her letters but also her emotional response to him: "Till this minute I had not opertunity of receiving your last letter, and twas a wonder I ever did. Had it falln into any body's hand but one, I had never seen it. I was walking in the Garden and expecting nothing lesse, when it was brought me by one that I did not know knew any thing of the matter, and was surpriz'd they should do me such a hazardous peice of service without my requiring it, or expecting any reward for it." She ends the letter with this fearful postscript: "How to send this I cant imagine. . . . If you write again, your Letters will certainly be stop'd and I shall never see them. I hope you would not do that Injury to a person that never design'd you one in her Life" (7 May 1710; 1:39–40).

Later in her life, once comfortably settled on the Continent, Lady Mary had to depend on a foreign post whose services were often erratic and whose delayed delivery increased both the emotional distance and the possibility that the letter itself might be lost. Mail was still sent on "post barks" or "packet boats" that were subject to bad weather, pirates, and interruptions resulting from wars, and even though ships' captains could be bribed to bring in correspondence, this method could never ensure delivery, a fact that also shaped Lady Mary's emotional responses. Living tucked away in an isolated Italian village, she was miles from the nearest post, and she complains to the Countess of Oxford, "I find the post has been very unjust to me, or perhaps my own Servants; being 25 mile from any post Town, I beleive [*sic*] they sometimes save themselves the Trouble of going when I send them, and throw away my Letters, by which they also put the franking in their pockets" (1 June 1753; 3:30). It was not unusual for Lady Mary, living in Italy, to wait for months for mail from London to arrive, a delay that she always interpreted in emotional terms—usually as crisis. In December 1752 she received a letter from Wortley dated 24 August of that same year and claims, "It reliev'd me from a great deal of pain occasion'd by your Silence" (3 December 1752; 3:19). The problem was also exacerbated by war. She laments to her friend Frances Steuart, "I can assign no reason for [the loss of a letter] but the uncertainty of the post. I am told many mails have been taken and the letters either thrown away or suppressed. We must suffer this, amongst the common calamities of war" (5 March 1762; 3:288). Lord Hervey also recognized the difficulties and cleverly complains about a series of lost letters: "I can not help saying a few Words by way of Solution to the Riddle of our writing constantly to one another without corresponding" (31/20 March 1741; 2:232).

The letter's indeterminate status is particularly apparent in government spies' practice of opening and reading private correspondence, both in England and abroad; thus the custom of addressing the letter to someone other than the intended recipient continued through the century. When an old priest came to visit Lady Mary and observed her folding a large letter to her daughter, he remarked upon the "great deal of Business" she had done that morning. Lady Mary claimed, "I made answer, I had done no business at all; I had only wrote to my Daughter on Family affairs or such triffles as make up Women's Conversation," but the priest refused to believe so large a letter could be taken up with "triffles." When Lady Mary offered to read him the letter, he demurred, saying, "If I did understand English I should not understand what you have written, except you give me the Key, which I durst not presume to ask." Indignant, she claimed the date to be the only "cypher" in the text, but he told her: "Cyphers were only us'd by Novices in Politics, and it was very easy to write intelligibly under feign'd names of persons and places to a correspondant in such a manner as should be almost impossible to be understood by any body else." Even though she described the incident as "very provoking," she appreciated the absurdity in the authorities' scrutinizing her letters and the humor of a situation in which "when I talk of my Grand children they are fancy'd to represent all the potentates of Europe" (10 October 1753; 3:41–42). Such an occurrence also indicates that the letter's secrets need not necessarily be "decoded," for one could simply appropriate the letter's status for an altogether different function.

Noting the problems presented by the materiality of the letter—its vulnerability, its uncertainties of status, and its difficulties of delivery— it seems almost miraculous that letters arrived at all and that people did not, in frustration, give up writing altogether. Yet the reverse is actually the case: after the Revolution, use of the post nearly doubled.[4] Once an avenue for relatively secure and frequent exchanges was paved, the best eighteenth-century writers took advantage of the historical circumstances that allowed them to make the familiar letter a self-conscious literary form and ushered in a new era in literary expression.

II

The letter as a means of writing the self into existence is often said to be related to the autobiography, the memoir, and the diary. Yet the dynamic predicated on transaction—the phenomenon of exchange that motivates letter writing—is profoundly important in separating this genre from those mentioned above. The autobiographer, reviewing a personal history and detailing the changing, kinetic self that was, writes out of the past tense to an amorphous, remote public; the memoirist, less interested in the self in flux, prefers to concentrate on events that, Marcus Billson argues, communicate "a moral vision" of the past.[5] In both forms, nostalgia for life gone by infuses a coherent narrative of the self and the past. The diarist, more akin to the letter writer, creates what H. Porter Abbott calls "a non-retrospective" text that depends more on the present and future tenses than on the past, a text that constitutes a "private drama of self-awareness." Yet even taking into account the possibility of future publication, the diarist writes ostensibly for the self, sketching a drama of the self for the self. In light of this "self-construction," Abbott cautions that diary writing—and, one should add, letter writing—is not composed without self-consciousness, for the formal equivalents of spontaneity neither guarantee self-knowledge nor prevent self-deception.[6] Walter J. Ong is more emphatic: "Masks are inevitable in all human communication, even oral. Role playing is both different from actuality and an entry into actuality," but "writing alone . . . will never bring us truly beneath to the actuality."[7]

Epistolary discourse provides an especially appropriate forum for the donning of such "masks." Alexander Pope created a series of roles in his correspondence, James Winn argues, roles that were dependent upon his recipient: Pope was rakish and passionate with women, deferential and elegantly submissive with his aristocratic friends, satiric and philosophical with the Scriblerians. In preparing his letters for publication, Pope revised his letters so that they showed him as he *wished* to appear: a witty writer, a serious thinker, a sensitive and sympathetic friend, and an educated practitioner of the epistolary form.[8] Roy Roussel says of Pamela and Squire B—— that "writing in this way becomes associated with the freedom to choose an identity by choosing a new relation to another, and this new identity, because it is the product of writing, comes in turn to be associated with fiction. It becomes something which has been literally written into existence."[9]

Yet notions about the genuineness of the self, the stripping naked of the psyche, and the "window in the bosom" persist. The writing closet, as the locus of subjective experience and introspection, supposedly allows a writer to use feelings as a mode of self-revelation, for it is difficult to write a really good letter if one is situated in the noise, color, and movement of a crowd. Richardson insists that "the pen is jealous of company. It expects, as I may say, to engross the writer's whole self; everybody allows the writer to withdraw: it disdains company; and will have the entire attention."[10] Eighteenth-century letter writers make much of retiring to their closets with pens, ink, and candles to scribble the hours away. Lady Mary apologizes to Anne Justice for her silence with this excuse: "I hope, Dear Nanny, you do not think I forget you, but I'll swear this town is such a place, and one is so hurryd about, tis with vast difficulty ⟨?⟩ to get pen, ink, and paper, and perhaps when they are all in readynesse, whip, there comes some impertinent visiter or another and puts all into Confusion again. So that—you must forgive me—that's the short on't" (3 February 1711; 1:70). Yet understanding that isolation is necessary for letter writing may have led Roy Roussel, in examining *Pamela,* to write that "the access to the writer's self which the letter allows the correspondent is not the removed and mediated relationship established by social usages, but instead the same kind of direct and intimate openness which love gives to the beloved." [11]

Such claims, however, erase the deliberateness of the act of letter writing, an attempt to articulate a part of the self already at some distance from the inner life. In the final analysis, a singular, fully authentic entity called "the self" is never recoverable in language; only the dramatic, expressive, and performative self resides in the letters. Bruce Redford's insightful analysis of six eighteenth-century letter writers, including Lady Mary, invokes the theatrical metaphor of "performance" to describe the "masks" of epistolary discourse. [12] The inherent motion, change, and sequence of the continuous epistolary exchanges found in a complete correspondence indicate its drama, its theatrical costuming of the self in various languages and styles that do indeed, as Redford insists, substitute for gesture. Yet he and other readers of the genre often abandon the metaphor in favor of the language of painting and portraiture, in part because the nature of the letter itself creates an easy segue. Individual letters, when studied in isolation, suggest that the letter writer creates for the moment a given "portrait" that can seem as static as any painting. Janet Altman uses an even more anchored metaphor drawn from geography: "To write a letter is to map one's coordinates—temporal, spatial, emotional, intellectual—in order to tell someone else where one is located at a particular time and how far one has traveled since the last writing." [13]

A reader of letters actually shifts back and forth between the continuous action of a complete correspondence and the individual scenes, frozen in tableau, that compose the collection as a whole. The process is reminiscent of the stylized posing of Restoration drama and the static posturing of the theatrical body that constitute the entirety of the play. In epistolary discourse, Shakespeare's "all the world's a stage" is less a metaphor than a reality, a fact of everyday existence recognized by Richard Steele, who devotes the whole of *Spectator,* No. 370, to the proposition that "the whole World acts the Player": "It is certain that if we look all round us, and behold the different Employments of Mankind, you hardly see one who is not, as the Player is, in an assumed Character. . . . Consider all the different Pursuits and Employments of Men, and you will find half their actions tend to nothing else but Disguise and

Imposture; and all that is done which proceeds not from a Man's very self is the Action of a Player." [14] Modern sociologist Erving Goffman and performance theorists have demonstrated how deep, systematic, and often unconscious are everyday forms of acting in a variety of settings and between both strangers and loved ones. Such acting occurs because an individual is always engaged, in Goffman's terms, in "impression management," an activity intended to create an often idealized image of the self performed in light of that individual's specific desires and needs within a particular relationship and for a specific "audience." [15] In epistolary terms, the letter writer first establishes his or her sometimes idealized but always constructed particularity in the transaction; as the relationship grows, such repeatable particularity authenticates the performance. Simultaneously the letter writer adds new facets to the role as an emergent self is constantly shaped. A break in the pattern may signal emotional difference, a shift in the role may indicate change, but the continuousness of the persona—the repeated transactions, or the "Commerce of Discourse," to use Steele's phrase—generates identity. Michael Ketcham has argued, in his study of *The Spectator,* that the social world demands a system of behavioral exchanges; [16] the epistolary world, a textually represented microcosm of the social world, demands a similar system of rhetorical exchanges, transactions directed toward others and providing a measure of the self.

Such a series of self-performances, inherently dramatic and change-able, is both a means of self-expression and a kind of role-playing for Lady Mary. She was a regular theatergoer, attending not only plays but also the opera and musical events. She assisted the play-writing career of her cousin Henry Fielding and read at the playwright's request a manuscript copy of Addison's *Cato,* responding with suggestions for revisions, some of which he apparently followed. Her only personal foray into play writing came after the 1734 Haymarket production of Marivaux's comedy, *Le Jeu de l'amour et du hasard,* which she translated and modified into an English comedy she called *Simplicity.* [17] Her sensibilities also indicate that such "theater" is, for her, an aristocratic phenomenon, especially when viewed in light of midcentury bourgeois narratives: the display, the costumes, the serial appearances demanded of aristocrats in the real world—bolstered by gestures mannered and refined—translate into a semiotics of public performance open to communal decoding and consensus.

The opportunity for the "creative reproduction" of a self is what defines all theatrical performance, according to Bruce Wilshire,[18] and such creative reproductions are clearly available in Lady Mary's epistolary performances. Just as costumes and gestures in the theater serve to point to a character's motives, the style of a letter—and especially the generic choices the writer makes—suggests the same aims and intentions. As the gestures of the actor bespeak his or her relationship with another character, so too does the style of a letter become the literary medium of emotional exchange; the literary trappings of a letter are the equivalent of the costumed body of the actor. More important, the letter functions as does a theatrical performance in its ability to make the illusory "real." Wilshire argues that "giving presence to absence is chiefly what characterizes theater,"[19] and this is precisely the letter writer's goal: to make the absent palpable, to allow one object or "body" to masquerade as another, and to substitute posture and gesture for identity.

III

The failure to account for the performative self has led modern scholars to apply a set of dichotomized standards to the art of letter writing, standards that isolate "thematic" concerns, or the biographical content of a given correspondence, from "formalistic" matters, or the stylistic qualities of the text itself. A new way of reading the eighteenth-century letter must account not only for performative "self" but also for the complications of transaction, for the interdependence between the writer and the recipient. Moreover, such a reading must acknowledge the literary and stylistic qualities of a letter without placing the letter in an ahistorical context; it must appreciate the experiential and biographical details of letters, without presuming that language is transparent and unmediated.

In an important essay concerning the de Sévigné scholarship, Louise K. Horowitz argues most persuasively for the insufficiency of the dichotomy that divides interpretations into "thematic" or "formalistic" methodologies.[20] "Thematic" approaches, which presume a lack of literary consciousness in the letter, focus on the biography of the writer who supposedly creates a self-referential epistolary universe. Such readings concentrate on the relationship the writer and the recipient create between them, tracing the psychology of shifting affect, the strategies for manipulation, and the pressures and coercive forces brought to bear. The "formalistic" methodology, on the other hand, examines the style and generic properties of a correspondence, outside of any particular context. This critical schism, while inadequate for generating a complete aesthetic for the letter, is understandable, given the dynamic of the letter-writing exchange. Because a writer addresses a single letter to an individual recipient, the epistolary universe seems a self-enclosed reference to the writer's lived experience and is, thus, "thematically" important; however, the document itself can also be lifted out of its personal and historical context as a means of examining a writer's literary acumen. Both kinds of readings also have their limited, if important, psychological functions: there is pleasure in examining the relationships writers create and in exploring the rhetorical strategies used by writers who supposedly lack literary consciousness; there is also a certain comfort in concentrating exclusively on the document as a stylistic exercise, for the generic choices and the literary devices displayed can be held up as "real" evidence, as opposed to the "traces" or "residue" of historical affect. However, such a division overlooks the power and the complexities of the phenomenon of epistolary exchange—a transaction generated not only through self-performance but also through an interdependence between the affective relationship the writer wishes to maintain with the recipient and a writer's literary style.[21]

Absence is the genesis of all letter writing: the correspondent, feeling the need to communicate with a friend or loved one, has only the letter to connect them. Mme de Sévigné valued her daughter's letters because they seemed to substitute for the young woman's presence.[22] The letter can exploit, even push the limits of, the elasticity of the epistolary form because, writers often claim, their epistles are merely trifles, humble attempts to please, gifts to these absent friends. Yet the fact of separation always intrudes, so much so that, rather than being a connection, the letter becomes, in Janet Altman's words, "an emblem of separation," a reminder—even a record—of absence.[23]

Partners in the epistolary cycle are also dependent on one another for the shape and substance of their letters; each document, whether a bridge or a record of absence, is a response to the letters that have gone before. The nature of the dynamic thus requires a special form of discourse, what Altman calls a "coded language" of partners who share a linguistic and symbolic system and a textual acknowledgment of the recipient's needs and expectations, an "addressee consciousness."[24] This language, however, has itself produced critical categories divided into binary opposites. Christina Gillis claims that the letter writer's experience is akin to the monologue, with the correspondent writing for the self, while Altman writes that the letter is an imagined dialogue between partners.[25] François Jost divides epistolary fiction into two categories: "lettres-confidence," where the writer emphasizes the "I" of the discourse (as in the monologue) and the receiver plays a relatively passive role; and "lettres-drame," where the action proceeds through the letters themselves and the participants emphasize the "you" of the discourse (as in dialogue) by manipulating, negotiating, and attempting to work through conflicts in the letter exchange.[26]

The category of "lettres-confidence" usefully describes those letters written by people who are relatively free from self-interest and desire, partners who write primarily to inform or to entertain one another as a means of sustaining a relationship. Lady Mary's letters written late in life to her daughter, for instance, display a relatively easy relationship of mutual affection and respect, a nurturing relationship that Lady Mary creates by describing her life, offering advice from her past (using herself as illustration), and confiding in her daughter. She will request of her daughter that she write "an Account [of] how you look, how you're dress'd, and in what manner your room is furnish'd. Nothing relating to you is trivial to me, and if the performance answers the engagement it will be a vast pleasure to your most affectionate Mother" (20 October 1755; 3:98). She will offer such encouraging and loving statements as these: "You need not go out of your own Walls [to entertain me]. You have within them ten strangers to me, whose characters interest me entreamly [*sic*]. . . . What proportion of Wit and Beauty has heaven allotted them? I shall be sorry if all the Talents have fallen into the male part of your Family" (1 April 1756; 3:105); and, "You have been the Passion of my Life. You need thank me for nothing; I gratify my selfe whenever I can oblige you" (7 July 1757; 3:130).

Real-life epistolary conflicts and attempted seductions, especially when the dramatic nature of partners in conflict is the focus, can also be usefully categorized as "lettres-drame." One reason the epistolary form is so conducive to fictional seduction and love plots is this very stimulus to action: the seducer sees the letter as a path leading to love, while the beloved sees the letter as a barrier, a form of distance and protection.

The pursuer wants to goad the loved one into a response—either a letter that substitutes for presence and reveals and gives of the self or an action that commits one partner to the other, a physical giving-over of the self. Lady Mary and the men in her life participate in such negotiations, where each tries to manipulate the other into some sort of action; when Lady Mary represents herself as a saintlike martyr in her desire to see Algarotti, the letter is both a written compliment emphasizing her affection and a demand that he gratify her desire: "My Lady Stafford and my selfe waited for you three Hours. Three Hours of expectation is no small Tryal of Patience, and I beleive some of your Martyrs have been canoniz'd for suffering less. If you have repentance enough to be enclin'd to ask pardon you may obtain it by comeing here to morrow at 7 o'clock" (April 1736; 2:101).

Such strife-ridden, manipulative correspondence need not be a male-female conflict. Mme de Sévigné, for instance, created between herself and her daughter, the Countess de Grignan, an epistolary system that manipulated the young woman into responding in ways demanded by her mother. Arguing that de Sévigné accomplished this "by forcing Mme de Grignan to consider her in nearly every aspect of her life and daily decisions," Gail Mensher claims, "[de Sévigné] tries to make herself felt and heard in Grignan despite the distance" by insisting that her very health and well-being are dependent on frequent and substantive exchanges from her daughter (and even going so far as to employ spies in Grignan's household to confirm or contradict her daughter's statements).[27] Such pressure placed a huge burden on the young woman to live up to her part of the exchange, yet de Sévigné's overwhelming obsession with maintaining contact with and authority over her daughter found quite suitable expression in the letter form: delays prohibited the acrimonious exchanges that they sometimes had in one another's company, and the separation gave her time to perfect the subtlest nuances designed for maximum effect.

Yet these categories are ultimately too restrictive for real-life letters because they ignore the wider context of letter writing. Lady Mary's letters to her sister, the Countess of Mar, or to her other close friends— the Steuarts, Lady Pomfret, the Countess of Oxford—are important instances where the emphasis rests on neither the "I" nor the "you" of a discourse that builds a relationship but on an assumed "we" of a partnership. Secure in their friendship, they turn their observations outward to focus on the comedy that their culture generates. For instance, Lady Mary gossips with her sister about their relatives and acquaintances: "My Father is going to the Bath, Sir Wm Wyndham is dying of a Fistula, Lady Darlington and Lady Mohun are packing up for the next World, and the rest of our Acquaintance playing the Fool in this, a l'ordinaire" (March 1725; 2:49); "A propos of family affairs, I had allmost forgot our dear and Aimable Cousin Lady Denbiegh, who has blaz'd out all this Winter. She has brought with her from Paris cart loads of Riband, surprizing fashions, and a complexion of the last Edition, which naturally attracts all the she and he fools in London, and accordingly she is surrounded with a little Court of both, and keeps a Sunday Assembly to shew she has learnt to play at cards on that day" (April 1727; 2:74). These letters contain no personal struggles between the correspondents, nor does Lady Mary focus primarily on herself. Instead, she concentrates on the comedy and absurdity of the behavior of her acquaintances: highlighted, such discourse creates a complicitous relationship with her correspondent, and together they confirm their mutual judgment and shared community.[28]

Because the recipient plays a generative role in the exchange, the actual writing is partially shaped by potential reading, and each writer must also be very much aware of the dynamic: the phenomenon requires the writer to construct the recipient—his or her desires and abilities—in a particular way. This means considering most carefully what the reader knows or does not know; because writing proceeds without the physical contact of an immediate exchange, knowledge about the degrees of admissible ignorance for readers is essential. In letter writing especially, the fictionalizing of both the writer and the recipient is subtle and specialized because it is dependent on a language that must be shared by the correspondents, a language that substitutes for familiar gestures.[29] Recognizing this phenomenon, Walter J. Ong goes even further to argue that any writer's audience is always a fiction: a writer casts the audience "in a made-up role and call[s] on them to play the role assigned," roles they have learned to know "not from daily life but from earlier writers who were fictionalizing in their imaginations . . . and so on."[30]

To her relatively sophisticated friend Lady Pomfret, Lady Mary writes wittily, employing the literary devices of the mock epic or the blasphemous wit of drama. She also entertains by poking fun at epistolary conventions: "I will say nothing of your complaints of your own dulness; . . . 'Tis impossible you should not be conscious that such letters as yours want not the trimmings of news, which are only necessary to the plain Spitalfields' style, beginning with *hoping you are in good health,* and concluding *pray believe me to be,* &c. &c. You give me all the pleasure of an agreeable author" (November 1738; 2:129–30). To her stuffier friend, the Countess of Oxford, Lady Mary *enacts* these conventions: she begins with this innocuous opening, "I have many thanks to give you for the agreable news of your Health (which is allways in the first place regarded by me)"; and she closes with this stiff postscript, "Your Ladyship will permit me to offer my compliments to the Duke and Duchess of Portland" (1 June 1744; 2:330). She is generally content simply to trade gossip with and to reiterate her continuing affection for the countess, a friend less sensitive and sophisticated than Lady Pomfret. The adjectives used here to describe the character and personality of Lady Mary's acquaintances are based on no historical evidence other than as it appears in the letters themselves in the way Lady Mary posits her correspondents' desires and abilities through the style and content she chooses.

Most important in disrupting the binary categories of letter writing is the fact that the epistolary universe is not self-enclosed. Some letters were read aloud as a form of communal sharing. Lady Mary's correspondence with her daughter indicates that she knew her son-in-law would read her letters, and thus she must apologize for suggestions she knows he will resist: "I cannot help writing a sort of Apology for my last letter, foreseeing that you will think it wrong, or at least Lord Bute will be extremely shock'd at the proposal of a learned Education for Daughters" (6 March {1753}; 3:25). This double-consciousness influenced not only the substance of her letters but also her stylistic and generic choices. Above, Lady Mary writes in the mode of the essay and exploits the rhetorical power of logic to argue for the benefits of female education in a way that might not strengthen her son-in-law's opposition. The comfortable but limiting critical dichotomy of "thematic" and "formalist" is effectively disrupted once the complications of transaction—especially the dynamics of an exchange predicated on an interdependence of performance between the writer and recipient—are understood.

IV

Attempts to define an aesthetic for the letter sometimes focus, ahistorically, on the literary elements present in the document; the larger cultural context of the production of the letter is sometimes overlooked in favor of an examination of its formalistic properties. Readers who do move beyond the margins of the document itself, in an attempt to account for the dynamic nature of epistolary exchange, often liken the letter to conversation, a similarity letter writers themselves frequently cite: Cicero claims, "I always accustom myself to write my letters in the language of conversation," while Pope calls it "Talking upon paper."[31] Keith Stewart and Bruce Redford cite Dr. Johnson's prescriptions for good conversation as the same standards for excellence in letter writing: "There must, in the first place, be knowledge, there must be materials;—in the second place, there must be a command of words;—in the third place, there must be imagination, to place things in such views as they are not commonly seen in;—and in the fourth place, there must be presence of mind, and a resolution that is not to be overcome by failures; this last is an essential requisite; for want of it many people do not excel in conversation."[32] While the qualities of knowledge, linguistic facility, imagination, and courage are certainly found in the best letters, such characteristics really describe the education and moral character of the letter writer rather than the letter itself.

Letters seem "like talk" in part because the overall structures of the best familiar letters are much freer than the strict rhetorical patterns long established for excellence in formal and informal discourse. Moreover, letter writers and readers learn to interpret certain written conventions as spontaneity—a "colloquial" or "conversational" style that employs shorter, more informal sentence structures and punctuation such as the exclamation point or the dash to create a sense of rapidity of movement.[33] Lady Mary herself makes use of these colloquial conventions, reserving the dash, for instance, for moments of emotional distress: surprised by a letter from Wortley after a long separation that appeared to be permanent, she writes, "I never thought to hear from you more.—Tis impossible to tell you my Surprize.—What would you have me say? There is a great deal of generosity and good nature in your Letter, but I know not how to answer it—" (20 August 1710; 1:53). Thus both writers and readers have agreed to interpret these conventions as indications of spontaneity, fluidity, and rapidity of movement—a style "dashed off" without deliberation. Recognizing the artifice in such conventions, however, leads others to describe letters as deliberate discourse that has been polished and revised for the greatest artistic effect. Howard Anderson and Irvin Ehrenpreis are characteristic: "Indeed, the letters that the eighteenth century judged its best are not thoughtless outpourings; their charm and their power, as well as their very appearance of spontaneity, are the result of considerable, if varied, art."[34]

The letter itself invites this privileging of either its ease or its artifice. William Cowper, also likening letter writing to conversation, uses a metaphor of the journey: "A letter is Written as a Conversation is maintained, or a Journey perform'd, not by preconcerted, or premeditated Means, by a New Contrivance, or an Invention never heard before, but merely by maintaining a Progress, and resolving as a Postillion does, having once Set out, never to stop 'till we reach the appointed End."[35] Cowper's "merely . . . maintaining a progress" is finally a more productive approach, for it points to an internal principle of associational logic according to which most letters proceed: because the letter has no prescribed formula, it seems spontaneous; yet, simultaneously, letters appear to be polished artistic exercises because writers exploit established literary tropes and genres.

An examination of the associational logic that drives one of Lady Mary's letters, sent to Sir James Steuart, can best determine the interplay between spontaneity and artifice in letter writing. Moreover, it reveals the interdependence between the generic and literary elements a writer specifically chooses for a particular recipient as a means of acknowledging and embodying the needs of both writer and reader. Finally, it displays the performative nature of the letter writer's identity as it is fashioned for the recipient through its artistry.

> You have made (what I did not think possible) writing to you uneasy to me. After confessing that you barbarously criticize on my letters, I have much ado to summon up courage enough to set pen to paper. Can you answer this to your conscience, to sit gravely and maliciously to examine lines written with rapidity and sent without reading over? This is worse than surprising a fine lady just sat down to her toilet. I am content to let you see my mind undressed, but I will not have you so curiously remark

the defects in it. To carry on the simile, when a Beauty appears with all her graces and airs adorned for a ball, it is lawful to censure whatever you see amiss in her ornaments, but when you are received to a friendly breakfast, 'tis downright cruelty or (something worse) ingratitude to view too nicely all the disorder you may see. I desire you would sink the critic in the friend, and never forget that I do not write to you and dear Lady Fanny from my head but from my heart. (18 October 1758; 3:182–83)

This passage displays an associational structure coupled with deliberate refinements of style, a deliberation clearly displayed for all Lady Mary's insistence on spontaneity. After chiding Sir James as too severe a critic of "lines written with rapidity and sent without reading over"—a claim difficult to believe when one considers that Lady Mary labored over her letters and kept copies of much of her correspondence—she counters with a metaphor dependent on gender: a letter is like a woman just sitting down to create her public persona. This image conflates the privacy of a woman's room with the performative quality of female display, invoking images both "natural" (the nonconstructed woman) and "theatrical" (Lady Wishforts sitting before their mirrors as the curtains rise).

This witty trope of the fine lady at her toilet may in fact have occurred to Lady Mary quite spontaneously, but the extension of the comparison required effort. Naturally enough, the mention of the toilet carries with it associations of undress, and the metaphor grows as Lady Mary insists she displays only a nakedness of the mind until, acknowledging the extended comparison she creates ("to carry on the simile"), she equates public, studied prose with "a Beauty" adorned for the ball, fully and artfully constructed, and ornamented with all the artifice at her command. Her own simple language, she claims, is merely the disordered, perhaps not fully conscious, but truthful discourse of a breakfast companion.

A modern reader, and presumably Steuart, is aware that such claims for simplicity and lack of artifice are contradicted on the very page. Lady Mary's metaphors—homey, domestic details of female dress and appearance—are clothed in the most suitable imagery, since she wants to make a point about her own personal style. But references to a woman's toilet and state of undress also require an intimate correspondent; in this case, the metaphor itself reinforces the intimacy. Her request that Steuart play the role of friend and not critic comes from a declaration that she writes out of affection, a strategy intended to erase the conscious literary elements she labored to produce even though such artifice is the greatest compliment she can bestow upon him: the style itself and the work required to produce it communicate her affection. Thus literary performance, while an essential component in the best eighteenth-century letters, when isolated and viewed alone is insufficient in generating a rhetoric for the letter, for these choices grow out of the writer's desire to create and sustain a particular relationship, itself revealed in the evidence of literary acumen. These literary devices depend as much on the affective relationship and the performative elements as they do on artistry.

Throughout her correspondence, Lady Mary carefully selects and tailors specific genres as one means of creating such performance and the resulting "impressions" and relationships she desires. In her best letters, there is no suggestion that her prose is intended as an example of unmediated consciousness; the pleasure for a reader, and presumably for Lady Mary herself, can be found in the shape the medium of self-performance takes, in the rhetorical strategies and literary conventions fashioned for a particular correspondent, incorporated within a particular emotional context, and proffering an individuated self. In the letter that suggests her granddaughters be educated beyond accepted custom, Lady Mary writes with the witty intelligence and perception of an essayist, establishing herself as moderate, rational, and clear-sighted in the hope of muting Lord Bute's resistance to her "progressive" notion:

> There is nothing so like the Education of a Woman of Quality as that of a Prince. They are taught to dance and the exterior part of what is call'd good breeding, which if they attain they are extroadinary Creatures in their kind, and have all the accomplishments requir'd by their Directors. The same characters are form'd by the same Lessons, which inclines me to think (if I dare say it) that Nature has not plac'd us in an inferior Rank to Men, no more than the Females of other Animals, where we see no distinction of capacity, thô I am persuaded if there was a Common-wealth of rational Horses (as Doctor Swift has suppos'd) it would be an establish'd maxim amongst them that a mare could not be taught to pace. (6 March 1753; 3:26–27)

The likening of a woman of quality to a prince is not the poetic metaphor that equates a prose style with a breakfast companion or a beauty attired for the ball; it is instead a comparison based on the reality of education.

Her final condemnation of a society that ill prepares its young women for life is couched in a literary reference whose humor might soften Lord Bute's dismay, even as it more sharply points to the ignorance of such a custom.

Lady Mary's letters also include epigrams, such as this ironic remark about the fate of those unhappily married: "I suppose we shall all come right in Heaven, as in a Country Dance, thô hands are strangly given and taken while they are in motion, at last all meet their partners when the Jig is done" (11 August 1721; 2:11). At moments of great exuberance or passion, she will burst into verse, both her own and others', as she does when writing the Steuarts about "us wretches who are condemned to petticoats," barred from the pleasure of love and vengeance:

> From whence is this unjust distinction shewn?
> Are we not formed with passions like your own?
> Nature with equal fire our souls endued,
> Our minds as lofty and as warm our blood.
> (19 July 1759; 3:219)[36]

Lady Mary uses character sketches of the great and small as exempla of moral rectitude: the death of the doge in Venice occasions a panegyric on his benevolence (22 July 1752; 3:13–15), praise matched only by her celebration of a humble physician who, dust-covered and weary, travels on foot throughout the Italian countryside ministering to the sick and injured (23 July 1754; 3:53). As a social commentator, Lady Mary describes the scandals of the English aristocracy in small prose narratives that take on the characteristics and power of drama, sometimes even accompanied by stage directions. In a dialogue sent to the Steuarts, she recounts one of her own dismal social performances and dramatizes her role as a besieged guest during an unpleasant drawing-room exchange at the house of her "enemy," John Murray:

"Why then (say my wise monitors) will you persist in reading or writing seven hours in a day?"—I am happy while I read and write.—"Indeed one would suffer a great deal to be happy," say the men sneering; and the ladies wink at each other and hold up their fans. A fine lady of threescore had the goodness to add—"At least, Madam, you should use spectacles; . . . I am really of [the] opinion they have preserved my sight, notwithstanding the passion I always had both for reading and draw-

ing."—This good woman, you must know, is halfe blind, and never read
a larger volume than a newspaper. I will not trouble you with the whole
conversation, tho' it would make an excellent scene in a farce. (19 July
1759; 3:216–17)

As a literary critic, she provides judgments concerning England's major
writers, especially the novelists, and adds her own short "novelistic" performances that sometimes offer direct rebuttals to the popular fiction of
the day. Thus claims that the letter mimics the essay or any other literary
form overlook the fact that, unlike the other, more rule-bound forms,
the letter has the capacity to incorporate and exploit *any* genre, because
the writer intends to fashion a document whose style contributes to the
communication of affect and to the production of a performative self.

Lady Mary sends her lifelong series of letters as offerings to friends
and absent loved ones, gifts that speak in passionate and powerfully
moving voices that modulate through the course of the correspondence
as she literally writes herself into existence in an epistolary form that
points to itself as artless, spontaneous, and natural, a form that works
to erase its fictive nature through the very structures of fiction. It is
the dynamic process—the complex interplay of performance, affect,
and art—that shapes and enlivens the letters of Lady Mary Wortley
Montagu.

Chapter Two

Intimate Negotiations

Early in a correspondence with Anne Wortley, the sister of the man she would ultimately marry, Lady Mary must respond to rumors that she is in love. Her first strategy is to disclaim all knowledge: "You tell me I'm in love; if I am, 'tis a perfect sin of ignorance, for I don't so much as know the man's name: I have been studying these three hours, and cannot guess who you mean" (21 August 1709; 1:10). She then downplays the significance of romantic love in a comic reference to that place where love, in all its extravagance, can be found:

> Tis against all form to have such a passion as that, without giving one sigh for the matter. Pray tell me the name of him I love, that I may (according to the laudable custom of lovers) sigh to the woods and groves hereabouts, and teach it to the echo. You see, being I am in love, I am willing to be so in order and rule; I have been turning over God knows how many books to look for precedents. (1:10)

Beyond this playful and self-deprecating handling of her own feelings, her satirical claim that women consult books in order to discover the proper conventions of love becomes reality in the epistolary relationships she sustains with three very different men: Edward Wortley Montagu, Alexander Pope, and Francesco Algarotti.

Unwilling to be only an object of male desire, Lady Mary seeks a measure of power and equality in the roles provided by literary heroines. As a means of foregrounding the roles a woman can play in romance, she chooses the literary language of the fictions of love, a language that both expresses and controls passion. Yet following the "order and rule" of such literary conventions, she soon discovers that epistolary style and social codes of behavior are perceived as equivalents. Thus she finds herself trapped by the very forms she chooses. With Wortley, she must moderate her witty Restoration heroine's discourse in response to his suspicion that wit indicates insincerity; she filters his fears by choosing the part of the "natural" philosopher. With Pope, she resists attempted seduction through a detached rhetoric of journalistic distance and through an insistence that they share the artistic role of poets. With Algarotti, a man who not only fails to objectify her but refuses even to engage in romantic discourse, she chooses a voice of female passion that becomes large and operatic, completely unrestrained. Even though all three epistolary encounters ultimately fail to produce sustained romantic relationships, she searches for a role and a discourse that allow her to exploit the elasticity of epistolary expression, to translate established, public, literary discourses into the private realm of affect. The result is a series of performances dependent on competing desires.

I

The courtship letters to Wortley, which span two and a half years, constitute a narrative of continued negotiations that culminates in an elopement risky for them both. Lady Mary's father rejected Wortley as a possible suitor because Wortley refused to agree to Lord Dorchester's financial settlement. Lady Mary's father insisted that Wortley's estate be entailed on the firstborn son, but Wortley refused, in part because it would have required an immediate ten thousand pounds, a huge burden on his estate, and, more important, because he insisted that the estate go only to a child who had proven himself worthy of the inheritance. Wortley was so committed to his own position that he sent notes to Steele for a *Tatler* essay outlining his arguments, and number 223 contains these ironic claims about the absurdity of the average marriage settlement: "And therefore, in full and perfect health of body, and a sound mind, not knowing which of my children will prove better or worse, I give to my first-born, be he perverse, ungrateful, impious, or cruel, the lump and bulk of my estate . . . wherein I resign my senses, and hereby promise to employ my judgment no farther in the distribution of my worldly goods from the day of the date hereof; hereby farther confessing and covenanting, that I am from henceforth married, and dead in law." [1] Lady Mary's father remained staunchly opposed to Wortley's Whiggish, antipatrilineal, even antiaristocratic views and commanded that Lady Mary remove Wortley from her sight and her affections. [2] Thus their courtship was forced to remain covert.

Occasionally hesitant, frequently filled with complaints, and usually fearful, their correspondence would seem on the surface to require a search for the courage necessary to overcome parental disapproval. Yet rather than focusing on these external pressures, their negotiation is in fact a continuous dispute about epistolary style—specifically, the incompatible language and identity that each imposes on the other. [3] Because Wortley's letters are extant, it is possible to chart the course of their epistolary confusion as each employs a contradictory rhetorical strategy: at one extreme, Wortley insists on the language of business out of a naive belief that meaning there is transparent; at the other, Lady Mary chooses a language of wit that allows her to create multiple meanings and subtle emotional shadings.

The danger posed by an epistolary relationship for a young woman, especially as it relates to the question of social decorum, is a concern in the very first letter she sends to him. Expressing doubts that writing to him or to any man is appropriate, and hoping to override the charge that she is too forward, she attempts to differentiate their relationship from those of other people: "Perhaps you'l be surprizd at this Letter. I have had manny debates with my selfe before I could resolve on it. I know it is not Acting in Form, but I do not look upon you as I do upon the rest of the world, and by what I do for you, you are not to judge my manner of acting with others. You are Brother to a Woman I tenderly lov'd. My protestations of freindship [*sic*] are not like other people's. I never speak but what I mean, and when I say I love, it is for ever" (28 March 1710; 1:24). Lady Mary locates their mutual specialness in a kinship mediated through another woman, her friend Anne Wortley. [4] Lady Mary intends this doubled distance to limit the sexual significance of their correspondence as she imposes a particular identity on Wortley, "Brother to a Woman I tenderly lov'd," and conflates what is ostensibly a reference to Anne—"When I say I love, it is for ever"—with a reference to Wortley himself.

Yet for all a woman's protestations, the "Form" is always a trap. Custom dictates that she not write to a man unless she is willing to surrender something. The letter itself is a giving over of an emblematic part of the self and could be interpreted as a prelude to other, more physical exchanges. Recognizing that the simple act of penning a letter to Wortley resonates with sexual implications, Lady Mary tries to contain that significance by labeling him "Brother" to the sister they both loved. Yet her strategy is doomed to failure: the very act of protesting against the sexual significance of their correspondence locates their relationship within that sexual context, and, more futilely, her claim that her behavior with him is extraordinary—that she does for him what she would not do for others—may initially flatter, but it proves to him that she *is* capable of ignoring the "forms" when she desires.

A more serious violation of social form is Lady Mary's choosing for herself a noncontractual alliance. Wortley tells her that marriage to him "can be on no other terms than of [her] being chang'd from a fine Court Lady into a plain Country Wife" (1:125), and he expresses his fears that she will regret the surrender of an aristocrat's financial security and the loss of social position: "It requires an uncommon greatness of Mind to chose to be reduc'd to less than a third part of your present Attendance, your Apartments, your Table, and be quite stript of what glitters more than all the rest of those Ornaments that are no part of You, the Train of Admirers" (1:26). His unease, growing out of culturally inscribed prejudices about women's love of money and their "natural" desire for increased social standing and male admiration, places Lady Mary in a difficult position: she can choose to defend all women, a strategy that would force her to combat the vices attributed to her entire sex, or she can insist on her "difference" from other women, a strategy that would force her to perform outside all cultural norms.

She chooses, instead, to answer Wortley by turning his own language against him. In a series of arguments contrasting private and public life—described as "nature" versus "custom"—she insists that her "natural" inclination is to choose a life of retirement, privacy, and love rather than the noise and hurry of "Greatnesse." Earlier in her correspondence with Anne Wortley, Lady Mary had written that she shuns fashion in favor of study and solitude: "I find the study [of dictionaries and grammars] so diverting, I am not only easy, but pleased with the solitude that indulges it. I forget there is such a place as London" (8 August 1709; 1:6). She calls these studies "those unfashionable diversions" and sums up her feelings about the beau monde in this way: "I believe more follies are committed out of complaisance to the world, than in following our own inclinations—Nature is seldom in the wrong, custom always" (1:6). She turns to literature—a *Tatler* essay that Wortley had sent to her—for her arguments with him:

> Mr. Bickerstaff has very wrong notions of our sex. I can say there are some of us that dispises charms of show, and all the pageantry of Greatnesse, perhaps with more ease than any of the Philosophers. In contemning the world they seem to take pains to contemn it. We dispise it, without taking the pains to read lessons of Morrality to make us do it. . . . Was I to chuse of £2,000 a year or twenty thousand, the first would be my choice. There is something of an unavoidable embarras in makeing what is calld a great figure in the world, [that] takes off from the happynesse of Life. I hate the noise and hurry inseparable from great Estates and Titles, and look upon both as blessings that ought only to be given to Fools, for tis only to them that they are blessings. (28 March 1710; 1:24)

She embraces the ideals of the eighteenth-century tradition of retirement—Wortley's "plain Country Wife"—as a "natural" philosophy. Such a strategy allows her not only to reject "custom" as constructed and artificial, in favor of the "natural" virtues that produce happiness, but also to exploit and then undermine the ideological male "truism" fundamental to Wortley's position. She does so by appealing to the almost universal strategy by which societies ensure the secondary social status of women: they align women with "nature" and men with "culture"; as a result, culture asserts itself to be not only distinct from but also superior to nature. As Sherry B. Ortner has argued, "that sense of distinctiveness and superiority rests precisely on the ability to transform—to 'socialize' and 'culturalize'—nature." Because women are placed "closer to" and described as "less transcendental of" nature, men take on the role as the keepers of symbols and artifacts, the proprietors of religion, ritual, and politics.[5] Lady Mary uses this cultural bias for her own ends: she appears to subordinate herself to the lesser realm of "nature," a strategy Wortley would be hard-pressed to dispute, while in reality she makes the "lesser" realm productive of the best in morality by elevating it to the aristocratic ideal of genteel retreat. She does not point to the fact that the very letter she pens is a product of "culture," a symbol and an artifact written according to the dictates of "custom"; instead, she appropriates Mr. Bickerstaff's discourse and Wortley's prejudices to her own advantage.

She continues to employ this argument, voiced in a tone of philosophical calm, in a letter that offers Wortley a definition, not of the perfect marriage, but of happiness. Such recourse to philosophy also expands the context of the too often claustrophobic quality of their negotiation:

> Happynesse is the natural design of all the World, and every thing we see done, is meant in order to attain it. My Imagination places it in Freindship. By Freindship I mean an intire Communication of thoughts, Wishes, Interests, and Pleasures being undivided, a mutual Esteem, which naturally carrys with it a pleasing sweetnesse of conversation, and terminates in the desire of makeing one or Another happy, without being forc'd to run into Visits, Noise, and Hurry, which serve rather to trouble than compose the thoughts of any reasonable Creature. (24 March 1711; 1:95)

This moderate, rational, philosophical discourse is reminiscent of the language of Shaftesbury's *Characteristics* (1711) and his arguments about the relationship between natural affections and happiness: "From all this we may easily conclude how much our happiness depends on natural and good affection. For if the chief happiness be from mental pleasures, . . . and are founded in natural affection, it follows 'that to have the natural affections is to have the chief means and power of self-enjoyment, the highest possession and happiness of life.' "[6] Such happiness in affection Lady Mary translates to Wortley in this way: "I take you to have Sense enough not to think this Scheme Romantic. I rather chuse to use the word Freindship than Love because in the general Sense that word is spoke, it signifies a Passion rather founded on Fancy than Reason, and when I say Freindship I mean a mixture of Tendernesse and Esteem, and which a long acquaintance encreases not decays" (1:95–96). Not simply rejecting love as "Passion" and "Fancy," she also makes him complicitous in her argument by presuming in advance his preference for "Freindship" and "Reason."

She is, however, capable of anger, irony, and even sarcasm when pushed past her limits. When this occurs, her frustration takes the form of exaggeration and mock self-deprecation. During one of their most turbulent periods, she purports to abandon her arguments for "natural" virtue by ironically claiming to "renounce all the Ideas I have so long flatterd my selfe with":

> How much wiser are all them women I have dispisd than my selfe! In placeing their Happynesse in triffles, they have plac'd it in what is attainable. I fondly thought Fine Cloaths and Gilt Coaches, Balls, Operas and public adoration rather the fatigues of Life, and that True Happynesse was justly defin'd by Mr. Dryden (pardon the romantic Air of repeating verses) when he says
>
>> Whom Heaven would bless it does from pomps remove,
>> And makes their Wealth in Privacy and Love.
>
> These Notions had corrupted my Judgment as much as Mrs. Biddy Tipkin's. According to this Scheme, I propos'd to passe my Life with you. (26 February 1711; 1:83–84)

The series of ironic assertions is predicated on two literary allusions. Through a reference to Biddy Tipkin, the heroine of Steele's *Tender Husband*, Lady Mary ironically compares her desire for retirement to the faulty judgment of a woman "corrupted" by reading romances. The lines of poetry, drawn from Dryden's *Aureng-Zebe*, may be preceded by Lady Mary's mock apology for "the romantic Air of repeating verses," but they provide her strongest statement about the "Privacy and Love" she had actually envisioned for them. Thus in the process of ironizing these hopes, Lady Mary again emphasizes her own good judgment, reasonable expectations, and superior set of values by equating her inclination for retirement with the "natural" wealth of human affection.

It is, however, this verbal richness, a texture layered and intellectual, that Wortley most suspects. Their negotiations about finding a mutually comprehensible epistolary style center around Lady Mary's need to create a voice that expresses with nuance and subtlety the emotional responses she is willing to reveal versus the plain and simple style Wortley wants to receive and demands that she write. Lady Mary points to the seriousness of their relationship and her fears that Wortley is merely toying with her affection in a whimsical reference to L'Estrange's fable of the frogs and boys. The fable itself reads, "A Company of Waggish

Boys were watching of *Frogs* at the Side of a Pond, and still as any of 'em put up their Heads, they'd be pelting them down again with Stones. Children (says one of the Frogs) you never consider, that *though this may be Play to you, 'tis Death to us*" (1:35n). Lady Mary's version reads, "All commerce of this kind between men and women is like that of the Boys and Frogs in L'Estrange's Fables.—Tis play to you, but tis death to us—and if we had the wit of the frogs, we should allwaies make that answer" (5 May 1710; 1:35). It is the very lightheartedness of the fable that reinforces its emotional impact. Yet this incongruous, witty comparison appears to Wortley as another sign of female disingenuousness. If, indeed, love is a serious undertaking, he insists, it should be spoken of as such: "I beg you will this once try to avoid being witty and write in a style of business, tho it shoud appear to you as flat as mine. Dont fancy it is below you to be as open and plain with me on such an occasion as you woud with an intimate friend" (4 November 1710; 1:63). Wortley's Whig sensibilities lead him to believe that one's language is a measure of sincerity, and so he finds appropriate expression in the language of business. This discourse, he implies, is solid and dependable, not open to misinterpretation. Although he is sensitive enough to label such transparency "flat," he insists that intimacy is located in a style "open and plain." His distrust of her playfulness, her mingling of voices, and her ability to live in a world referenced by the literary is translated into complaints about a lack of proper linguistic decorum, and he therefore easily equates Lady Mary's wit with an inconsistent, unstable, and unreliable character.

Her feelings about love and marriage, which she expresses warily to Wortley, are treated very differently in letters sent to her women friends. In a much more expansive and energetic language, she and Philippa Mundy play a game that includes an intimate private language to describe the kinds of marriages they foresee: "Paradise," marriage to a beloved partner, may be replaced by "Purgatory," a man neither desired nor offensive; "Hell," of course, is the despised partner imposed upon the woman by necessity. Lady Mary's fears of being forced to marry an unacceptable man are equalled only by the horrors of spinsterhood, or "leading the Apes," as she calls it. When her father contracts a marriage for her, against her wishes, to Clotworthy Skeffington, the son of an Irish peer, she expresses both of these fears to her friend in heightened descriptive and metaphoric language. Her imagination sees the spinster's future vividly embodied in a rotting tree outside her window:

> I have a Mortal Aversion to be an old Maid, and a decaid Oak before my Window, leavelesse, half rotten, and shaking its wither'd Top, puts me in Mind every morning of an Antiquated Virgin, Bald, with Rotten Teeth, and shaking of the Palsie. . . . Paradise is in your veiw, fresh, young and blooming. . . . A little rats' bane is all the remedy can be given me. For want of that I go to Hell—Fire, brimstone, Frosts and burnings, Favours, a Parson and wedding Cloaths. (12 December 1711; 1:112–13)

The grotesque physical degeneration of a useless part of nature, submitting to the forces of entropy, stands as a constant reminder of the kind of life Lady Mary fears; it is imaged in the particularly graphic depiction of the decayed oak, which communicates her fears not simply about old age but about the condition of the "Antiquated Virgin." However, against these images Lady Mary juxtaposes a description of the bad marriage that includes all the conventional trappings of Hell (fire, brimstone, burnings) coupled with all the finery of the wedding ceremony (a parson and bridal gown). Lady Mary does not hesitate to send this pair of seemingly incongruous images to Philippa Mundy, because the two young women shared similar expectations and fears. Lady Mary need not worry about being opaque or misunderstood, for rotting virgins and hellish marriages are images both find mutually repugnant. In a letter to Wortley concerning her planned marriage to Skeffington, Lady Mary emphasizes, in the unembellished way he demands, her sense of duty and the burden it represents: "I am perswaded the Man they force me to is of a humour to suffer me to do what I please, but what is Liberty to one that carrys her goaler in her breast? My Duty is more a chain to me than all others that could be impos'd on me" (15 June 1712; 1:124–25). She expresses her fear of wifely duties in this mild metaphor of prison to Wortley; to Philippa Mundy, "Favours" are coupled with "Frosts and burnings," and the result is a rich and hellish metaphor quite unlike the unease expressed to Wortley.

Lady Mary offers to Frances Hewet a second, very different kind of "old maid" story, a narrative that expresses a young woman's fears about the gravity of marriage through straightforward ridicule combined with a bemused appreciation of, even a genuine sense of wonder about, the vagaries of the human heart. The subject concerns a late-in-life marriage that a penniless spinster contracted with "a Man of £7,000 per Annum and they say £40,000 in ready money." The motives for the marriage are mystifying to Lady Mary, for "never was man more smitten with these Charms, that [had] lain invisible this forty year"; the groom himself is "so filthy, frightful, odious and detestable I would turn away such a footman for fear of spoiling my Dinner while he waited at Table." More surprising still is the visible satisfaction of this union. The couple, married on a Friday, attended church on Sunday, and Lady Mary, sitting in the same pew, observed "Mrs. Bride fall fast asleep in the middle of the Sermon and snore very comfortably, which made several women in the Church think the bridegroom not quite so ugly as they did before" (13 February 1710; 1:21–22). Lady Mary can treat the mystery of sexual satiety humorously with a woman friend, for there is no risk of being misinterpreted, no fear of future ramifications that might demand an explanation, no suspicion that the satire will be unappreciated.

The palpable intelligence in this wit, its attraction and powerful seduction, Wortley equates with Lady Mary's beauty; yet a disturbing ambivalance about these two qualities—which drew him to her in the first place—colors his desires. He fears that the external power of her beauty, coupled with her inherent intellectual gifts, will serve to make her attractive to all manner of men, and Lady Mary must search for a rhetorical strategy that combats his repeated expressions of jealousy without crushing his desires or silencing her own. She chooses wit and a metaphor drawn from high and low literary culture to reassure him and to claim certain freedoms for herself: "The pritty Fellows you speak of, I own entertain me sometimes, but is it impossible to be diverted with what one dispises? I can laugh at a puppet shew, at the same time I know there is nothing in it worth my attention or regard. General Notions are generally wrong. Ignorance and Folly are thought the best foundations for Virtue, as if not knowing what a Good Wife is was necessary to make one so. I confess that can never be my way of reasoning" (28 March 1710; 1:24). Reading their relationship through the literary structures of the theater, she uses the puppet-show metaphor to contrast the high drama of their own courtship with the fleeting pleasure of "low culture" entertainment. Yet she also claims the right to the amusement such comedy provides, without sacrificing those things "worth my attention and regard." The airy bravado of her performance is reminiscent of that of the witty heroines of Restoration comedy: like Celimene in Molière's *Misanthrope,* Lady Mary lives within a social whirl, and part of the attraction Wortley must feel for her surely comes from the energy that the flurry of coaches, fine clothes, and witty exchanges generates. Lady Mary also echoes Millamant's answer for the pleasure she takes in the follies of her world: when asked by Mirabell, "How can you find delight in such society?" Millamant replies, "I please myself:—besides, sometimes to converse with fools is for my health" (2:ii). Like Congreve's heroine, Lady Mary refuses to give in to her suitor's fears and instead claims a right to full participation in society by devaluing the meaning of the "lesser" pleasures but refusing to cloister herself from their very real attractions.

Yet Wortley's fear is so palpable that, in one of his most passionate letters, written after he learns she has been ill, he actually expresses joy in imagining her beauty disfigured:

> An Aversion may possibly be remov'd, but the loss of you woud be irretrievable; there has not yet bin, there never will be, another L. M. You see how far a man's passion carries ⟨his⟩ reflexions. . . . I am not the least concern'd to fancy your Colour may receive some Alteration. I shoud be overjoy'd to hear your Beauty was very much impair'd, cou'd I be pleas'd with any thing that wou'd give you displeasure, for it woud lessen the number of your Admirers, but even the loss of a feature, nay of your Eyes themselves, wou'd not make you seem less beautiful. (20 April 1710; 1:28)

These sentiments, which Wortley intends as a compliment, are actually a painful indication of his insecurity, for the fantasy of real violence directed against her person reveals only the disturbing depth of his distrust.

This insecurity, and Lady Mary's response to it, can best be seen in a series of three letters: a compliment from Wortley generates an aggressive, negative response from Lady Mary, which produces an equally aggressive reply from Wortley. The debate begins with Wortley's insistence that epistolary style, more than female fashion, best displays a woman's feelings for her lover. Underlying the sentiment is his suspicion that a woman's romantic "performance" can be falsified through costume, whereas her "style" will reveal her sincerity: "Should you write to me it woud not be a greater Compliment. Every woman wou'd write instead of dressing for any lover she had not resolv'd to strike out of her list, that coud persuade herselfe she did it halfe so well as you. I know that when you write you shine out in all your beauty" (10 August 1710; 1:52). Wortley's desire for a particular kind of epistolary performance is nevertheless a request that Lady Mary display herself for him personally, that she "shine" in his private company in the stylistic "costume" he desires.

Lady Mary immediately responds by taking the offensive, first by disclaiming the importance of letter writing and then by positing a desire in Wortley that she proceeds to deny: "As to writeing, that any woman would do that, thought she writ well, now I say, no woman of common good sense would. At best, tis but doing a silly thing well, and I think tis much better not to do a silly thing at all" (22 August 1710; 1:55–56). She then takes the rather general metaphor offered by Wortley—that epistolary style and fashion are equivalent—and turns it into a concrete image: "You compare it to dressing. Suppose the comparison Just, perhaps the Spanish dresse would become my face very well, yet the whole Town would condemn me for the highest Extravagance if I went to Court in't, tho' it improv'd me to a Miracle. There are a thousand things not ill in themselves which custom makes unfit to be done." She then goes on to interpret Wortley's "compliment" as a demand for extravagant romantic language and insists that statements of personal feeling are entirely inappropriate in a young woman's epistolary discourse, especially in letters sent to a suitor who has yet to contract a real marriage settlement with her father: "You would have me say I am violently in Love. That is, finding you think better of me than you desire, you would have me give you a just cause to contemn me. I doubt much whither there is a creature in the world humble enough to do that." No matter how attractive the dress and the discourse might be under private circumstances, Lady Mary knows that a woman cannot contain the significance of her correspondence with a man; she will be open to censure, not just from her family and society but from her gallant himself if she allows her passions to overcome her "common good sense."

More important, she likens romantic protestations of feeling to self-mutilation: "I should not think you more unreasonable if you was in love with my Face and ask'd me to disfigure it to make you easy. I have heard of some Nuns that made use of that Expedient to secure their own happynesse, but amongst all the popish Saints and Martyrs I never read of one whose charity was sublime enough to make themselves deformd or ridiculous to restore their Lovers to peace and quietnesse." Echoing the "loss of feature" that Wortley imagined in the letter sent four months before, Lady Mary sees the marring of her beauty—the external, visual impact she has in the world—as equivalent to the besmirching of her reputation—the communal consensus of her internal value; and she refuses the self-inflicted diminishment.

At this point, it appears that the correspondents are at an impasse. Wortley, however, finds a way around Lady Mary's clever comparison when he qualifies her Spanish-dress metaphor and then takes advantage of the strategy she introduced: historical precedent. In doing so, he assumes the pedant's tone, a voice difficult for a young woman denied an extensive education to overcome:

> I have heard from good hands that many [women] have writ and have writ to declare that Passion which you are not the least acquainted with. I yield to you so far as to own it has not yet happend to myselfe. I dare say I never hinted to you I desird any such thing, but you suppose I do, only for an occasion of assuring me you dont value me overmuch. Your Comparison of the Spanish dress is not, I think, well appli'd. I agree a woman woud not go to Court in one, but woud certainly find out the means to be seen in it by the man she woud marry if she thought that woud secure him. You are out too in your Spanish story, for a young man did mangle his face that it might not charm any more. (24 October 1710; 1:59)

This letter is intended to embarrass her. First Wortley accuses her of misreading his intentions, of demanding protestations of love, when—in all innocence, he implies—he merely offered her a compliment on her style. More unpleasant still is his critique of her metaphor as "not well appli'd," an argument that reveals the most extreme instance of his objectifying Lady Mary into the embodiment of his desires, evidence of which he wants to see in her letters: because their correspondence is an entirely private matter, he insists that she should be willing to "dress up" for him in a language equivalent to a Spanish costume, that she should be willing to "perform" for him as she would not for others. Lady Mary is wise enough to know that such an argument is both naive and coersive. Her reputation and perhaps the course of the rest of her life are at stake in this correspondence, and, protestations to the contrary, neither she nor Wortley can keep their epistolary relationship entirely private.

This struggle and failure to find a mutually comprehensible language and compatible styles becomes the subject of a letter Lady Mary sends after meeting Wortley at the Steeles'. These moments together, which required elaborate planning and secret preparations, could be interpreted as Lady Mary's complying—in the real, not the epistolary, world—with the very demand Wortley makes above. However, rather than smoothing out their differences, their meeting acts to increase Wortley's suspicions. Lady Mary's frustration and anger grow out of their failure to interpret events similarly, their inability to share a common language:

> What recompence have I for all this? Have I the pleasure of obliging a Man that I esteem? On the contrary, you think me more inexcusable than [the Steeles] do, and that I would do the same for every Man in the world. After your Manner of thinking, every fresh instance of kindnesse is a New Crime.—How can you use me so? You call all things Criminal; my Confusion (which I know not how to overcome when I see you) is Peevishnesse, and my very sincerity is design. Am I to think you love me? I must come over to the Opinion of my Sister and own that (at least) I ought not to think so. (22 February 1711; 1:81–82)

The issue of sexual faithfulness is intimately linked with the problem of rhetorical sincerity, and each suspects the other of disingenuousness because language itself is the locus of conflict. The antithetical nature of their dialogue reveals that they are in many ways speaking entirely different languages. Lady Mary's "obliging" is an action "inexcusable" to Wortley. Her "kindness" becomes a "criminal" action in his mind. Worse still, they participate in completely contrary interpretive strategies: what Lady Mary interprets as a "sincere" act of love becomes a scheming "design" in Wortley's vocabulary.

The continual phenomenon of misunderstanding is recognized by both. Lady Mary complains, "Your last letter (which came safe to me by miracle) I don't understand a word of" (5 May 1710; 1:35). To this, Wortley replies, "If I mistake the meaning of [your letters] I hope you will give your selfe the trouble of explaining" (6 May 1710; 1:37). Complaint is so often answered by complaint that Wortley commands, "Tell me how to mend the stile if the fault is in that. If the Characters are not plain I can easily mend them" (3 March 1711; 1:87). After posing this easy solution without emotional content—perhaps it is his handwriting that is at fault—he plainly states his desire: "I always comprehend your expressions, but woud give a great deal to know what passes in your heart." Aware that in his mind there are two appropriate forms of discourse—plain business style, or language unembellished and therefore sincere, and writing that echoes the heart, or effusive protestations of romantic feelings—Lady Mary cannot risk this language of passion, for it could be ruinous to her reputation and make her vulnerable to him. She insists that she is writing as plainly as she can, and yet her clever, densely textured prose does not fit comfortably into the stylistic categories Wortley creates. He finds her "expressions" comprehensible but incompatible with her feelings, and, even though she chooses a moderate, often philosophical language only occasionally enlivened by wit and metaphor as the language most suitable to communicate her hopes and affections, he will not allow her that middle ground.

One might wonder why these two people continued to pursue a relationship so at odds, so full of misunderstandings, so seemingly incapable of mutual accord. Yet at times they could express their feelings tenderly. Wortley's passion takes the form of a vow: "The greatest part of my life shall be dedicated to you. From every thing that can lessen my Passion I will fly with as much speed as I shoud from the Plague. I shall sooner choose to see my heart torn from my breast than divided from you. . . . I now declare to you that I am already, if you please, marri'd to You" (7 August 1712; 1:145). And immediately before their elopement, he writes of her value to him: "I shall go to meet you with more joy than I shoud to take possession of Riches, Honour or Power; nay, then I shoud to meet you if you brought 'em along with you because I coud not so well convince you how much I value you" (11 August 1712; 1:152). These sentiments are echoed in Lady Mary's expressions of satisfaction with her lover: "I had rather be confine'd to a desart with you than enjoy the highes⟨t of⟩ Rank and fortune in a cou⟨rt with⟩ him I am condemn'd to" (17 July 1712; 1:129). There is no misunderstanding about what each surrenders in the union.[7] Wortley turns his back on the "Riches, Honour, and Power" of a marriage settlement, while Lady Mary foresees her own "desart" of solitude and lessened rank and fortune. The topos of deprivation, however, is outweighed by Lady Mary's affection: "I have an Esteem for you, with a mixture of more kindnesse than I imagin'd. That kindnesse would perswade me to abandonn all things for you, my Fame, my Family, the Settlement they have provided for me, and rather embark with you through all the hazards of perhaps finding my selfe reduce'd to the last extremes of Want (which would be heavier on me than any other body) than enjoy the certainty of a plentifull Fortune with another" (15 August 1712; 1:157). Yet even on the brink of their elopement, they cannot abandon their fears. Lady Mary worries about her dependence on him: "Refflect now for the last time in what manner you must take me. I shall come to you with only a Nightgown and petticoat, and that is all you will get with me" (16 August 1712; 1:160–61). Wortley succinctly commands silence: "If we shoud once be in a coach let us not say one word till we come before the parson, least we should engage in fresh disputes" (8 August 1712; 1:148).

The high seriousness of their epistolary courtship, however, culminated in an elopement that proved worthy of farce. Having discovered her correspondence with Wortley and intending to ensure that she marry the Irish suitor with whom he had signed a marriage contract, Lady Mary's father attempted to secret her away from Wortley's attentions by moving her miles away to Wiltshire. Yet when she and her party stopped for the night at an inn, unbeknownst to either of them, Wortley and his servant took rooms there as well. Guests at the inn, thinking that the men downstairs were highwaymen, were frightened by the commotion, but no one suspected that Wortley would eventually spirit her away. Exactly how they eloped and even when or where the ceremony was performed are not known, but two days later, when Wortley visited Steele, the marriage had become official, and Lady Mary had alienated herself from her family, most especially from her father, who refused to speak to her for years.

Yet silence ultimately becomes the source of Lady Mary's greatest displeasure with Wortley after the marriage. Her first letter as wife echoes Millamant's directive to Mirabell while it continues to acknowledge their uncertainty about epistolary style: "I don't know very well how to begin; I am perfectly unacquainted with a proper matrimonial stile. After all, I think tis best to write as if we were not marry'd at all. I Lament your Absence as if you was still my Lover, and I am impatient to hear you are got safe to Durham and that you have fix'd a time for your return" (22 October 1712; 1:168). The gradual dwindling away of whatever passion the two might have felt is clear in the course of a matrimonial correspondence that slowly shifts in style. Lady Mary takes a real interest in Wortley's political career, offering advice and strategies: "I am very sorry you have not yet a more sure place than Newark. The Tory Interest there is very strong. The Duke of Newcastle (who you know had more than double the power of Lord Pelham there) set up Brigadeir Sutton there a few years ago, and he lost it, after an Expence of £1,200 as I heard him say" (17 September 1714; 1:224–25). But because he settled her alone in the country shortly after the marriage, her advice goes generally unacknowledged.

As time goes by, two issues bring forth consistent emotion from her: anger at Wortley's abandoning her and his lack of interest in their young son. Lady Mary expresses her loneliness in the forms of concern for Wortley's health and fears that he no longer loves her; she writes, "I cannot forbear any longer telling you I think you use me very unkindly. I don't say so much of your absence as I should do if you was in the Country and I in London, because I would not have you beleive I am impatient to be in town when I say I am impatient to be with you. But I am very sensible I parted with you in July, and tis now the middle of November. As if this was not hardship enough you do not tell me you are sorry for it" (24 November 1714; 1:236). Sometimes her loneliness, when felt less keenly, she describes in the witty language of old, but these letters contain an edge that emphasizes her isolation: "I walk'd yesterday 2 hours on the Terrace. These are the most considerable Events that have happen'd in your absence, excepting that a good Natur'd Robin red breast kept me companny allmost all the afternoon, with so much good humour and Humanity as gives me faith for the peice of charity ascrib'd to them little Creatures in the Children in the Wood, which I have hitherto thought only a poetical Ornament to that history" (4 December 1712; 1:172). Wortley, rather than empathizing with her plight, takes the offensive by reiterating his old jealousy: "I can think of no other reason for your silence but your having better company than the Robin, who woud not have hindred you in writing. Whoever was with you, sure your absence might have bin excus'd for a minute to tell me of your health" (11 December 1712; 1:175). About their son, Lady Mary is more vehement. She ends two letters with complaints about Wortley's lack of interest in their child, one a sarcastic reminder and the other a piece of information Wortley should have solicited: "You have forgot, I suppose, that you have a little Boy" (January 1714; 1:204); "I will tell you the child is well thô you don't ask after it" (1 October 1714; 1:228).

Ultimately, even these squabbles, which indicate a degree of emotional involvement between the two, are replaced by the flat language Wortley had once hoped to hear from her. They become people who merely share mutual domestic concerns: "The hire of 2 Coach horses and a postillion from hence to London is £6 if they bear their own charges, and 5 if I do. You can Judge which is cheaper, to hire them here or from London. I have taken a Coachman for present use, but I have had him but 3 days, so can make no Judgment what he will prove. . . . Let me know if you would have me keep him, or whither you have hir'd another" (6 December 1714; 1:239). Their struggle for intimacy finally dwindles to this—letters that treat only plans for Lady Mary's move to London or the renting of a house and domestic goods. And while they continue, throughout the whole of their marriage, to correspond in an always civilized fashion, their passionate and involved negotiations about the proper style, acceptable decorums, and the necessary forms result only in distance as Lady Mary and Wortley become strangers living in the same house and using the language of business or living apart and speaking the rhetoric of acquaintances who wish one another, from time to time, good health and happiness.

II

In 1715 Lady Mary and Alexander Pope commenced a friendship that began with their mutual interest in poetry and their shared community of friends; their relationship became entirely epistolary, however, when Lady Mary left for Turkey in 1716.[8] This second "romantic" encounter with a man is an equally dramatic conflict of established discourses, and the progress, or lack of progress, in their relationship can be traced in their differing epistolary styles. Calling this series of letters a "farce of incomprehension," Patricia Meyer Spacks argues most persuasively that Pope writes to Lady Mary out of an established literary convention: the effusively romantic voice of Voiture. Yet her conclusion—that Lady Mary was always complicitous in Pope's romance and had only "the antiromantic, antitender, self-presentation of refusal"[9]—overlooks the other rhetorical devices Lady Mary exploits. To Pope's representation of himself as the romantic gallant and to his attempts to locate her in the role of "Woman" in an established "public" voice, Lady Mary answers in the "private" discourse of Royal Society empiricism, a language that offers to him individual experience and observation—the products of her perception, but not her heart.

The bookish flavor of their correspondence is present in the very first letter he sends: "I attend you in Spirit thro' all your Ways, I follow you in Books of Travells thro' every Stage, I wish for you and fear for you thro' whole Folio's. You make me shrink at the past dangers of dead Travellers" (20 August 1716; 1:356). Because his declarations of feeling are so overt, Lady Mary has no need to defend herself from jealousies or accusations about her irregularities, for Pope fashions extravagant compliments intended to free her from all restraining decorums. Eventually, he will dare to "liberate" even her body, but not before he compliments her virtue. To Lady Mary's graphic descriptions of the treacherous territory and the very real dangers ahead of her, Pope points to what the world would lose were tragedy her destiny: "For God's sake, value Yourself a little more, and don't give us cause to imagine that such extravagant Virtue can exist any where else than in a Romance" (October 1716; 1:364).

This "virtue" is central in his romantic "plot," and, when she is told that only extraordinary fictional heroines are her equals, she is willing on occasion to play the romance game with him—but only on her terms. When she expresses her own fears concerning the possible dangers along the road, she romantically enhances her depictions of the threatening countryside, but she assigns herself the part, not of the virtuous heroine, but of the courageous *hero:* "I ought to bid Adeiu to my freinds with the same Solemnity as if I was going to mount a breach, at least if I am to beleive the Information of the people here, who denounce all sort of Terrors to me; and indeed the Weather is at present such as very few ever set out in. I am threaten'd at the same time with being froze to death, bury'd in the Snow, and taken by the Tartars who ravage that part of Hungary I am to passe" (16 January 1717; 1:296–97). While she takes the part of the active subject, Pope offers compliments and exaggerated declarations of his feelings and intentions, a performance that places him in a "passive" position. To his insistence on her virtue he adds this description of himself: "I tremble for you the more, because (whether you'll believe it or not) I am capable myself of following one I lov'd, not only to Constantinople, but to those parts of India, where they tell us the Women best like the Ugliest fellows, as the most admirable productions of nature, and look upon Deformities as the Signatures of divine Favour" (October 1716; 1:364). While Lady Mary appropriates a courageous, active womanhood—the role of the female traveler and accomplished writer—the premier poet of the land must sit at home waiting, attempting to elevate his "biological irregularities" into the realm of the divine.

Pope's insistence that Lady Mary speak of herself and what she feels grows out of his representing her departure as his own personal loss, and Lady Mary herself contributes to his anxiety. Her description of a "most remarkable Accident," the near overturning of her coach, includes a none too subtle desire to be immortalized as the female Orpheus. She writes that, had the coach actually overturned into the Hebrus, her death might have been celebrated:

> If I had much regard for the Glorys that one's Name enjoys after Death I should certainly be sorry for having miss'd the romantic conclusion of swimming down the same River in which the Musical Head of Orpheus repeated verses so many ages since. . . . Who knows but some of your bright Wits might have found it a subject affording many poetical Turns, and have told the World in a Heroic Elegy that
>
> As equal were our Souls, so equal were our fates?
>
> I dispair of ever having so many fine things said for me as so extrodinary a Death would have given Occasion for. (1 April 1717; 1:330–31)

Positioning herself as one who has metamorphosed into the poet empowered to sing the mysteries, she can quite legitimately wish for "a Heroic Elegy" if she fails to return home.

To express his anxiety about her safety and his sense of loss, Pope has his own poetic rhetoric of passion on which to draw. Geoffrey Tillotson has argued that the loss of Lady Mary's presence evokes in Pope the melancholy death would occasion and that at least some portion of Pope's "Elegy to the Memory of an Unfortunate Lady" comes out of his fears about Lady Mary's safety: "The ambition Pope speaks of [in the poem] seems to be heroic, the spirit of the angels, gods, kings, and heroes. Pope may have had Lady Mary's heroic dangers in his mind. He probably wrote the poem when for all he knew she might be dead." [10]

Pope also composed *Eloisa to Abelard* during her absence, and the rhetoric of emotional extreme found in Eloisa's language has its echoes in Pope's letters.[11] He sent Lady Mary a copy of the poem while she was in Turkey and included a note saying, "There are few things in [his *Works*] but what you have already seen, except the Epistle of Eloisa to Abelard; in which you will find one passage, that I can't tell whether to wish you should understand, or not?" (June 1717; 1:407). The passage to which he refers is very likely the conclusion of the poem:

> Such if there be, who love so long, so well,
> Let him our sad, our tender story tell;
> The well-sung woes will soothe my pensive ghost;
> He best can paint them who shall feel them most.

Separation and death, feelings of absence and loss, produce the two conflicting impulses out of which he writes. In the first, Pope sees Lady Mary as a disembodied spirit, an ethereal creature, even an angel. Shortly after the death of his father, Pope writes to her that "a Letter from you sooths me in my Reveries; 'tis like a Conversation with some Spirit of the other world the least Glympse of whose Favour setts one above all taste of the Things of this. Indeed there is little or nothing Angelical left behind you. The Women here are—Women" (1718; 1:469). The specialness that Lady Mary had so hoped to convince Wortley she possessed is not only recognized but exploited by Pope in the following elaborate compliment to her extraordinary nature: after comparing his letters to her with "addresses only to Invisible & distant Beings," he writes, "If I hear from you, I look upon it as little less than a miracle, or extraordinary Visitation from another world; Tis a sort of Dream of an agreable thing, which subsists no more to me, but however 'tis such a Dream as exceeds most of the Dull Realities of my Life" (June 1717; 1:406). The fact that a man so often compliments her virtue, her angelic spirit, her uniqueness—rather than repeatedly insisting that she is "irregular" and worthy of suspicion, as Wortley had—might lead a less sensitive woman to respond in kind, pleased to be celebrated and valued. However, Lady Mary understood that Pope was implicating her in his romance by imposing upon her the role of his heroine.

Rather than rejecting these moves outright, Lady Mary will occasionally play the part of "absent spirit" with Pope. After receiving the letter where he supposes her "dead and bury'd," she writes that "I have already let you know that I am Still alive, but to say Truth I look upon my present Circumstances to be exactly the Same with those of departed Spirits. The Heats of Constantinople have driven me to this place which perfectly answers the Description of the Elysian fields" (1:365). The letter goes on, however, to provide, not a romantic answer to Pope's hopes, but a detailed description of life in Belgrade, including the fruit trees, fountains, walks, the sea, and the inhabitants. Even when she does express an emotion, it is a backhanded compliment to the life Pope leads in England:

> To Say Truth, I am Sometimes very weary of this Singing and dancing and Sunshine, and wish for the Smoak and Impertinencies in which You toil, thô I endeavour to perswade my Self that I live in a more agreeable Variety than You do, and that Monday Seting of partridges, Tuesday reading English, Wednesday Studying the Turkish Language (in which, by the way, I am already very learned), Thursday Classical Authors, Friday spent in Writing, Saturday at my Needle, and Sunday admitting of Visits and hearing Musick, is a better way of disposing the Week than Monday at the Drawing Room, Tuesday Lady Mohun's, Wednesday the Opera, Thursday the Play, Friday Mrs. Chetwynd's, etc.: a perpetual round of hearing the same Scandal and seeing the same follies acted over and over, which here affect me no more than they do other dead people. (17 June 1717; 1:366–67)

She will accept Pope's fears about her safety, but she will not answer him as the female Voiture. The image of a spirit that he imposes on her she clearly modifies to suit her purposes: inhabiting the world of the dead, she can interpret the frivolity of English life as stifling and trivial in its regularity in contrast to the pleasures of her intellectual work, including becoming "very learned" in Turkish.

Pope's second and more daring strategy grows out of an opposite impulse. Rather than an ethereal spirit, she becomes the embodiment of his desires. He writes, "You have already (without passing the bounds of Christendom) outtraveld the Sin of Fornication, and are happily arrived at the free Region of Adultery" (10 November 1716; 1:368). He urges that their geographical separation allows them to ignore epistolary decorums, and the result is his locating Lady Mary's value in her progressively naked body:

I foresee that the further you go from me, the more freely I shall write, & if (as I earnestly wish) you would do the same, I can't guess where it will end? Let us be like modest people, who when they are close together keep all decorums, but if they step a little aside, or get to the other end of a room, can untye garters or take off Shifts without scruple. (1716–17; 1:384)

This metaphor of stripping off one's clothes runs directly counter to Wortley's suggestion that Lady Mary "dress up" for him, yet each man insists that he can best direct Lady Mary's epistolary style. Like Wortley, Pope wants more from her than she is willing to give, and, perhaps in frustration or perhaps out of simple wish fulfillment, Pope asks her four times to find and bring back a Circassian slave girl—one who looks exactly like her—so that he can serve as both slave and master to this pseudo–Lady Mary: "She, whom my Imagination had drawn more amiable than Angels, as beautiful as the Lady who was to chuse her by a resemblance to so divine a face; she, whom my hopes had already transported over so many Seas and Lands, & whom my eager wishes had already lodg'd in my arms & heart" (October 1716; 1:364). If he cannot in reality ask her to untie her garters or import a slave girl, he can "innocently" enough express his desire to see her body naked by disguising it in the language of the soul. In an extraordinarily specific expression of this hope, he imagines her return to England: "I expect to see your Soul as much thinner dressd as your Body; and that you have left off, as unwieldy & cumbersome, a great many damn'd European Habits. Without offence to your modesty be it spoken, I have a burning desire to see your Soul stark naked, for I am confident 'tis the prettiest kind of white Soul, in the universe" (1 September 1718; 1:494). This process of "paganizing" Lady Mary herself takes its most concrete form late in Lady Mary's travels, when Pope expresses his hope that she has metamorphosed from an English matron into an exotic, non-Christian, uninhibited female body eager to indulge in pleasure:

I doubt not but I shall be told, (when I come to follow you thro' those Countries) in how pretty a manner you accomodated yourself to the Customes of the True-Believers. At this Town, they will say . . . here she was bathd and anointed; & there she parted with her black Full-bottome. At every Christian Virtue you lost, and at every Christian Habit you quitted, it will be decent for me to fetch a holy Sigh, but still I shall proceed to follow you. . . . Lastly I shall hear how the very first Night you lay at Pera, you had a Vision of Mahomet's Paradise, and happily awaked without a Soul. From which blessed instant the beautiful Body was left at full liberty to perform all the agreeable functions it was made for. (10 November 1716; 1:369)

She, however, refuses to play the part of sexual object in Pope's imagination, simply by failing to mention his request for a slave-girl or his vision of her liberated sexuality. The power of silence, coupled with distance and absence, is a strategy of rejection impossible for Pope to overcome.

The rhetoric she offers instead insists that she is an artist and intellectual equal. She also has the powerful advantage of living in and writing about exotic locales, historical sites, and privileged information denied to him and other writers. Pope's hope for intimate discourse therefore confronts Lady Mary's role as informed insider. Pope will plead, "For Gods sake Madam, when you write to me, talk of your self, there is nothing I so much desire to hear of: talk a great deal of yourself, that She who I always thought talk'd best, may speak upon the best subject. The Shrines and Reliques you tell me of, no way engage my curiosity. I had ten times rather go on Pilgrimage to see your Face, than St. John Baptist's Head" (10 November 1716; 1:368). But she responds with perfectly impersonal reportage:

We pass'd over the feilds of Carlowitz, where the last great Victory was obtained by Prince Eugene over the Turks. The marks of that Glorious bloody day are yet recent, the feild being strew'd with the Skulls and Carcases of unbury'd Men, Horses and Camels. I could not look without horror on such numbers of mangled humane bodys, and refflect on the Injustice of War, that makes murther not only necessary but meritorious. Nothing seems to me a plainer proofe of the irrationality of Mankind (whatever fine claims we pretend to Reason) than the rage with which they contest for a small spot of Ground, when such vast parts of fruitfull Earth lye quite uninhabited. (12 February 1717; 1:305)

In Maynard Mack's words, her response is a "well-observed but low-key and quite impersonal travelogue, bristling with enough exotic details of costume and custom to make the heart of a less determined swain quail." [12] She will not be Pope's personal tour guide, nor will she enter

into his closed, sexual universe; instead she plays the empowered observer who writes philosophically, offering universal interpretations for
what she sees.

Most especially, she is living the literature about which Pope can only
read. From Adrianople, she sends an evocative letter about the truth of
the pastorals in Turkey:

> I have often seen [the inhabitants] and their children siting on the banks
> and playing on a rural Instrument perfectly answering the description of
> the Ancient Fistula. . . . The Young Lads gennerally divert themselves
> with makeing Girlands for their favourite Lambs, which I have often seen
> painted and adorn'd with flowers, lying at their feet while they sung or
> play'd. It is not that they ever read Romances, but these are the Ancient
> Amusements here, . . . I no longer look upon Theocritus as a Romantic
> Writer; he has only given a plain image of the Way of Life amongst the
> Peasants of his Country. (1 April 1717; 1:331–32)

Erudite and perceptive, she even presumes to demystify the classics
for him, calling the literary landscape merely a "Way of Life" that can
still be observed. She compliments, again in a backhanded fashion,
Pope's translation of *The Iliad* by claiming that the text is enriched by
her personal experiences in the classical landscape: "I read over your
Homer here with an infinite Pleasure, and find several little passages
explain'd that I did not before entirely comprehend the Beauty of, many
of the customs and much of the dress then in fashion being yet retain'd"
(1:332). She goes on to cite the snowy veils of Helen as still fashionable,
the embroidered belts and golden claps worn by Menelaus as still in evidence, and the great ladies working their looms, exactly as Andromache
had. Pope's fantasies of romance are answered with data, information
that Lady Mary implies might enrich his own poetic endeavors.

She even presumes to teach him in the arena that was almost entirely
his public province: poetry. Not only does she write to him about the
Turkish poetry she reads, but she also sends one of her own translations
of a contemporary Turkish poem as accompaniment. She rather pedan-
tically informs him that Turkish poetry is written in an "exact scripture
stile" called the "Sublime," and she presumes that he "would be pleas'd
to see a genuine example of this." The pleasure she expresses concerns
her "power to satisfy [his] Curiosity" by sending a copy of the verses that
Ibrahim Bassa, the reigning favorite, had made for the young princess.

Citing the poem's likeness to the Song of Solomon, she offers him her own "litteral Translation" which has "receiv'd no poetical Touches from {her interpreters'} hands":

Stanza 1st

1   V. The Nightingale now wanders in the Vines,
      Her Passion is to seek Roses.

2   I went down to admire the beauty of the Vines,
      The sweetness of your charms has ravish'd my Soul.

3   Your Eyes are black and Lovely
      But wild and disdainfull as those of a Stag.

Stanza 2nd

1   The wish'd possession is delaid from day to day,
      The cruel Sultan Achmet will not permit me to see those
         cheeks more vermillion than roses.

2   I dare not snatch one of your kisses,
      The sweetness of your charms has ravish'd my Soul.

3   Your Eyes are black and lovely
      But wild and disdainfull as those of a Stag.

Stanza 3rd

1   The wretched Bassa Ibrahim sighs in these verses,
      One Dart from your Eyes has pierc'd through my Heart.

2   Ah, when will the Hour of possession arrive?
      Must I yet wait a long time?
      The sweetnesse of your charms has ravish'd my soul.

3   Ah Sultana, stag-ey'd, an Angel amongst angels,
      I desire and my desire remains unsatisfy'd.
      Can you take delight to prey upon my heart?

Stanza 4th

1   My crys peirce the Heavens,
      My Eyes are without sleep;
      Turn to me, Sultana, let me gaze on thy beauty.

2   Adeiu, I go down to the Grave;
      If you call me I return.
      My Heart is hot as Sulphur; sigh and it will flame.

3   Crown of my Life, fair light of my Eyes, my Sultana,
         my Princesse,
      I rub my face against the Earth, I am drown'd in scalding

60

Tears——I rave!
Have you no Compassion? Will you not turn to look upon me?

(1:334–35)

She then comments on the poem by judging the image of the "stag-
ey'd" Sultana as "a very lively image of the Fire and indifference in his
mistrisse's Eyes," but this reference to the passion of the subject—an
emotional context Lady Mary has, in the rest of the correspondence,
taken pains to avoid—locates her in the role he selects. Thus she is
faced with competing desires: to establish her own poetic territory, she
must control the beautifully sensuous and romantic subject through the
detached but empowered intelligence she wants to project.

She comes up with two dazzlingly clever solutions. First, by comparing their mutual experiences as translators, she attempts to downplay
the passion by claiming that one cannot judge the lofty sentiments by
the music in ancient verses: "You are so well acquainted with Homer,
you cannot but have observ'd the same thing, and you must have the
same Indulgence for all Oriental Poetry." Then, in a sidelong comment
on Pope's emotional outpourings, and perhaps in a covert reference to
Eloisa to Abelard, Lady Mary claims that these verses are more passionate
at the conclusion "as 'tis natural for people to warm themselves by their
own discourse, especially on a Subject where the Heart is concern'd."
Her second strategy occurs in a smooth, almost artless transition. She
comments that the opening of the poem is "much the same thing as if an
English poem should begin by saying: Now Philomela sings—Or what
if I turn'd the whole into the stile of English Poetry to see how twould
look?" And she does just that:

Stanza 1
Now Philomel renews her tender strain,
Indulging all the night her pleasing Pain.
I sought the Groves to hear the Wanton sing,
There was a face more beauteous than the Spring.
Your large stag's-eyes where 1,000 glorys play,
As bright, as Lively, but as wild as they.

2
In vain I'm promis'd such a heavenly prize,
Ah, Cruel Sultan who delays my Joys!
While pierceing charms transfix my amorous Heart

I dare not snatch one kiss to ease the smart.
Those Eyes like etc.

3

Your wretched Lover in these lines complains,
From those dear Beautys rise his killing pains.
When will the Hour of wish'd-for Bliss arrive?
Must I wait longer? Can I wait and live?
Ah, bright Sultana! Maid divinely fair!
Can you unpitying see the pain I bear?

Stanza 4th

The Heavens relenting hear my peircing Crys,
I loath the Light and Sleep forsakes my Eyes.
Turn thee, Sultana, ere thy Lover dyes.
Sinking to Earth, I sigh the last Adeiu—
Call me, my Goddesse, and my Life renew.
My Queen! my Angel! my fond Heart's desire,
I rave—my bosom burns with Heavenly fire.
Pity that Passion which thy charms inspire.

Regularized into heroic couplets, Lady Mary's English version becomes a traditional courtly love complaint, complete with the conventions of the genre—Philomel sings of "pleasing Pain" in groves where "wretched Lover[s]" sigh, rage, and die. In her most pointed strategy to mute the poem's passion, she apologizes for the "deficiencies" of their shared native language: "I cannot determine upon the whole how well I have succeeded in the Translation. Neither do I think our English proper to express such violence of passion, which is very seldom felt amongst us; . . . You see I am pritty far gone in Oriental Learning, and to say truth I study very hard. I wish my studys may give me occasion of entertaining your curiosity" (1:337). Concluding that their mutual Englishness is not conducive to passion, she satisfies Pope's intellectual curiosity, not his erotic fantasies, and appropriates for herself the poetical territory of contemporary Eastern love poetry, a commodity to which he has no access.

The battle of poetical wills, and perhaps the beginning of the end of their friendship, is signaled by Pope's sending to Lady Mary a copy of his epitaphs on the deaths of two rural lovers. He writes sentimentally of the two lovers having taken shelter from a storm only to be struck by lightning and killed: "John with one arm about his Sarah's neck, and the other held over her face as if to screen her from the Lightning. They were struck dead, & already grown stiff and cold in this tender posture" (1 September 1718; 1:495). Pope claims the critics prefer "the godly" version of his epitaphs, but he wishes that Lady Mary had been in England "to have done this office better":

> When Eastern Lovers feed the fun'ral fire,
> On the same Pile their faithful Fair expire;
> Here pitying Heav'n that virtue mutual found,
> And blasted both, that it might neither wound.
> Hearts so sincere, th' Almighty saw well-pleas'd,
> Sent his own Lightning, & the Victims seiz'd.
>
> I.
>
> Think not, by rig'rous Judgment seiz'd,
>   A Pair so faithful could expire;
> Victims so pure Heav'n saw well-pleas'd,
>   And snatchd them in celestial fire.
>
> 2.
>
> Live well, & fear no sudden fate:
>   When God calls Virtue to the grave,
> Alike 'tis Justice, soon, or late,
>   Mercy alike, to kill, or save.
> Virtue unmov'd, can hear the Call,
> And face the Flash that melts the Ball.
>
> (1:495)

Pope laments Lady Mary's absence from England, supposing that she, too, might have written a fine epitaph, but he closes by preferring a "Tear from the finest eyes in the world" as her honored monument to the lovers. This is the final instance of his locating Lady Mary's value in the body: he "touches" her and evokes a response, not in her writing but in her tears.

In one of the last extant letters from Lady Mary to Pope, she replies to this tribute to the fallen lovers. Rather than answering him on sentimental terms, however, she again presents to him a more detached vision of English love. After commenting that young John's endeavor to shield his beloved from the lightning "was a natural Action and what he would have certainly done for his Horse if he had been in the same situation" and after recounting the young people's death, Lady Mary asks:

> Who knows if 'twas not kindly done?
> For had they seen the next Year's Sun
> A Beaten Wife and Cuckold Swain
> Had jointly curs'd the marriage chain.
> Now they are happy in their Doom
> For P[ope] has wrote upon their Tomb.
> (September 1718; 1:446)

This prediction of wife beating and adultery serves as her final rejection of Pope's romanticizing of their relationship. Her response has been labeled cynical and hard-hearted by Sherburn, for instance, who feels the need to apologize for Lady Mary, claiming that her "callousness" was occasioned by her preoccupation with preparations for the journey home (1:522). But even Edith Sitwell, a staunch apologist for Pope and usually one of Lady Mary's strongest detractors, in this case actually appreciates her response, seeing in it "a fund of common sense, a good deal of natural cynicism, and a certain coarse good humor." [13] Pope himself was not always so straightforwardly emotional about the deaths of these lovers. He sent the following couplet to Martha Blount and to John Caryll, but *not* to Lady Mary: "Here lye two poor Lovers, who had the mishap / Tho very chaste people, to die of a Clap" (1:349). That he considered Lady Mary the object of his romantic fantasies has no clearer indication than this; he will not allow her to join the ranks of flesh and blood women. Lady Mary is for Pope the Spirit, the naked soul of his fantasies. For Lady Mary, Pope is fellow artist and friend. She never wavers in her rejection of his imposed role of heroine; she never surrenders her project to meet him on artistic terms.

It is not surprising, then, that the friendship reached only a stalemate, for each is playing a different game according to a different set of rules. The breakup of their friendship and the subsequent poetic wars waged in public are too familiar to recount here. But this early battle of the seducer and the seduced ended in stasis. Neither of the strong-willed correspondents was willing to relinquish the right to create a personally fashioned performance, and in the fight for the position of subject neither wins, because each maintains the status of subject simply by ignoring the other's objectification.

III

Lady Mary's midlife infatuation with Francesco Algarotti, a handsome young Italian who had made a reputation in the sciences and in belles lettres, reveals a side of her seen nowhere else in her correspondence. The two first met in London in April 1736, when Algarotti was welcomed, on an introduction from Voltaire, into intellectual and social circles. The Royal Society and the Society of Antiquaries, especially impressed by his translation of Newton's *Optics* into scholarly Italian dialogues, invited his membership. He was appreciated for his charm and wit not only by Lady Mary but by Lord Hervey, who subsequently became her rival for the attentions of this man half her age.

She seems not to have recognized Algarotti's unsuitability as the object of her passions: he was predominantly homosexual in his romantic attachments, ambitious for advancement in the political and intellectual arenas, personally cool and detached. Yet Lady Mary immediately began a correspondence with him and continued to pursue him even after he sailed with Lord Baltimore for Saint Petersburg. There he cultivated the patronage of Frederick of Prussia and was ultimately ennobled as Count Algarotti. After nearly three years of correspondence, Lady Mary left England in 1739 and quietly settled in Italy, hoping to create a life close to him. At the time, she had few family responsibilities in England: her sister's care had been taken over by the Mar family; her daughter had married and was living in Scotland; her son was safely tucked away in Holland with a tutor. But after waiting for nearly two years for his return to Italy, she was forced to acknowledge, after a 1741 meeting, that all her plans had been mere fantasy. She chose, however, to remain in Italy and take up her life again, alone.[14]

In letters to him, she loosens all restraints and writes—often in French—effusively, passionately, expectantly, and despairingly. She is freed to do so with Algarotti because she is not the object of male attention: she is not constantly besieged, as she was with Wortley, having to insist repeatedly that her prose is as plain and sincere as she can create; nor does she desire to distance herself, as she did with Pope, by emphasizing what she sees and thinks. Algarotti becomes the object of her romantic quest, and thus she exchanges the rhetoric of the philosophical negotiator and the accomplished artist for the language of operatic excess. In taking the part of the active subject, the agent who seeks to woo and win her beloved through the power of a woman's discourse, Lady Mary writes letters that reveal an identity in tumult, even in crisis. She roams the literary landscape, seizing temporarily and sequentially a series of models for love and desire, trying to discover the discourse that will unlock his passion. Unfortunately, none of his letters from this period survives, and so the dramatic nature of their epistolary dialogue is not recoverable; yet her need to chide him for his silence and his continued absence are clues to his lack of interest, and it is this resistance that becomes the most important force shaping her rhetoric.

In the extremity of her desire, she often turns to classical antecedents; the *Heroides* especially allows her to appropriate and exploit the extravagant rhetoric of abandoned heroines lamenting the loss of their beloveds. This rhetorical strategy leads her, quite naturally, into positioning Algarotti as an absent but powerful, and even spiritual, presence, and thus she moves equally easily into the language of religion to make him a beautiful icon. This topos of courtly love necessarily provokes startling role reversals and an almost blasphemous religious wit. Most important, by taking on the role of subject in this "romance," representing herself as heroic in her pursuit and ardent in her quest, she generates the discourse by moving into her own imagination where the very act of writing fuels her emotions: the letters—especially in the absence of Algarotti's correspondence—seem directed into the void, and there, echoing and reverberating back, they generate even greater emotional intensity.

Surrendering philosophical control for what she promises is the transparency Wortley had once demanded, Lady Mary assures Algarotti that her letters will reveal to him what he has never seen before: the soul of a woman.

> Vous verrez (ce qu'on n'a pas vûe jusqu'ici) le fidele portrait d'un Coeur de femme sans detour ou deguisement, peint au naturel, qui se donne pour ce qu'elle est, et qui ne vous cache ni vous farde rien. Mes foiblesses et mes emportemens doivent attirer au moins vostre curiosité en vous presentant la vraie disection d'une Ame femelle. On dit que Montagne plait par cette naiveté qui decouvre jusqu'a ses defauts, et j'ai cette merite si je n'ai point d'autres aupres de vous.

> [You will see (what has never been seen till now) the faithful picture of a woman's Heart without evasion or disguises, drawn to the life, who

presents herself for what she is, and who neither hides nor glosses over anything from you. My weaknesses and my outbursts ought at least to attract your curiosity, in presenting to you the accurate dissection of a female Soul. It is said that Montaigne pleases by that naturalness which reveals even his faults, and I have that merit if I have no others in your eyes.] (20 September 1736; 2:107, 503) [15]

Echoing Pope's "window in the bosom," Lady Mary uses an image drawn from the sciences and appropriate to Algarotti's own intellectual interests, "la vraie disection d'une Ame femelle," as illustration of the minute exactness she will bring to the examination. The portrait "drawn to life" does not, however, concern her external beauty: she does not "dress up" as Wortley had wished, nor is she nakedly displayed as Pope had hoped. She claims instead to send him "a faithful picture of a woman's Heart" in an unmediated and transparent discourse that, because it cites even her faults, contains a paradoxical kind of purity. Yet her notions of "sans detour ou deguisement" are not altogether clear to her, for in this instance she immediately appropriates another *writer's* naturalness ("naiveté") as her own, hoping that the pleasure Montaigne generates will translate similarly to Algarotti. Through the course of the correspondence, she seizes examples of love and the extremes of passion found in art and literature as models, and thus she makes the satiric letter sent to Anne Wortley years before—where she claimed ironically to look for love's precedents in books—a reality.

The most powerful antecedents to which she has recourse, for both herself and Algarotti, are those found in classical literature. The grandeur of the Golden Age emerges in her representation of Algarotti as Apollo. In a letter that opens with complaints about a toothache as well as the noise, political divisions, and sickness in the city, she contemplates his return and is revived:

'Tis enough that you can make me insensible either to pain or politics, but I must necessarily be dull when the Sun and you are both so distant from me; may the spring bring a return of both.

You, Lovely Youth, shall my Apollo prove,
Adorn my Verse, and tune my Soul to Love.
(24 February 1738; 2:115)

Her feelings, which function as a kind of narcotic against the pains of human existence, also provide poetic inspiration. To Pope, she will send her translations of Eastern poetry while simultaneously denying any personal connection with the sensuality they convey, and she never offers poetry to Wortley, except ironically. It is only with Algarotti that she permits herself to cultivate, in extravagant fashion, male desires—in the main because she is uncertain about the very existence of such desires. She does so, however, by concentrating on her own. Thus the epistolary cycle, which usually demands that one write while considering the recipient's needs as much as one's own, becomes a self-contained, self-sustaining cycle: by magnifying Algarotti into this mythic figure, she places him out of her reach; his distance serves only to increase the intensity of her desires, and so she picks up her pen again.

To his Apollo, Lady Mary offers a series of literary equivalents drawn from classical heroines who endured the pain of separation and the grief of absence. Algarotti's silence and her own uncertainty about his well-being find an echo in an Homeric parallel: "J'ai été la Penelope de vostre absence, negligant tous les objets que je voyez pour m'entretenir sans cesse des charmes d'un fugitif dont je ne sçavois pas mesme la demeure, et me doutoit quelque fois de l'existence" ["I have been the Penelope of your absence, neglecting all the objects that I saw in order to dwell every moment on the charms of a fugitive whose abode I did not even know, and whose existence I sometimes doubted"] (11 July 1738; 2:116, 504). In this startlingly revealing expression of the degree of her objectification of him, she claims to neglect "les objets que je voyez" in favor of "des charmes d'un fugitif"—thus making him present, if only in her imagination. Her characterization of him as a "fugitive" also resonates perhaps in ways unbeknown to her, for this Odysseus seems as much to flee from her Circe-like calling as struggle to return to Penelope patiently weaving at home.

Dido, however, stands as Lady Mary's most important literary antecedent, for this heroine best represents her feelings about her beloved's resistance. Shortly after Algarotti returned to Italy in 1736, she sends a letter that opens with a long Latin quotation from the *Aeneid* that describes the peaceful slumbers of the land: "The woods and wild seas had sunk to rest—the hour when stars roll midway in their gliding course, when all the land is still, . . . and they that dwell in fields of tangled brakes, couched in sleep beneath the silent night, [and with hearts forgetful of toil, laid aside their troubles]." [16] Juxtaposed to this tranquility is Dido's distress: "But not so the soul-racked Phoenician queen; she never sinks to sleep, nor draws the night into eyes or heart. Her pangs redouble, and her love, swelling up, surges afresh." Such poetic emotion, heightened and exaggerated, places her lament in the tradition of the *Heroides,* texts that provide Lady Mary with a voice that foregrounds female subjectivity, validates female passion, and confers female power. [17] Examining the heroic epistle, Gillian Beer claims that the classical heroines write out of the hope that precedes despair in a form that accords importance to women's erotic experience and to their assertive rhetorical expressions. Calling the poems "ceremonies of passion" where the heroines write in an attempt to move their partners, Beer concludes that these heroines, lamenting the "loss of plenitude," experience emotions that become "gigantic" because they are not shaped by a reply: "The grotesque amplification of heroic epistle shows emotions ballooning outward to fill empty space, language unmitigated by response." [18]

Lady Mary's own passions, ceremoniously recounted and answered by silence, balloon out in just this fashion as she feeds on his absence and on her own expressions of longing. The dramatic nature of the heroic epistle, a performative quality long recognized as inhering in the genre, is an especially attractive element for Lady Mary, whose theatrical expressions of desire are dependent on Algarotti's distance. Daniel Gunn goes so far as to liken the epistle to the "big" scenes from the grand French neoclassical dramas, *Phèdre* in particular, and he claims that Pope's *Eloisa to Abelard* employs a rhetoric "consciously heightened and exaggerated" that serves to intensify Eloisa's confusion about a desire she is unable either to satisfy or to renounce. [19] As evidenced above, Lady Mary was altogether resistant to Pope's expressions of his desire and confusion, but she does not hesitate to appropriate such discourse as a model for her own. And even though she promises Algarotti the unmediated product of her consciousness—"the soul of a woman"—in reality she offers him the same shaped and performative declarations spoken by the tragic heroines.

Yet after opening the Dido letter with the images of the repose of the landscape and the anxiety of the "soul-racked Phoenician queen," Lady Mary then claims to possess a soul greater than that of the classical heroine:

Je suis mille fois plus a plaindre que la triste Didon, et j'ai mille fois plus des raisons de me donner la mort. . . . Je me suis jetté a la tête d'un étranger tout comme elle, mais au lieu de crier parjure et perfide quand mon petit Aenée temoigne qu'il a envie de me quitter, j'ÿ donne les mains par un sentiment de Generosité dont Virgile n'a pas crû les femmes capable.

[I am a thousand times more to be pitied than the sad Dido, and I have a thousand more reasons to kill myself. . . . I have thrown myself at the head of a foreigner just as she did, but instead of crying perjurer and villain when my little Aeneas shows that he wants to leave me, I consent to it through a feeling of Generosity which Virgil did not think women capable of.] (2:104–5, 501)

In positing that her unhappiness is more extreme than Dido's and by claiming a "generosity" with which Virgil supposed women unacquainted, she performs a doubly powerful rhetorical feat: she suggests the limitations of the fictional heroines on whom she could draw and creates a representation of herself as superior to her classical models. Robert Halsband suggests that Lady Mary's "paraphrasing her own emotions with classical poetry was to elevate them, to endow them with spacious dignity for Algarotti as well as for herself,"[20] but such sentiments more importantly provide her with an illusion of control: her most extravagant turn, the claim that her female strength of generosity takes the form of granting "little Aeneas" his freedom, is intended to function as a means of domesticating her "foreigner," but it is clear that he, like Dido's Aeneas, is beyond the power of her rhetoric.

Moreover, like the heroines of old, Lady Mary does not speak; she writes, in a language she hopes will "seal up the gap between body and language, between enactment and desire, between memory and the present moment."[21] Forced to believe that such language is power, she intends her intense responses to provoke the same in Algarotti. Yet even as her voice echoes as intensely declarative as Ariadne's, she claims such emotional upheaval to be as "foreign" as Algarotti, and she paints her extremity as a battle between head and heart: "Ma raison me fait voir tout l'extravagance, et mon Coeur me fait sentir toute l'importance. Foible Raison! qui choque ma passion et ne le détruit pas, et qui me fait voir inutilement toute la folie d'aimer au point que j'aime sans esperance de retour" ["My reason makes me see all its absurdity, and my Heart makes me feel all its importance. Feeble Reason! which battles with my passion and does not destroy it, and which vainly makes me see all the folly of loving to the degree that I love without hope of return"] (10 September 1736; 2:105–6, 502).[22]

The very fact that her passion is "sans esperance" points to the most important psychological reality that underlies all her expressions: Algarotti is merely the local moment, the impetus to expressions of desire. The act of writing is the genuine source of her pleasure: "You have taken from me not only the taste but the sufferance of those I see, but in recompence you have made me very entertaining to my selfe, and there are some moments when I am happy enough to think over the past till I totally forget the present" (2:109). In his study of the *Heroides,* Howard Jacobson cites the heroine's use of writing as a means to satisfy desire as one of the defining characteristics of the genre: "Powerless women who are helpless to influence their own lives must resort to vicarious (and futile) acts to provide psychic satisfaction in the absence of potency, be it weeping, complaining, or verbal suggestion. In other words, the very act of letter-writing is itself little more than an attempt at psychic gratification."[23] Because she is in reality in love with her own rhetoric, Lady Mary can live in her imagination, recounting the pleasures of her past moments with him. Such intense concentration leads her to claim that the present has no meaning, even though her present is taken up with epistolary expressions of desire for him:

Je m'abbandonne donc a mon penchant et me rappelle tous mes aimables chimeres au mepris de tout ce que m'environne, et je veux me laisser aller a la douce illusion que me represente que vous pensez quelque fois a moi, toute éloigné que vous ettes, et tout incertain que je suis quand je vous verray. C'est la seule Idée que puisse me plaire. J'avoue je suis surpris de me trouver des Sentimens si extrodinaire. J'ai un Coeur fait pour entretenir un Sylphe.

[So I abandon myself to my inclination and recall all my pleasant phantoms, disdaining all that surrounds me, and I choose to abandon myself to the sweet illusion which tells me that you think of me sometimes, distant as you are, and uncertain as I am when I shall see you. It is the only

Idea that can please me. I confess I am surprised to find in myself such extraordinary Feelings. I have a Heart made to sustain a Sylph.] (15 June 1738; 2:116, 504)

Purporting to be surprised yet delighted by her emotions—desires literally written into existence—she is honest enough to acknowledge that she chooses the theatrical acts of abandonment she cites above: "Je n'ai nulle but que de me satisfaire en te disant qu je t'aime" ["I have no purpose except to satisfy myself by telling you that I love you"] (10 September 1736; 2:105, 502).

Thus it comes as little surprise, when Lady Mary sets off in 1739 to meet Algarotti in Italy, that she claims coidentity with that literary figure made both mad and heroic by his imagination: "Me voici aux pieds des Alpes, et demain je franche le pas qui doit me conduire en Italie. Je me recommande a vous dans tous les perils comme Don Quichotte a sa Dulcinée, et je n'ai pas l'imagination moins échauffée que lui" ["Here I am at the feet of the Alps, and tomorrow I take the step which is to lead me into Italy. I commend myself to you in all perils like Don Quixote to his Dulcinea, and I have an imagination no less inflamed than his"] (6 September 1739; 2:147, 508). This inward turn to an "inflamed" imagination, with its quixotic hints of a madness in the pursuit, is one of many instances when Lady Mary appropriates the male role. In likening herself to Don Quixote, not only does she suggest that the illusory nature of his quest is the equivalent of her own, but she also acknowledges the near impossibility of forming a lasting romantic attachment with a much younger, ambitious, perhaps exclusively homosexual man. The remark also functions to highlight the degree of her own transgression of her status as an older, aristocratic, married woman. Most important, she assumes the male role as a means to empower herself to *action,* an action prohibited by the *Heroides,* whose heroines, according to Karen Alkalay-Gut, are the antithesis of the epic heroes in that they are superior neither to their environments nor to men.[24]

Thus, in this madness, she focuses all her energies upon an absent but powerful, almost godlike force. Because her "Dulcinea" is so distant and so illusory, Lady Mary can translate her emotions through the language and imagery of religion, a strategy that allows her to represent the sojourn to Italy as a spiritual pilgrimage, a journey to salvation, the first step toward paradise:

Enfin je pars demain avec la Resolution d'un homme bien persuadé de sa Religion et contente de sa conscience, rempli de foye et d'esperance. Je laisse mes amis pleurant ma perte et franche le pas hardiment pour un autre monde. Si je vous trouve tel que vous m'avez juré, je trouve les champs élissée et la Felicité au de la de l'imagination.

[At last I depart tomorrow with the Resolution of a man well persuaded of his Religion and happy in his conscience, filled with faith and hope. I leave my friends weeping for my loss and bravely take the leap for another world. If I find you such as you have sworn to me, I find the Elysian Fields, and Happiness beyond imagining.] (24 July 1739; 2:140, 508)

As she equates herself with the resolute man and imagines herself as taking the first step into another world, she chooses the extraordinary transformative powers of religion and its rhetoric of translation as the only discourse befitting the new life she envisions.

In painting her desire as a form of worship and exploiting the discourse of the courtly love tradition to describe a zeal equal to that of a religious novice, Lady Mary rejects Pope's use of Eastern religious wit in favor of the language and iconography of Catholicism, rhetoric particularly fitting for the Italian Algarotti. Such a rhetorical strategy allows her to represent him as a religious icon—beautiful, remote, and silent—in an image that emphasizes the depths of her adoration and points to the singularity of her devotion. In the first extant letter she sends to him, she represents herself as fit for sainthood, a canonization in reward for waiting three hours for him and his failure to meet her: "I beleive some of your Martyrs have been canoniz'd for less. If you have repentance enough to be enclin'd to ask pardon you may obtain it by comeing here to morrow at 7 o'clock" (April 1736; 2:101). Such ironic language may provide some measure of distance from the disappointment that saddens her, but it also indicates the fervor she brings to the pursuit. Speaking the language of religion and romance, wooing and objectifying him, she takes another, altogether startling male role in repeatedly representing Algarotti as the Virgin Mary and herself as his supplicant: "You are ever present to my thoughts, and halfe those aspirations to the B[lessed] V[irgin] would deserve her personal appearance to encourrage so sincere a Votary" (December 1736; 2:111). Even more specifically, she takes on the impassioned role of zealot:

J'ai une devotion pour vous plus zelé qu'aucun des adorateurs de la Vierge a jamais eû pour elle. Je croi que tous ces messeiurs ont eû un peu de vanité dans leur devoûement, où ils ont esperé des grandes recompenses de leurs oraisons. Me voici en oraison à vous sans esperance que vous m'en teniez le moindre comte, et je passe des heures entiere en mon Cabinet absorbé dans la contemplation de vos perfections.

[I have a devotion for you more zealous than any of the adorers of the Virgin has ever had for her. I believe that all these men have had a little vanity in their devotion, or they hoped for great rewards for their prayers. Here am I praying to you without hope that you will give me any credit at all for it, and I spend whole hours in my Study absorbed in the contemplation of your perfections.] (10 September 1736; 2:105, 501–2)

This confusing of the language of religion and desire also has its echoes in *Eloisa to Abelard,* a theatrical performance demanding the gestures of the supplicant in a legitimate religious ritual.[25] By using the very hopelessness of her situation—praying without hope of reward—to elevate her absorption into the realm of divine contemplation, she can claim that the "common" worshipper has neither her zeal nor her lack of self-interest.

Moreover, like Eloisa, she can easily equate her renunciation with desire, another instance of a retreat into the solitary that itself intensifies and heightens her emotions. Such a strategy also allows her to ameliorate some of the guilt stemming from her most transgressive violation: the seeming promise to break her wedding vows. Employing the language of religion, she skirts the edges of real blasphemy as she seeks to convince herself that other women have tawdry affairs, mere physical couplings, while she, such imagery implies, has access to the transcendent, a realm of resurrection and rebirth. After the stifling life she has led in England—emotionally estranged from her husband, useless to her children, no longer amused by the follies of her friends—Lady Mary takes refuge in a language that points her not toward adultery but toward salvation. Exchanging a staid religion and its retribution of sins for the transformative power of an emotional renewal, she attempts to erase the guilt in this "criminal" act and create a clear conscience through the very act of writing: her epistolary confessions bring absolution, and his desire produces her rebirth.

Once settled on the Continent, however, Lady Mary discovers no Elysian Fields. She expresses only impatience with Algarotti's absence and his silence; as the delay grows, her frustration builds. Her unhappiness must surely have been reinforced by her correspondence with Lord Hervey, a man who became her rival for Algarotti's affections. As she set off for Italy, she had shared her desire to live in proximity to Algarotti with only one friend—Lord Hervey himself. The openness with which she expressed her affections for their young friend can be seen in a "game" of poetry played by Lady Mary and Lord Hervey. According to Isobel Grundy, they discussed her infatuation in verse, "recording a conversation in which intimate dissection of the feelings of one party proceeded in metre and rhyme, the handwriting of each alternating" (237). Part of Lady Mary's poem includes the following extraordinary expressions of the extremity of her affection:

> With useless Beauty my first Youth was crown'd,
> In all my Conquests I no pleasure found,
> The croud I shunn'd, nor Applause was vain
> And Felt no pity for a Lover's pain.
>
> . . . .
>
> Now that contempt too dearly repaid,
> Th'impetuous Fire does my whole Soul invade.
> O more than Madness!—with compassion View
> A Heart could only be enflam'd by You.

She ends the poetic lament with this poignant line: "Look on my Heart, and you'll forget my Face." The poem also contains, as Grundy notes, two role reversals. In the first, Lady Mary calls herself Pygmalion and equates his having "warmed" his "Ivory maid" to life with her own desire for a similar awakening in Algarotti; more tellingly in the second, she likens herself to Iphis—a young woman, raised as a boy, who fell in love with Ianthe and, after praying to Isis, was transformed into a man.[26]

Lord Hervey, however, plays rather cruel games with her after she leaves England. While he initially encourages her journey, telling her that she is "in the right to take the Pilgrim's Staff in Hand," he later refuses to divulge much information about Algarotti once the young man returns to England: "Our Friend is in London; he dined with me to day. I did not say I had hear'd from you, because you gave me no Directions to do so" (13/2 November 1739; 2:160). Particularly frustrating for her must have been comments such as the one that follows, written

by Hervey just as Algarotti walked into his rooms: "I did not tell ⟨him⟩
to whom I was writing, and as you decline giving me any Directions
for my Conduct, am at a Loss to know what sort of Conduct I should
hold; . . . [I] shall not tell ⟨him⟩ what I really believe, which is that as
⟨a Venetian⟩ when you was at London made you forget every Englishman, so a Piedmonteze at Venice will make you forget every Venetian"
(11 January 1740; 2:167).[27]

Alone in exile but aware of Algarotti's pleasures in the social world,
Lady Mary writes of a disappointment that takes the form of a contrast
between the warm reception she has received in Italy and his cool ingratitude, a complaint she pens as she sits alone on Christmas Eve: "Je
menerai une vie assez douce s'il elle n'etoit troublé par le souvenir d'un
ingrat qui m'a oublié dans un Exil qu'il a causé" ["I should lead a peaceful enough life if it were not troubled by the remembrance of an ingrate
who has forgotten me in an Exile which he caused"] (24 December 1739;
2:164, 509). He, however, enjoying court life and winning esteem in
intellectual circles, was in no hurry to rush to her side. Only after she
had endured almost two years of his absence do they have their long-
awaited meeting, a completely unsatisfying reunion that forces her to
write what she has known all along: that her hopes for a life with him
were mere fantasy.

This devastating encounter, however, results in a letter dazzling with
indignation and intelligence.[28] Gone is the language of passion drawn
from literature; replacing it is imagery drawn from science, primarily
Newton's *Optics*. Her dream of herself as a romance heroine turns into
the scientist's search for cause. Opening by telling him that she has
begun "a mepriser vostre mépris," she harks back to the time when she
desired to please him, an event she describes as "toute l'impossibilité,"
and launches into her rejection:

Je vous a étudié, et si bien étudiée, que le Chevalier Newton n'a pas
disecté les raions du Soleil avec plus d'exactitude que j'ai dechiffré les
sentimens de vostre ame. Vos yeux m'ont servi de Prism pour demeler
les Idées dans vostre esprit. J'ÿ ay regardois avec une si grande Aplica-
tion, je me suis presqu'aveuglée (car ces prisms sont fort éblouïssante).
J'ai vû que vostre ame est rempli de mille belles imaginations mais tout
ensemble ne forme que de l'indifference. Il est vrai que separement, met-
tez cet Indifference (par exemple) en sept parties, sur des objets a des

certains distances, on verroit le gout le plus vif, les sentimens les plus fin, l'imagination la plus delicat etc. Chaqu'une de ces qualitez sont réelement en vous. Sur les manuscripts, sur les statues, sur les Tableaux, les vers, le vin, la conversation, on vous trouveroit toujours du gout, de la Delicatesse, et de la vivacité. Pourquoi donc est ce que je ne trouve que de la grossierité et de l'indifference? Ce que je suis assez épais pour n'exciter rien de mieux, et je voye si clairment la nature de vostre ame que j'ai tout autant de Desespoir de le toucher que Mr. Newton avoit d'augmenter ses decouvertes par des Telescopes, que par leur propres Qualités dissipent et changent les raions de la Lumiere.

[I have studied you, and studied so well, that Sir (Isaac) Newton did not dissect the rays of the sun with more exactness than I have deciphered the sentiments of your soul. Your eyes served me as a Prism to discern the Ideas of your mind. I watched it with such great Intensity that I almost went blind (for these prisms are very dazzling). I saw that your soul is filled with a thousand beautiful fancies but all together makes up only indifference. It is true that separately—divide that Indifference (for example) into seven parts, on some objects at certain distances—one would see the most lively taste, the most refined sentiments, the most delicate imagination etc. Each one of these qualities is really yours. About manuscripts, statues, Pictures, poetry, wine, conversation, you always show taste, Delicacy, and vivacity. Why then do I find only churlishness and indifference? Because I am dull enough to arouse nothing better, and I see so clearly the nature of your soul that I am as much in Despair of touching it as Mr. Newton was of enlarging his discoveries by means of Telescopes, which by their own Powers dissipate and change the Light rays.] (May 1741; 2:237, 514)

In representing herself as a scientist, not a romantic literary heroine, she radically shifts the ground of observation from her internal nature to his outward charms. Like Newton, she takes the part of the objective observer, in this case an empiricist not of her own soul but of Algarotti's character. With the same intensity that Newton dissected the sun's rays, Lady Mary claims finally to have "deciphered" him: while he is still metaphorically "the sun," he no longer provides life's essential warmth; instead he becomes truly an object, one not to be revered but to be observed. Honestly assessing her own psychology, she describes herself as initially blinded by the brightness in the prisms of his eyes, but this image of Algarotti, while dazzling, is equally grotesque and even monstrous.

Stripped of the veil of fantasy and hope, she plays the mathematician, dividing his soul into seven equal parts. Thus fragmented and scattered, without the power of an integrated identity, Algarotti shrinks from his mythic stature, a diminution that finally allows Lady Mary to see him clearly. Parts of him are tasteful and delicate in his appreciation of art and the sensuous pleasures of life—manuscripts, poetry, and wine— but other parts are churlish and indifferent to the gift of her own sensuous, artistic self. The concluding sentence, particularly poignant in its lament, equates her despair with Newton's: neither the telescope nor her own understanding can bring the object of scrutiny any closer; as distant and beautiful as the sun's rays, Algarotti's charms dissipate because, like the telescope, the instrument of Lady Mary's inquiry—the language of passion and the heart—actually distorts the thing it views.[29]

Lady Mary's romantic encounters provoke a particular kind of epistolary discourse, for romance, by its very nature, involves her in a struggle to find a language that allows her to be a feeling and speaking subject. Although her attempts to generate and maintain intimacy, to be that speaking subject, fail on all three occasions, in the process of working through her romantic entanglements she discovers the powers and the limits of epistolary discourse in romantic performance.

By employing three very different strategies, she creates three equally different styles, each dependent only partly on male objectives and expectations. Even though the emotional, complicated discourse of the Wortley correspondence turns into the flat language of business and everyday domestic concerns, Lady Mary discovers the subtle varieties of meaning that a witty and textured discourse can produce. She also discovers the limits of the power of epistolary persuasion, for Wortley's silence is a strategy she has no way to overcome. While the language of the empowered observer she presents to Pope goes as completely ignored as his persona of romantic gallant, she appropriates and exploits Wortley's power of silence even as she learns to represent herself—to Pope and to herself—as a writer. And although her passionate seducer's rhetoric with Algarotti is unanswered, seemingly unappreciated, and ultimately shunned, she expresses delight in and recognizes the sorrows of epistolary expressions of desire.

Most important, in exploring the elasticity of epistolary discourse, Lady Mary exploits the multiplicities of a performative female identity. She experiments with shaping her discourse through modifying the expressions of literary heroines and developing the possibilities presented by literary genres. In this, supposedly the most private kind of correspondence, she can play with the literary and the performative because they are possibilities offered by a sanctioned division between public and private. She can trust Algarotti's discretion precisely because she has seen so little evidence of his desire. With Wortley, she insists that their correspondence is public, for all his protestations to the contrary, and thus she refuses to accept his naive and coercive attempts to modify her private style in a correspondence she fears will be made public. With Pope, she presumes that her performance is public and layers her letters with all her literary acumen.

This public performance with Pope, however, is only one small part of the correspondence she produces from Turkey, a country lying perhaps at the farthest extreme from English life. The Turkish Embassy Letters, the focus of the chapter that follows, provoke Lady Mary's most dazzling, most polished, and most public correspondence. From this dangerous and exotic culture, she produces the letters that will generate for her genuine public fame.

Chapter Three

❦

The Veil of Romance:
The Turkish Embassy Letters

In August 1716, Lady Mary embarked on an extraordinary odyssey. With her infant son in tow, she accompanied Wortley, who had been made ambassador to Turkey, through various eastern European states before stopping to visit the baths in Adrianople and ultimately settling in Pera. Wortley rented a palace fully staffed by a retinue of servants, and Lady Mary spent her time managing the house, seeing the Turkish sights (frequently traveling in native costume), and, she claims, learning the Turkish language. As the wife of an important European ambassador, she was treated with great civility and exploited the opportunities that her aristocracy and her womanhood created for her to gain access to realms entirely uncharted by male travelers. She secured permission to visit a mosque, accepted invitations to the homes of prominent Turkish citizens, entered into the luxury of the women's baths, and dined with a high-ranking sultana. She also devoted a great deal of time to corresponding with absent friends. And when she acquires a Turkish love letter, it is an event noteworthy enough to write about.

Her Turkish love letter is "si curieux," she says, "que je ne puis assez admirer la stupidité des Voyageurs de n'en avoir pas encore aporté en

Europe" ["that I cannot sufficiently marvel at the stupidity of Travellers in not having brought any back to Europe before"] (1 April 1718; 1:404, 459). The value of the letter resides in its ability to communicate only partially through language, for the "letter" is "composed" of small natural objects that are placed in a purse with an accompanying traditional verse. A pearl translates as "Fairest of the young," and a jonquil means "Have pity on my passion"; a pear becomes "Give me some hope," while a match signifies "I burn I burn, my flame consumes me" (16 March 1718; 1:388–89). Paper, soap, coal, straw, cloth, cinnamon, a rose, a gold thread, a grape, and gold wire constitute the whole, but a postscript, in the form of a pepper, means "Send me an answer." The natural world—all that is visible and external—contains significances not immediately apparent but meanings one can be taught to understand: "There is no colour, no flower, no weed, no fruit, herb, pebble, or feather that has not a verse belonging to it; and you may quarrel, reproach, or send Letters of passion, freindship, or Civillity, or even of news, without ever inking your fingers" (1:389). Lady Mary so values the communicative power of these objects that she suggests the Turkish practice is superior to that of the English, for the former results in gifts one can touch, symbols that are sensuous and powerfully evocative.[1]

The whole of the natural, objective world in Turkey shimmers with just such significance for Lady Mary. Common objects become representations, and the natural translates into the aesthetic. Turkey is a landscape where things metamorphose into meaning, where objects are suffused with significances not to be found in dull, one-dimensional English life. This process of transformation is the singular force shaping Lady Mary's perceptions about life in Turkey, a force that often takes the form of what she calls "a female spirit of contradiction," an impulse that generates her insistence that Turkish women are the "freest" in the world or that the sultan is enslaved by his janissaries. Such claims not only contradict earlier travelers' reports but also function as a means of equating Turkish practices with their European counterparts: her suggestion that Islam is just a version of Western deism serves to level difference and deflate English superiority. More powerful still are the literary elements that inform her judgments. The romance, which has a generative force in this correspondence, allows Lady Mary to see power in Turkish women's lives, but it also seduces her into believing that the fictional constructs are real. As a result, she fails to perceive the violence and pain endured by some women in Turkey because she views female sorrow through the veil of romance.

I

The embassy letters extant today, fifty-two in all, are not the letters Lady Mary actually sent but a compilation carefully preserved in her own autograph and copied into two small albums. Robert Halsband reports that among the Wortley manuscripts is a document, written in Lady Mary's hand and endorsed by Wortley as "Heads of L. M.'s Letters from Turky," which contains her correspondents' initials accompanied by brief summaries of the letters. While she drew on her letters to create the embassy collection, other evidence indicates that she edited out the personal references and rearranged information: descriptions sent to one correspondent, for example, appear in the albums to have been sent to another. Halsband calls the collection "pseudo-letters, dated and addressed to people either named or nameless." As such, the embassy correspondence is Lady Mary's most polished and self-conscious epistolary performance—a document deliberately shaped, edited, and fine-tuned for nuance and subtlety. That she always intended the letters to be published is clear: she carried the albums with her throughout her twenty-two-year, self-imposed exile on the Continent; upon her return to England after Wortley's death, she stopped in Rotterdam and presented the manuscripts to the Reverend Benjamin Sowden, telling him that they were "to be dispos'd of as he [thought] proper." The letters were published in May 1763 (less than a year after her death) without the family's permission and from an imperfect manuscript copy.[2]

For all its inaccuracies, the collection elicited an overwhelmingly positive response to Lady Mary's literary skills. Smollett, citing the common observation that the grace and elegance of women's correspondence make it infinitely superior to men's, wrote that her letters "were never excelled, we might venture to say, never equalled by any letter-writer of any sex, age, or nation. They are, to say the truth, so bewitchingly entertaining, that we defy the most phlegmatic man upon earth to read one without going through with them." Voltaire echoed these sentiments, claiming that the letters were superior even to Madame de Sévigné's because they were written for all nations, not simply her own. The only work Dr. Johnson read simply for pleasure, according to Mrs. Piozzi, was Lady Mary's: "I have heard him say he never read but one book, which he did not consider as obligatory, through his whole life (and Lady Mary Wortley's Letters was the book)." Edward Gibbon's praise was particularly positive: "What fire, what ease, what knowledge of Europe and of Asia! Her account of the manners of the Turkish women is indeed different from any thing we have yet seen."[3] Her readers recognized that the extraordinary quality of these letters resulted from her knowledge of the international scene and her ability to entertain.

Yet, as Gibbon's perceptive comment reveals, Lady Mary also presents information that was indeed "new." Such exotic information resides in a world previously invisible to other travelers—the domestic, female, hidden side of life in Turkey:

> Now do I fancy that you imagine I have entertain'd you all this while with a relation that has (at least) receiv'd many Embellishments from my hand. This is but too like (says you) the Arabian tales; these embrodier'd Napkins, and a jewel as large as a Turkey's egg!—You forget, dear Sister, those very tales were writ by an Author of this Country and (excepting the Enchantments) are a real representation of the manners here. (10 March 1718; 1:385)

Even a "real representation" of life in a place as little understood and as infrequently visited as Turkey is open to charges of exaggeration and "Embellishments," for the real life Lady Mary sees in Turkey could have been lifted from *The Arabian Nights*. Her correspondents expected to hear tales of splendor in the East—wealth beyond imagination, beautiful girls enslaved in the sultans' harems, barbarous and uncivilized social customs, atheists and renegades—because they were familiar with the cultural histories of the past and the contemporary artistic representations of Turkey. Lady Mary herself views everyday Turkish activity through the lens of that most extravagant of arts: "All I see is so new to me, it is like a fresh scene of an opera every day" (1 April 1717; 1:309). Living in a land where remote settings, sprawling action, and adventure are ready-made, she inhabits a world that comfortably incorporates both the quotidian and the extraordinary: her discussions with Turkish women about love, courtship, and marriage also include tales of love potions and "majic," stories of lovers' cruelty and widows' constancy. Lady Mary presents this "real representation" of Turkey in the rhetorical form most common to all travelers: the "sheer, overpowering, monumental descriptions" that Edward Said points to as characterizing most Western accounts of the Orient.[4]

Yet for all her formal protests about "naturalness" and for all her claims to enact the empiricist's imperative—to record in minute detail and to observe as closely as possible—her descriptions are almost always aesthetic appreciations, especially when Turkish people attempt to modify nature, artificially decorating not only animals but also themselves. Thus she exploits the conventional "strange, therefore true" paradox that Michael McKeon sees as underlying the eighteenth-century traveler's discourse.[5] Camels and buffalo, for instance, provide an opportunity for Lady Mary to play the pedant with Anne Thistlethwayte:

> You never saw Camels in your Life and perhaps the Description of them will appear new to you. . . . They seem to me very ugly Creatures, their heads being ill form'd and disproportion'd to their bodys. They carry all the burdens, and the Beasts destin'd to the Plough are Buffolos, an Animal you are also unacquainted with. They are larger and more clumsey than an Oxe. They have short black Horns close to their heads, which grow turning backwards. They say this horn looks very beautifull when tis well polish'd. . . . The Country people dye their Tails and the Hair of their foreheads red by way of Ornament. (1 April 1717; 1:340–41)

When the "natural" ugliness of the camel is contrasted with the "enhanced" beauty of the polished horns of the buffalo, simple workcreatures metamorphose into objects worthy of aesthetic contemplation.

Lady Mary is equally fascinated when women treat themselves as aesthetic objects. She arrives in Turkey expecting Turkish women to be more beautiful than their Western counterparts, and her expectations are confirmed: "It must be own'd that every Beauty is more common here than with us. 'Tis surprizing to see a young Woman that is not very handsome" (1 April 1717; 1:327). This beauty is partially a result of the transformative powers of cosmetics. Turkish women shape their eyebrows and "have a custom of putting round their Eyes on the inside a black Tincture that, at a distance or by Candle-light, adds very much to the Blackness of them. I fancy many of our Ladys would be overjoy'd to know this Secret, but tis too visible by day. They dye their Nails rose colour; I own I cannot enough accustom my selfe to this fashion to find any Beauty of it" (1:327). While she rejects the eyeliner and the nail polish as "unnatural" and too "visible by day," she does agree to enact the scientist's imperative by experimenting on herself with a Turkish "beauty treatment" called the balm of Mecca. This substance was reputedly the source of the physical attribute Lady Mary most admired in Turkish women, "the most beautifull complexions in the World" (1:327), and a potential restorative for her own complexion, damaged by smallpox.

Lady Mary's English friends plead with her to send them the balm, longing for its miraculous effects,[6] but Western beauty proves to be impervious to Eastern magic: "I have had a present of a small Quantity (which I'll assure you is very valuable) of the best sort, and with great joy apply'd it to my face, expecting some wonderfull Effect to my advantage. The next morning the change indeed was wonderfull; my face was swell'd to a very extrodinary size and all over as red as my Lady ⟨?⟩'s. I remain'd in this lamentable state 3 days, during which you may be sure I pass'd my time very ill" (17 June 1717; 1:368–69). After enduring Wortley's reproach for her "indiscretion," Lady Mary finally returns to normal, but without an improved countenance, and she ends with this vow: "For my part, I never intend to endure the pain of it again;—let my Complexion take its natural course and decay in its own due time. I have very little Esteem for med'cines of this Nature; but do as you please, Madam, only remember before you use it that your face will not be such as you'l care to shew in the drawing room for some days after" (1:369). She agrees to send the balm back to England, knowing that no matter how much she protests her friends will trust the "reality" of the myths found in the texts of the past more than her firsthand experience.

Lady Mary does take exception, however, to Turkish women's love potions and "majic," for—unlike the empirical data to be gleaned from an experiment with a beauty treatment—this transformation has no visible effects. Turkish women claim that when beauty alone is insufficient, charms and enchantments can be used to make a woman irresistible. As "evidence," her Turkish friend points to a host of examples of "ridiculous marriages that there could be no other reason assign'd for" (1:369). Lady Mary provides a more ironic explanation: "I assur'd her that in England, where we were entirely ignorant of all Magic, where the Climate is not halfe so warm nor the Women halfe so handsome, we were not without our ridiculous Marriages; and that we did not look upon it as any thing supernatural when a Man plaid the fool for the sake of a Woman" (1:369). Her friend, annoyed with her refusal to believe, protests that "no Enchantments would have their Effect on [her], and that there were Some people exempt from their power, but very few" (1:370). Lady Mary owns a hardheaded Western insistence on empirical evidence, saying she is "not very apt to beleive in Wonders." Yet she does place great faith in and even stakes her reputation on one truly transformative procedure she discovers in Turkey and brings back to England: inoculation.

Her personal anxiety—even terror—about smallpox turns into wonder and then commitment when she is presented with proof that the deadly disease can be eradicated. This instance is the most extreme and potentially dangerous case of the modification of the natural, for this change requires a metamorphosis of a fundamentally physical nature. It is, however, an internal change with visible results. Lady Mary offers a clinical description of the "engrafting," as the Turkish people call it, which is performed by an old woman who gathers together fifteen or sixteen patients and then, with a nutshell full of smallpox, asks which vein the patient wishes to use:

> She immediately rips open that you offer to her with a large needle (which gives you no more pain than a common scratch) and puts into the vein as much venom as can lye upon the head of her needle, and after binds up the little wound with a hollow bit of shell, and in this manner opens 4 or 5 veins. . . . [On the eighth day] the fever begins to seize 'em and they keep their beds 2 days, very seldom 3. They have very rarely above 20 or 30 in their faces, which never mark, and in 8 days time they are as well as before their illness. Where they are wounded there remains running sores during the Distemper, which I don't doubt is a great releife to it. (1 April 1717; 1:339)

Her description is a measured and intentional balance between the pain of the procedure (the inoculation itself is a "scratch"; the running sores provide "releife") and the extraordinary results (patients recover to become "as well as before their illness" and their skin is not marked—an essential element for Lady Mary, scarred as she was by the disease). To further mute the anxiety a Westerner would feel, she creates likeness by citing corroborating "outside" Western evidence: "Every year thousands undergo this Operation, and the French Ambassador says pleasantly that they take the Small pox here by way of diversion as they take the Waters in other Countrys" (1:339). Deadly smallpox is thus transformed into a fashionable malady, no worse than a cold or sore throat overcome by a visit to the pleasures of Bath.[7]

That one could conquer a disease by inviting it in must have struck the average eighteenth-century mind as wrong indeed, for it certainly did not prove true with typhoid or syphilis. Yet calling herself "a Patriot," Lady Mary vows to bring inoculation back to England, even though she presumes that the greatest resistance will come from English doctors who will reject the technique because it will lessen their profits. Lady Mary predicts, "Perhaps if I live to return I may, however, have courrage to war with 'em."[8] Like her contemporary Voltaire, she positions herself in a broader Enlightenment tradition, joining those intellectuals committed to exploring the new frontiers of medicine. Yet she does so through a belief in inoculation that is directly tied to her interpretive strategies for Turkish life: the transformation of the natural into the aesthetic leads "naturally" to a belief that the body itself can be transformed. The metamorphosis played out in her consciousness—object into beauty—finds a comfortable counterpart in the modification of the disease into health. She closes the letter by pointing to the "Heroism in the Heart" that such belief requires while simultaneously elevating herself into one who braves the danger for the good of the individual and collective "body." In this instance most particularly, Lady Mary removes Turkish reality from the barbarous and degraded world previous travelers described by placing its "folk" medicine in an Enlightenment context. Styling herself as a modern, open-minded, Western observer, Lady Mary seeks to raise and recuperate the Turkish culture through the empiricist's methodology.

II

This refutation of charges of Turkish barbarism is one of Lady Mary's self-conscious programs, and her praise for the practice of inoculation is only one such instance. Toward that end, she is sensitive to her "strategic location," the dialogue among texts that Edward Said claims has created the Western vision of the Orient.[9] Keenly aware that her observations exist in a specific historical context, that she and her correspondents measure her descriptions against previous travelers' texts, she creates minute, particular, eye-witness descriptions of what she observes. Yet she acknowledges that the strategy is problematic in a land as remote and exotic as Turkey: "We Travellers are in very hard circumstances. If we say nothing but what has been said before us, we are dull and we have observ'd nothing. If we tell any thing new, we are laugh'd at as fabulous and Romantic, not allowing for the difference of ranks, which afford difference of company, more Curiosity, or the changes of customs that happen every 20 year in every Country" (10 March 1718; 1:385). Understanding that she enjoyed opportunities denied to seventeenth-century travelers such as Paul Rycaut and George Sandys, whose work constitutes what she calls the "dull" and repetitive discourse of the past, Lady Mary recognizes that her class and gender create her special access to Turkey. In this context, she scoffs specifically at the inaccurate reports of Jean Dumont:

> [He] has writ with equal ignorance and confidence. Tis a particular plea-sure to me here to read the voyages to the Levant, which are generally so far remov'd from Truth and so full of Absurditys I am very well di-verted with 'em. They never fail giving you an Account of the Women, which 'tis certain they never saw, and talking very wisely of the Genius of the Men, into whose Company they are never admitted, and very often describe Mosques, which they dare not peep into. (17 June 1717; 1:368)

Lady Mary's status as an aristocrat secured her permission to visit a mosque and to form a friendship with at least one man of genius, Effendi Achmet Beg.[10] She is authorized to give "an Account of the Women" because she has access to entirely uncharted—female—realms. Her unique vantage point, she insists, will correct the information falsified by others: "Tis certain we have but very imperfect relations of the manners and Religion of these people, this part of the World being seldom visited but by merchants who mind little but their own Affairs, or Trav-ellers who make too short a stay to be able to report any thing exactly of their own knowledge" (1 April 1717; 1:315). Turkish people are "too proud" to converse familiarly with bourgeois merchants who "can give no better an Account of the ways here than a French refugée lodging in a Garret in Greek street could write of the Court of England."

Her insistence that an aristocrat and the wife of an ambassador has access to a "truth" denied the "common" visitor highlights her difference from earlier travelers. Acting as gatherers of information and distancing themselves from the local inhabitants through a process of othering, sixteenth- and seventeenth-century visitors to Turkey often labeled the inhabitants "inferior" and "primitive." Later nineteenth-century writer-explorers, according to Mary Louise Pratt, saw as their goal the enumeration of the traits of native inhabitants, especially as these customs differed from the observers' own manners. John Barrow's information gathering becomes a form of othering that grows out of an unconscious ideology of colonialism and produces descriptions of people "homogenized into a collective 'they.'"[11] While Lady Mary never escapes from the impulse to see difference as "other," she does reject the earlier strategy of relying on European customs as the sole measure of appropriate standards. Instead, she perceives equivalents—a leveling of differences, an expository form of "wit" rather than "judgment"—that result in a form of cultural relativism: she celebrates both the merits and the demerits of Turkish *and* European culture. She gleans most of this information during conversations with the privileged Effendi Achmet Beg, who flatters her by presuming she is a scholar and by giving her the "opertunity of knowing their Religion and morals in a more particular manner than perhaps any Christian ever did" (1 April 1717; 1:317). The status of this wealthy, powerful Muslim friend, whom she describes as a scholar-priest, appeals directly to Lady Mary's own aristocratic identity. She claims that, as a class, the effendi "are the only men realy considerable in the Empire" and that the sultan "never presumes to touch their lands or money, which goes in an unintterupted succession to their Children. . . You may easily judge the power of these men who have engross'd all the Learning and allmost all the Wealth of the Empire" (1 April 1717; 1:316–17).

When aristocrat meets aristocrat, there is no need to disguise or soften the "truth," as in the instance when Achmet Beg employs an argument "from use" to confess forthrightly that he drinks liquor: "The prohibition of Wine was a very wise maxim and meant for the common people, being the Source of all disorders amongst them, but that the Prophet never design'd to confine those that knew how to use it with moderation" (1 April 1717; 1:318). The effendi, however, assures Lady Mary that he never drinks in public, echoing Paul Rycaut's description of alcohol consumption among the great men: "Because in office, [these men] are more careful how the world discovers the delight they take in that Liquor, lest the miscarriages of their office should be attributed to the excess of Wine; or the knowledge of their use of that which deprives them of their reason, render them uncapable of their trust and dignity." [12] Mimicking aristocrats everywhere, Achmet Beg outwardly observes the forms created by his class to improve the morality of the common people, but in private he creates his own standards. Lady Mary implies that those with secular power can rise above dogma and enter a shared Enlightenment realm of good sense and rationality; aristocrats of all cultures, she reasons, share a kinship of insight and a mutual but separate set of "higher" standards.

In appreciating Turkish culture in this manner, Lady Mary shares with other "early Orientalists" a vision of the East that becomes, according to Said, "a salutary *dérangement* of European habits." [13] Striking at the heart of European economic practices, Lady Mary perceives the Eastern custom of adoption as far superior to European legal fictions concerning family inheritances. Because Turkish estates cannot be left to friends or even distant relatives (the sultan acquires all properties for whom there is no direct heir), wealthy Turks, Greeks, and Armenians choose "some pritty child" from among the "meanest people" and declare the child an heir: "The adopting Fathers are generally very tender to these children of their Souls, as they call them. I own this custom pleases me very much better than our absurd following our Name. Methinks tis much more reasonable to make happy and rich an infant whom I educate after my own manner, brought up (in the Turkish Phrase) upon my knees, and who has learnt to look upon me with a filial respect, than to give an Estate to a creature without other Merit or relation to me than by a few Letters" (May 1718; 1:410). Echoing Wortley's arguments to Lady Mary's father during the marriage-contract negotiations, Lady Mary appreciates the transformative power by which one of the "meanest" sort is made "happy and rich," but it is secondary to the power of the process to replicate the aristocracy: children of the soul, brought up on "privileged" knees, learn filial respect and internalize aristocratic values.

Lady Mary also chooses religion, a particular source of Western superiority and pride, as a focus of such *dérangement,* in part because such Western notions were shaped by the discourse of previous travelers such as Paul Rycaut, whom Lady Mary calls "mistaken (as he commonly is)"

(1:318) for labeling the Turks atheists. He writes that the word *Muserin* signified "the true secret is with us," the secret being "no other then [*sic*] the absolute denial of a Diety." [14] George Sandys's remarks are even more condemnatory:

> The *Mahometan* religion, being derived from a person in life so wicked, so worldly in his projects, in his prosecutions of them so disloyall, trecherous, & cruell; being grounded upon fables and false revelations, repugnant to sound reason, & that wisedome which the Divine hand hath imprinted in his workes; alluring men with those inchantments of fleshly pleasures, permitted in this life and promised for the life ensuing; being also supported with tyranny and the sword (for it is death to speake there against it;) and lastly, where it is planted rooting out all vertue, all wisedome and science, and in summe all liberty and civility; and laying the earth so waste, dispeopled and uninhabited; that neither it came from God (save as a scourge by permission) neither can bring them to God that follow it. [15]

To this unyielding insistence on tyranny, vice, and wickedness, Achmet Beg presents a gentler, less threatening version of the Muslim faith and thus provides her with a means of refuting the barbarous reputation of the Turks by placing them in the seemingly open-minded context of cultural relativism.

Such relativism proves to be particularly powerful in her program for rehabilitation, because Lady Mary can argue for the mildness, civility, and rationality of the Turkish religion by placing it in a comfortable Enlightenment context. Many of the great seventeenth- and eighteenth-century thinkers, including Locke and Berkeley, used travelers' reports to gain a new perspective on Western religious practices, and deists particularly welcomed reports of the "natural religion" of peoples assumed to be entirely godless and uncivilized. The Reverend Lancelot Addison, father of Joseph Addison, writes in the preface to his *West Barbary* (1671) that he intended to make visible "the Justice and Religiousness of a People esteemed Barbarous, Rude, and Savage" in order to urge Christians to reexamine their belief that theirs was the only true religion. [16] Thus when Achmet Beg calls the Alcoran "the purest morality deliver'd in the very best Language," Lady Mary is led quite easily to see Islam merely as an Eastern version of Western deism: "But the most prevailing Opinion, if you search into the Secret of the Effendis, is plain Deism, but this is kept from the people, who are amus'd with a thousand Different notions according to the different interests of their Preachers" (1 April 1717; 1:317–18). This insistence on the Turkish religion as "enlightened deism" is also representative of a flattening out of difference, an erasure of otherness, for Lady Mary's and the effendi's shared aristocracy allows her to tame the threatening and to make the strange understandable through recourse to the familiar. The various sects of Islam, for example, remind Lady Mary that Christianity is splintered into different groups whose disagreements are just as strong: "The Zidi, Kadari, Jabari, etc. put me in mind of the Catholic, Lutheran, Calvinist, etc., and are equally zealous against one Another" (1:317).

In fact, Lady Mary more emphatically emphasizes the religious differences between her Anglicanism and the Catholicism of her friend and correspondent, the Abbé Conti. She writes to a Catholic priest that the effendi "was pleas'd to hear there were Christians that did not worship images or adore the Virgin Mary. The ridicule of Transubtantiation appear'd very strong to him" (1:317). She will even skirt the edges of blasphemy when she treats the status of women in Turkey. Speaking as though she is personally familiar with the prophet himself, Lady Mary comments on the Western belief that Muslim women are denied paradise: "[Mohammed] etoit trop galant homme & aimoit trop le beau Sexe, pour le traiter d'une maniere si barbare. Au contraire, il promet un trèsbeau Paradis aux femmes Turques. Il dit, à la verité, que ce sera un Paradis separé de celuy de leurs Maris: mais je crois que la pluspart n'en seront pas moins contentes pour cela." ["Mohammed] was too much a Gentleman, and lov'd the Fair Sex too well, to use 'em so barbarously. On the contrary, he promises a very fine Paradise to the *Turkish* Women. He says indeed, that this Paradise will be a separate Place from that of their Husbands: But I fancy the most Part of 'em won't like it the worse for that"] (February 1718; 1:375–76, 455).[17] Continuing by claiming that only through being fruitful and multiplying will women gain entrance to this paradise, Lady Mary presents this question to a Catholic clergyman:

Que deviendront vos *Saintes Catherines, Thereses, Claires,* & toute la bande de vos pieuses *Vierges & Veuves?* lesquelles, etant jugées par ce Systeme de vertu, sont des infames, qui ont passé toute leur vie dans un libertinage effroyable.

[What will become of your Saint *Catharines,* your Saint *Theresas,* your Saint *Claras,* and the whole Bread-roll of your *holy Virgins and Widows?* who, if they are to be judged by this System of Virtue, will be found to have been infamous Creatures, that past their whole Lives in a most abominable Libertinism.] (February 1718; 1:376, 455)

Religion is transported into the drawing room, where comedy serves to confine some of the anxiety such "alien" notions present to her, especially concerning the question of female virtue, an issue that in the West is always linked to chastity and in the East is dependent on its opposite: continuous sexual activity, indulgence, and fertility.

It is information of just this kind—observations about daily female rituals, the domestic concerns, the "womanly" elements long hidden from view—that clearly differentiates Lady Mary's accounts from those of earlier travelers. Mary Astell, one of the first of Lady Mary's friends to see the manuscript copy of the letters and immediately to recognize their genius, comments on the fundamental difference between male travel writers' dullness, uniform predictability, and univocal style and Lady Mary's energy, elegance, and finer sensibilities:

> I confess I am malicious enough to desire that the World shou'd see to how much better purpose the LADYS Travel than their LORDS, and that whilst it is surfeited with Male Travels, all in the same Tone and stuft with the same Trifles, a *Lady* has the skill to strike out a New Path and to embellish a worn-out Subject with variety of fresh and elegant Entertainment. For besides that Vivacity and Spirit which enliven every part and that inimitable Beauty which spreds thro the whole, besides that Purity of Style for which it may justly be accounted the Standard of the *English* Tongue, the Reader will find a more true and accurate Account of the Customs and Manners of the several Nations with whom the Lady Convers'd than he can in any other Author. (1:466)[18]

This "New Path" takes Lady Mary beyond the narrow range of subjects about which earlier male travelers wrote. Paul Rycaut, whose information Lady Mary trusts only when it requires "that tis very easy to procure lists of" (1:412), divides his *Present State of the Ottoman Empire* into discussions of government, religion, and the military. Under the heading of religion, he makes passing references to domestic and social matters, but the bulk of his writing treats the "gentlemanly" concerns of politics and war. As the reception of the first printed version of Lady Mary's letters indicates, readers of both genders were interested not simply in the traditional realms of government and philosophy but also in the female domestic world and the minutiae of daily life.

Lady Mary also sees these hidden, inaccessible elements of life in Turkey as subject to transformation. One such hidden side of Turkish life was the institution of slavery. The topic was of powerful interest to Lady Mary and her English friends, in part because it was a historical reality and in part because it was central in the conventions of contemporary fiction. Lady Mary is occasionally exasperated by her English friends' "misinformation" about Turkish slaves:

> I heartily beg your Ladyship's pardon, but I realy could not forbear laughing heartily at your Letter and the Commissions you are pleas'd to honnour me with. You desire me to buy you a Greek slave who is to be mistrisse of a thousand good Qualitys. The Greeks are subjects and not slaves. Those who are to be bought in that manner are either such as are taken in War or stole by the Tartars from Russia, Circassia or Georgia, and are such miserable, aukard, poor Wretches, you would not think any of 'em worthy to be your House-maid.[19]

She is always a staunch apologist for Turkish slavery, and her habit of translating Eastern customs into Western equivalents allows her to perceive the institution only as it is like Western servitude: "I know You'l expect I should say something particular of that of the Slaves, and you will Imagine me half a Turk when I don't speak of it with the same horror other Christians have done before me, but I cannot forbear applauding the Humanity of the Turks to those Creatures" (10 April 1718; 1:401). Her sense of herself as "half a Turk" is only partially accurate. She should have said "half a Turkish aristocrat," for she speaks positively about the status of Turkish slaves precisely because she records no conversations with slaves themselves. Therefore she can insist that Turkish slaves are gently treated: bought at the age of eight or nine, they are "educated with great care to accomplish 'em in singing, danceing, Embroidery, etc. . . . . Their Patron never sells them except it is as a Punishment for some very great fault. If ever they grow weary of 'em, they either present them to a freind or give them their freedoms" (17 June 1717; 1:368). Her use of the aristocratic term "Patron" is an attempt to remove the practice from a system of commodification and to place it in the privileged system of beneficence: kindess for the deserving, charity for the needy. Likewise, she interprets Turkish slavery—visible, clearly delineated, and institutionalized—as a more honest assessment of the same status hierarchy present in all cultures. The life of a Turkish slave is "no worse than Servitude all over the world" (10 April 1718; 1:402), and, as for the notion that Turkish men buy women "with an Eye to Evil," Lady Mary responds, not with horror at such a barbarous thought, but by insisting that women "are bought and sold as publickly and more infamously in all our Christian great Citys" (1:402).

She also responds to Rycaut's claim that polygamy is freely practiced with a statement about class and moral imperatives. Rycaut wrote that "every one may freely serve himself of his Women Slaves, with as much variety as he is able to buy or maintain; and this kind of Concubinage is no wayes envyed or condemned by the Wives, so long as they can enjoy their due maintenance, and have some reasonable share in the Husbands bed, which once a week is their due by the Law, for if any of them hath been neglected the whole week before, she challenges *Thursday* night as her due, and hath remedy in that case against her Husband by the Law" (152). Lady Mary makes the taking of more than one wife an aristocratic question of bad manners, for she insists that polygamy is never practiced by people of quality. She is acquainted with only one man, the *tefterdar*, or treasurer, who "keeps a number of she slaves for his own use (that is, on his own side of the House, for a slave once given to serve a Lady is entirely at her disposal) and he is spoke of as a Libertine, or what we should call a Rake, and his Wife won't see him, thô she continues to live in his house" (1 April 1717; 1:329). Adultery in Turkey is flattened into mere libertinism and rejected as a matter of decorum.

Polygamy and the enslavement of lower-class women in Turkey had, in the imaginations of Westerners, an aristocratic equivalent: the seraglio. Yet Lady Mary argues, paradoxically, that it is the sultan himself who is enslaved—by his military forces: "The Government here is entirely in the hands of the Army, and the Grand Signor with all his absolute power as much a slave as any of his Subjects, and trembles at a Janizary's frown" (1:322). Because military loyalty overrides government and religious imperatives, the army has the power to induce terror not simply in the most abject peasants (Lady Mary often laments the violence done to the inhabitants of the countryside) but also in the sultan himself: "That Sultan (to whom [the army] all profess an unlimited Adoration) sits trembling in his Apartment, and dare neither defend nor revenge his favourite. This is the blessed Condition of the most Absolute Monarch upon Earth, who owns noe Law but his Will" (1 April 1717; 1:322).

Western notions about the power of the sultan and the practice of royal concubinage were much more exotic: the institution fascinated Westerners, who envisioned extraordinarily beautiful women, bound in servitude to the whim of the sultan, simultaneously elevated into privilege. The most lavish welcome Lady Mary received came from the Sultana Hafise, favorite of the late Mustafa II, and from this real-life resident of the seraglio Lady Mary gleans most of her information about life in the harem.[20] This subject, too, saturated popular imagination, both as historical reality and romance convention.[21] Paul Rycaut had earlier described the sultan's choosing of his bedmate this way:

> When the Grand Signior resolves to choose himself a Bed-fellow, he re-
> tires into the Lodging of his Women, where (according to the story in
> every place reported, when the Turkish *Seraglio* falls into discourse) the
> Damsels being ranged in order by the Mother of the Maids, he throws
> his handkerchief to her, where his eye and fancy best directs, it being
> a token of her election to his bed. The surprised Virgin snatches at this
> prize and good fortune with that eagerness, that she is ravished with joy
> before she is defloured by the *Sultan,* and kneeling down first kisses the
> handkerchief, and then puts it in her bosom, when immediately she is
> congratulated by all the Ladies of the Court, for the great honour and
> favour she hath received. (39)

The sultana's description of the method the sultan uses to choose his bedmate, as Lady Mary records it, does not include such breathless phrases as "surprised Virgin," "snatches at this prize," or "ravished with joy." Instead, the sultana rejects Rycaut's report by calling the old story "altogether fabulous" and by describing the process as a private, not a public, matter: "The manner upon that occasion [is] no other but that he sends the Kuslir Aga to signify to the Lady the honnour he intends her. She is immediately complemented upon it by the others, and led to the bath where she is perfum'd and dress'd in the most magnificent and becoming Manner. The Emperor precedes his visit by a Royal present and then comes into her apartment" (10 March 1718; 1:383). Moreover, the sultana specifically denies Western reports that the woman must crawl to the sultan from the foot of his bed.[22] Lady Mary refutes Rycaut's report by tempering some of the more titillating aspects of the old story while at the same time providing an account that appears more authoritative in its eye-witness authenticity but is itself not without the drama of selection, bathing, and gift giving.

When the sultana admits that the favorite incurs the envy of other women, Lady Mary surmises, "This seem'd to me neither better nor worse than the Circles in most Courts where the Glance of the Monarch is watch'd and every Smile waited for with impatience and envy'd by those that cannot obtain it" (1:383–84). Lady Mary attempts to make the Turkish custom seem less alien and perhaps less reprehensible to English notions of morality by comparing the sultan's interest to a European monarch's glance—a similarity her correspondents would immediately recognize. Such a strategy also serves simultaneously to undercut whatever moral superiority her English friends might feel when first presented with such alien customs and to elevate Turkish practices by casting them in a familiar light.

Yet Lady Mary's remarks about marriage, childbearing, and Turkish women's "freedom" form a contradictory mix. Her positive response to Turkish women's culture is reinforced by the splendor of their homes, the richness of their garments, and the extraordinary personal beauty that is embodied quite literally in their persons. Her descriptive strategies, in the case of women, exemplify the "quantitative completeness" that Said sees as the primary rhetorical strategy of Western discourse about the East: minute, particularized, external, visible, detailed catalogs constitute an inventory of Eastern magnificence. For instance, it is the Sultana Hafise's costume, rather than her personal beauty, that attracts Lady Mary. The dress far exceeds any expectations a Westerner might bring to Turkish riches:

Round her neck she wore 3 chains which reach'd to her knees, one of large Pearl at the bottom of which hung a fine colour'd Emerald as big as a Turkey Egg, another consisting of 200 Emeralds close joyn'd together, of the most lively Green, perfectly match'd, every one as large as a halfe Crown piece and as thick as 3 Crown pieces, and another of small Emeralds perfectly round. But her Earrings eclips'd all the rest; they were 2 Diamonds shap'd exactly like pears, as large as a big hazle nut. Round her Talpoche she had 4 strings of Pearl, the whitest and most perfect in the world, at least enough to make 4 necklaces every one as large as the Dutchesse of Marlbrô's, and of the same size, fasten'd with 2 roses consisting of a large ruby for the middle stone, and round then 20 drops of clean di'monds to each. . . . She wore large Di'mond bracelets and had 5 rings on her fingers, all single Di'monds (except Mr. Pit's) the largest I ever saw in my Life. (10 March 1718; 1:382)

Lady Mary's correspondents would have been astounded, as she obviously was, to know that such wealth could be found in the possession of one woman and displayed in this form. Lady Mary supposes that the dress must be valued above one hundred thousand pounds sterling, an astonishing sum to pay to decorate one's person, and the voluptuous excesses and vast wealth of the East are here personified in the figure of the bejeweled widow. What Lady Mary fails to mention, however, are the oppressive weight, the encumbrance, and the discomfort such a costume must have posed for the sultana, a woman who must endure the pressures of her own magnificence.

The tension inherent in this portrait of excess is even more apparent in Lady Mary's descriptions of women's domestic duties. She is told that marriage is essential for a woman in Turkish culture because a woman's only real duty is to bear children—"'Tis more despicable to be marry'd and not fruitfull, than 'tis with us to be fruitfull befor Marriage" (4 January 1718; 1:372)—and she claims that, while her acquaintances who have been married for ten years usually have twelve or thirteen children, older women boast of having twenty-five or thirty children. Men, too, are respected in proportion to the number of children they have sired.[23] Lady Mary believes that childbearing is fundamentally a religious matter: "Any Woman that dyes unmarry'd is look'd upon to dye in a state of reprobation. To confirm this beleife, they reason that the End of the Creation of Woman is to encrease and Multiply, and she is only properly employ'd in the Works of her calling when she is bringing children or takeing care of 'em, which are all the Virtues that God expects from her; and indeed their way of Life, which shuts them out of all public commerce, does not permit them any other" (29 May 1717; 1:363). Concerned for the welfare of so many children, she asks these women how they will provide for so great a number, and "they answer

that the Plague will certainly kill half of 'em; which, indeed, generally happens without much concern to the Parents, who are Satisfy'd
with the Vanity of having brought forth so plentifully" (4 January 1718;
1:372). Lady Mary never comments negatively about this female vanity
or lack of maternal sentiment, nor does she openly acknowledge such
perpetual childbearing as another form of slavery. Yet when she herself
gives birth to her daughter in Turkey, there are only two, artificially off-
hand references to her condition. Lady Mary refers to her pregnancy in a
letter to Anne Thistlethwayte by apologizing for the lack of entertaining
information: "I am at this present writing not very much turn'd for the
recollection of what is diverting, my head being wholly fill'd with the
preparations necessary for the Encrease of my family, which I expect
every day" (4 January 1718; 1:371). After the birth of her daughter, she
writes an account very much at odds with her celebration of Turkish
women's fertility:

> L'Oisiveté est la mere des vices (comme vous sçavez) & n'ayant rien de
> meilleur à faire, j'ai fait une fille. . . . Dans ce païs ci, il est tout aussi
> necessaire de faire voir des preuves de jeunesse, pour être reçûë parmi les
> beautez, que de montrer des preuves de Noblesse pour être reçû parmi
> les Chevaliers de Malte. J'etois très fâchée de cette necessité; mais, remar-
> quant qu'on me regardoit avec un grand air de mépris, je me suis mise
> enfin à la mode, & je suis accouchée comme les autres.

> [Idleness is the mother of vices (as you know) and having nothing better
> to do, I have produced a daughter. . . . In this country, it is just as nec-
> essary to show proofs of youth, to be recognized among beauties, as it is
> to show proofs of Nobility to be admitted among the Knights of Malta.
> I was very angry at this necessity; but, noticing that people looked at me
> with a great air of contempt, I finaly complied with the fashion, and I lay
> in like the others.] (April 1718; 1:403–4, 458)

Pretending in this rather breezy manner merely to be enacting an aristocratic duty and to be complying with fashion, Lady Mary nevertheless
cites the force of others' contempt as noteworthy, even though her personal feelings of coercion and the anger it produces never extend to
Turkish women.

This general habit of mind—appreciating Turkish culture by viewing
it in terms of European equivalents—is very likely responsible for the
most controversial claim Lady Mary makes in the embassy letters: she

repeatedly insists that aristocratic Turkish women are "freer than any Ladys in the universe, and are the only Women in the world that lead a life of unintterupted pleasure, exempt from cares, their whole time being spent in visiting, bathing, or the agreable Amusement of spending Money and inventing new fashions" (May 1718; 1:406). Katharine Rogers applauds Lady Mary's insistence on Turkish women's liberty when it "functions as a wicked comment on the Englishman's complacent assumption that England was 'the paradise of wives.'" Yet, Rogers continues, "it is upsetting to note that she defined woman's liberty in terms of spending money and carrying on adulterous affairs with impunity." [24] It is true that Lady Mary writes of Turkish gentlewomen's adultery with amusement, even enthusiasm. Drawing on a quotation from Aphra Behn's *Emperor of the Moon,* when the Harlequin states that morality on the moon is no different from morality on earth, Lady Mary refers to Turkish "Ladys" sexual behavior only as a means of establishing likeness: "As to their Morality or good Conduct, I can say like Arlequin, 'tis just as 'tis with you, and the Turkish Ladys don't commit one Sin the less for not being Christians" (1 April 1717; 1:327).[25]

Yet just as she equated the sultan's choosing of his bedmate with a monarch's glance, her pronouncements about freedom for Turkish gentlewomen are, on the one hand, genuine appreciations of the different liberties these women enjoyed and, on the other hand, complaints about English gentlewomen's imprisonment. Lady Mary builds her argument for sexual "freedom" based on what she calls Turkish women's "disguise"—the veils, head coverings, and dresses that, she claims, do not allow one to distinguish a fine lady from her slave. Such attire creates a "perpetual Masquerade [which] gives them entire Liberty of following their Inclinations without danger of Discovery" (1:328). She insists that assignations are easily arranged and that the men themselves rarely discover the identity of their women partners:

> The Great Ladys seldom let their Gallants know who they are, and 'tis so difficult to find it out that they can very seldom guess at her name they have corresponded with above halfe a year together. You may easily imagine the number of faithfull Wives very small in a country where they have nothing to fear from their Lovers' Indiscretion, since we see so many that have the courrage to expose them selves to that in this World and all the threaten'd Punishment of the next, which is never preach'd to the Turkish Damsels. Neither have they much to apprehend from the

resentment of their Husbands, those Ladys that are rich having all their money in their own hands, which they take with 'em upon a divorce with an addition which he is oblig'd to give 'em. (1 April 1717; 1:328–29)

Lady Mary cites specific advantages to the Turkish system: unlike their English counterparts, Turkish men are discreet (because they are ignorant of their lovers' identities), and, unlike divorced Englishwomen, Turkish women need not surrender large percentages of their fortunes to their husbands.[26]

Lady Mary's account of Turkish women's freedom is reinforced by Abū Tālib Khan, an Indian of Perso-Turkish origin employed by the British as a revenue officer, who traveled to England in the eighteenth century. The account is summarized by the historian Bernard Lewis, who speculates that Abū Tālib Khan (although he wrote in Persian) may have tailored his account to please an English audience:

[Englishwomen] are kept busy with a variety of employments in shops and elsewhere—a situation which Abū Tālib Khan attributes to the wisdom of English legislators and philosophers in finding the best way to keep women out of mischief—and are further subject to a number of restrictions. For example, they do not go out after dark and do not spend the night in any house other than their own unless accompanied by their husbands. Once married, they have no property rights and are completely at the mercy of their husbands, who may despoil them at will. Muslim women in contrast are far better off. Their legal position and property rights, even against their husbands, are established and defended by law. . . . Hidden behind the veil, he notes with some distress, they can indulge in all kinds of mischief and wickedness, the scope for which is very great.[27]

Even when we take into account that Abū Tālib may have had his eye on possible British readers, his description clearly emphasizes the restraints placed on Englishwomen; as cultural relativists, both Lady Mary and Abū Tālib celebrate the legal and financial security as well as the greater personal freedom enjoyed by Turkish women.

III

When Lady Mary finds no Western equivalents to applaud or lament, she most fully exploits the romance of the exotic character of Turkey in her rich and detailed descriptions of Turkish beauty, descriptions that are the clearest instances of the particular kind of "othering" found in the embassy letters. On one unusual occasion, Lady Mary is allowed the privilege of visiting the women's baths, and from there she sends what is probably the first Western description of a place about which male travelers could only speculate. Lady Mary calls her account "a sight as you never saw in your Life and what no book of travells could inform you of," because " 'tis no less than Death for a Man to be found in one of these places" (1 April 1717; 1:315). *The Monthly Review,* appreciating the "masculine" character of Lady Mary's prose—"There is no affectation of female *delicatesse,* there are no *prettynesses,* no *Ladyisms* in these natural, easy familiar Epistles"—goes on to label this letter "one not to be paralleled in the narrative of any *male* Traveller." [28]

The event opens with Lady Mary's entering a sensuous room, and her aesthetic pleasure in the architecture of the bagnio concentrates on the thermal contrasts—marble basins fill continuously with both hot and cold running water as the melody of the streams flows from room to room:

> It is built of Stone in the shape of a Dome with no Windows but in the Roofe, which gives Light enough. . . . The next room is a very large one, pav'd with Marble, and all round it rais'd 2 Sofas of marble, one above another. There were 4 fountains of cold Water in this room, falling first into marble Basins and then running on the floor in little channels made for that purpose, which carry'd the streams into the next room, something less than this, with the same sort of marble sofas, but so hot with steams of sulphur proceeding from the baths joyning to it, twas impossible to stay there with one's Cloths on. The other 2 domes were the hot baths, one of which had cocks of cold Water turning into it to temper it to what degree of warmth the bathers have a mind to. (1:312–13)

While the grand and spacious dome, with its profusion of marble sofas, and the steamy rooms bespeak a luxury entirely different from English grandeur, Lady Mary insists that she is acquainted with "no European Court where the Ladys would have behav'd them selves in so polite a manner to a stranger" (1:313).

Even though it is Lady Mary's womanhood that allows her to enter the baths, dressed in her Western riding outfit, she is quite clearly an Englishwoman and an outsider. This distance allows her to view not only the magnificent structures of the bath but also the two hundred bathers themselves as aesthetic objects:

> The first sofas were cover'd with Cushions and rich Carpets, on which sat the Ladys, and on the 2nd their slaves behind 'em, but without any distinction of rank by their dress, all being in the state of nature, that is, in plain English, stark naked, without any Beauty or deffect conceal'd, yet there was not the least wanton smile or immodest Gesture amongst 'em. They Walk'd and mov'd with the same majestic Grace which Milton describes of our General Mother. There were many amongst them as exactly proportion'd as ever any Goddess was drawn by the pencil of Guido or Titian, and most of their skins shineingly white, only adorn'd by their Beautifull Hair divided into many tresses hanging on their shoulders, braided either with pearl or riband, perfectly representing the figures of the Graces. (1:313–14)

For all the particular physical details of Turkish women's braided hair and shining skins, the power of this passage lies in its allusions. Lady Mary views these women through layers of art and, as a result, perceives them not as unequal, inferior "others" but as quintessential examples of ancient womanhood: the Graces and Eve. The allusions locate the women in their proper non-Western geographical setting while simultaneously endowing them with the weight of Western classical culture. Their "otherness" has mythic dimensions: they are original, prelapsarian, beautiful. Painters, too, provide Lady Mary with a frame of reference. The lush oils of Guido Reni and the sensuous portraits of Titian, who was especially famous for his depiction of goddesses in languid repose, communicate some of the essential qualities of this luxurious womanhood, but Lady Mary laments that modern Western painters have lost the ability to paint equally evocatively. Wishing that Jervas (who created a portrait of Lady Mary in a shepherdess's costume) could have been there, invisible, to observe the scene, Lady Mary describes what he could have learned: "I fancy it would have very much improv'd his art to see so many fine Women naked in different postures, some in conversation, some working, others drinking Coffee or sherbet, and many negligently lying on their Cushions while their slaves (generally pritty Girls of 17 or 18) were employ'd in braiding their hair in several pritty manners" (1:314).[29]

For Lady Mary, beauty is embodied quite literally in the physicality of these women. Unused to seeing the flesh of two hundred women—especially considering the veils and the "Ferigée" that completely concealed all but a Turkish woman's eyes—Lady Mary marvels at their nakedness. The corporeality of these women, which Lady Mary never actually describes, is so palpable to her that she agrees with those who argue that, if it were the fashion to go naked, the face would be ignored. She judges that "the Ladys with the finest skins and most delicate shapes had the greatest share of my admiration, thô their faces were sometimes less beautifull than those of their companions" (1:314). More telling still is Lady Mary's response to the opportunity that would have allowed her not simply to view Turkish women's lives but to participate in their rituals: when invited to join the Turkish women in their bath—the epitome of her privilege as a female traveler—she refuses, preferring instead to satisfy some part of their curiosity by opening her skirt and revealing her stays. With amusement she notes, "They beleiv'd I was so lock'd up in that machine that it was not in my own power to open it, which contrivance they attributed to my Husband" (1:314). Here, in an unexpected reversal, "enslaved" Turkish women suppose a European woman imprisoned by her husband in a "modern" chastity belt.

It is her status as onlooker that leads Lady Mary to transform these women into objets d'art, and her "othering" lies in the distance of aesthetic appreciation. Mary Louise Pratt uses the word *bodyscapes* to describe travelers' language of this kind, arguing that the particularity and present-tense mode create a normalizing discourse: the observer writes as though the unique "scene/seen" of his or her experience is representative rather than personal. As a result, the native inhabitants observed are situated in a timeless present rather than a particular historical moment.[30] Such timelessness certainly exists in the description above, yet it is also the same timelessness that a viewer of a painting might experience. This phenomenon is so apparent that Lady Mary herself not only describes her own point of view as that of the observer but also invokes painters as references. These timeless moments became commonplace in postmedieval painting, according to Wendy Steiner, because Renaissance artists reasoned that an atemporal medium should represent atemporal subject matter. Accordingly, such painters participated in a self-conscious shift in aesthetics that resisted and finally rejected the collections of representations that characterize medieval narratives: "In a painting with vanishing-point perspective and chiaroscuro, the assumption is that we are observing a scene through a frame from a fixed vantage point *at one moment in time.*" Steiner further argues that Renaissance painters rejected unfolding identity, contingency, history, and desire (as they were depicted in the multiple panels of medieval narrative) and concentrated instead on design, atemporality, and the single moment arrested in time, a moment that depicts an eternal essence: "By prohibiting repeated subjects, painting could depict identity as either a single frozen moment or an eternal essence, but not as a continuity constantly modified by time. Thus, the Renaissance system reinforced the distinction between the isolated or transcendent self and the self modified by circumstance." [31]

This distinction between the two kinds of selves can also be found in the literary romance, a form itself composed of "stopped-action scenes" where the heroine is often suspended either in prison or in some other state of immobility. Both pictorial representations and romance narratives emphasize a transcendent moment at the end of a journey from the physical to the spiritual. The romance narrative—which often concentrates on a woman who loses her identity, enters a world of chaos, and emerges with a heightened sense of identity and order—concludes with the heroine arrested at that moment of reemergence into self and transcendence. [32] Lady Mary, too, sees such moments in the lives of Turkish women. The pleasure she finds in the freedoms she interprets as institutionalized for Turkish women grows in part out of the enchantment she feels in their company, in the splendor of their homes and costumes, and in the beauty of their bodies. However, she finds most compelling their surprising life stories—romance narratives of adventure and even heroism which often contain moments of transcendence that mimic contemporary fiction.

For instance, when taken to meet Fatima, the wife of the vizier's second in command, Lady Mary is introduced to a woman whose history could have been lifted from a seventeenth-century romance. This encounter begins when Lady Mary first enters a melodious and sensuous house. A large "Pavilion," as she calls it, was built round with gilded sashes, and the jasmine and honeysuckle vines emitted "a soft perfume encreas'd by a white Marble fountain playing sweet Water in the Lower part of the room, which fell into 3 or 4 basons with a pleasing sound" (1:349). The young woman herself is even more astonishing. Lady Mary claims at first to be rendered speechless by the young woman's beauty but then produces a positively ecstatic description (containing more ex-clamation marks than any other letter in the correspondence): "That surprizing Harmony of features! that charming result of the whole! that exact proportion of Body! that lovely bloom of Complexion unsully'd by art! the unutterable Enchantment of her Smile! But her Eyes! large and black with all the soft languishment of the bleu! every turn of her face discovering some new charm!" (1:350). As she did with the bathers, Lady Mary turns Fatima into an object of aesthetic contempla-tion, claiming that she took more pleasure in looking at the "beauteous Fatima than the finest piece of Scupture" (1:351).

She is most fascinated, however, by Fatima's life story, which emerges when the Greek interpreter accompanying Lady Mary whispers that she cannot believe Fatima—whose graceful manner and air of cultivated civility—could be Turkish by birth. Lady Mary is loath to repeat the remark, fearing that "[Fatima] would have been no better pleas'd with the Complement than one of our Court Beautys to be told she had the air of a Turk" (10 March 1718; 1:386). Yet the young woman, charmed by the comment, explains her cross-cultural heritage with a life story that could have been lifted from fiction: "My Mother was a Poloneze taken at the Seige of Caminiec, and my father us'd to rally me, saying he beleiv'd his Christian Wife had found some Christian Gallant, for I had not the Air of a Turkish Girl" (1:386). The most beautiful woman Lady Mary encounters in the entire course of her travels turns out to be a product of the spoils of war.

Stories of women being captured and sold into Turkish servitude were staples of the romance, of course, but Lady Mary's descriptions of Fatima also identify her with another conventional romance figure: the native as naturalized European aristocrat. Lady Mary's heroine, with her extraordinary beauty and personal grace—a woman half-European by birth and comfortably Western in deportment—stands as a living symbol of the confluence of Turkish reality and romance convention. Her life history, coupled with her high-ranking social position, allows Lady Mary to focus not on difference or "otherness" but on similarity and shared values. This likeness is an instance of leveling different from Lady Mary's claims for Turkish women's freedom in that Fatima validates Lady Mary's own Western standards of courtesy and civility.

Such difference (Fatima's beauty) and likeness (a graceful union of Turkish and European cultures) are here held in tension. But one par-ticular letter, composed as Lady Mary was about to leave Turkey in May

1718, moves beyond this balance and reveals that romance conventions actively shape Lady Mary's positive perceptions: by concentrating on the elements of romance, she downplays the harsher reality she has indeed seen. Opening with a complaint about male travel writers, Knolles and Rycaut specifically ("I am more enclin'd, out of a true female spirit of Contradiction, to tell you the falsehood of a great part of what you find in authors" [1.405]) and reiterating her familiar claim that Turkish women are freer than other women, Lady Mary moves to Turkish truth telling and generosity; she ends with a complaint about the Christian Armenians and their marriage customs. Embedded in the heart of this long letter is a three-part discussion that, proceeding according to a logic of association, moves in continuous paragraphs from a description of a Turkish bride to two instances of violence. Filtered through the conventions of romance, such violence is diluted and comes ultimately to serve the cause of female power.

The first event concerns the premarriage ceremonies for a Turkish bride. Dazzled by the occasion considered the most significant in any Turkish woman's life, Lady Mary again sees literary precedents. She likens this bride and her activities to the epithalamium for Helen by Theocritus, perhaps remembering these lines:

> And so in Sparta long ago the maids,
> With blooming hyacinth their locks among,
> . . . In one accord
> They sang, with measured beat and woven steps,
> While loud the halls rang with the marriage-lay.[33]

After the Turkish women meet at the bagnio and all two hundred arrange themselves on marble sofas, the virgins throw off their clothes, meet the bride at the door, and proceed to present the young woman to her mother: "[The bride] was a Beautifull Maid of about 17, very richly drest and shineing with Jewells, but was presently reduce'd by them to the state of nature. 2 others fill'd silver gilt pots with perfume and begun the procession, the rest following in pairs to the number of 30. The Leaders sung an Epithilamium answer'd by the others in chorus, and the 2 last led the fair Bride, her Eyes fix'd on the ground with a charming affectation of Modesty. In this order they march'd round the 3 large rooms of the bagnio" (1:407). Here, too, Lady Mary is the nonparticipating outsider who views the innocence inscribed on the bodies of these young women. However, the charming sweetness of the scene—the naked-

ness, the modesty, and the vulnerability of the bride—leads Lady Mary
to remember an incident involving a less fortunate young woman.

The second description opens with Lady Mary's comment that the
wit, civility, and liberty of Turkish women—which give them an opportunity to gratify "their evil Inclinations (if they have any)"—also
place them "very fully in the power of their Husbands to revenge them
if they are discover'd." [34] The recent death of a young woman, described
in graphic detail, proves the point:

> About 2 months ago there was found at day break not very far from my
> House the bleeding body of a young woman, naked, only wrapp'd in a
> coarse sheet, with 2 wounds with a knife, one in her side and another in
> her Breast. She was not yet quite cold, and so surprizingly Beautifull that
> there were very few men in Pera that did not go to look upon her, but it
> was not possible for any body to know her, no woman's face being known.
> She was suppos'd to be brought in dead of night from the Constantinople
> side and laid there. Very little enquiry was made about the Murderer,
> and the corps privately bury'd without noise. Murder is never persu'd by
> the King's officers as with us. Tis the busyness of the next Relations to
> revenge the dead Person; and if they like better to compound the matter
> for Money (as they generally do) there is no more said of it. One would
> imagine this deffect in their Government should make such Tragedys
> very frequent, yet they are extreamly rare, which is enough to prove the
> people not naturally cruel, neither do I think in many other particulars
> they deserve the barbarous character we give them. (1:407–8)

Lady Mary's ambivalence is apparent, even if she does not fully recognize it. She intends the incident to refute the argument that the Turks
are "naturally cruel" and "barbarous" in their treatment of women. [35]
However, her juxtaposition of the description of the splendid bride,
nakedly displayed for all her women friends to see, with that of the
naked body of an equally beautiful dead woman—who has become the
object of male examination—actually serves as a dreadful comment on
the position of women in Turkey. Even more lamentable is the anonymity of the dead woman. That Lady Mary ends the paragraph by
claiming that such incidents are rare does not overcome the powerful
visual impact: the figure of the dead woman is inevitably superimposed
on the image of the innocent bride. The freedom to engage in adultery,
a freedom she had earlier delighted in, comes to this end—seemingly
without specific comment from her. Yet this description of death and

burial is immediately followed by a much longer narrative about the history of a Spanish woman of quality with whom she became acquainted. Lady Mary's decision to place this story last in the trio is her means of overpowering the images of violence and vulnerability with the real-life history of a woman whom Lady Mary paints as creating triumph out of seeming tragedy.

The Spanish woman's troubles began when she and her party were attacked, boarded, and taken by a Turkish admiral. Lady Mary asks, "How shall I modestly tell you the rest of her Adventure? The same Accident happen'd to her that happen'd to the fair Lucretia so many Years before her, but she was too good a Christian to kill her selfe as that heathenish Roman did" (1:408). Her comment echoes Augustine's complaint that Lucretia, in choosing suicide, failed to join the ranks of the *feminae Christianae* who chose to live with their shame,[36] and she goes on to confer upon her heroine a heroic stature surpassing that of a classical martyr: the Spanish woman's decision involves a fight for the kind of female honor that Mark Bannister sees at work in French heroic novels—the heroine must maintain her *vertu* in order to create moral independence[37]—and she finds a solution that will allow her to live, but honorably.

As the events unfold, it appears that the Spanish woman will be saved from making such a decision because the admiral, charmed by her beauty and long suffering, immediately released the Spanish woman's brother, who later sent four thousand pounds sterling as ransom for his sister. The admiral then granted the young woman her freedom and returned the money to her as well. Liberty was not, however, without its price:

> The Lady very discreetly weigh'd the different treatment she was likely to find in her native Country. Her Catholic Relations, as the kindest thing they could do for her in her present Circumstances, would certainly confine her to a Nunnery for the rest of her Days. Her Infidel Lover was very handsome, very tender, fond of her, and lavish'd at her feet all the Turkish Magnificence. She answer'd him very resolutely that her Liberty was not so precious to her as her Honnour, that he could no way restore that but by marrying her. (1:408–9)

Lady Mary contrasts an honorable married life in an aristocratic Turkish household with an equally honorable but cloistered life in a Western nunnery: the Spanish woman would be forever lost if she were to return home, whereas marriage to a Turkish admiral protects her moral independence. It gives her, Lady Mary reports, "the satisfaction of knowing no Man could boast of her favours without being her Husband" (1:409).

That the Spanish woman made the proper choice, by Lady Mary's standards, is reinforced in the conclusion of the story. As her final reward, when she offered the money as her portion, the admiral refused it, saying that he was "too happy in her Possession." After the marriage, the admiral never took another wife and, at his death, left the Spanish woman one of the richest widows in Constantinople. Of course, a happy ending for such a story is one of the most important elements of romance because, as Gillian Beer has argued, the romance makes "apparent the hidden dreams of that world" and fulfills desires that cannot find "controlled expression within a society."[38] Lady Mary and her correspondents were probably relieved (perhaps even pleased) to see the Spanish woman rewarded with an "Infidel Lover" transformed into a handsome, tender, generous, faithful, loving, and rich husband. The Spanish woman is the perfect object of sympathetic identification for Lady Mary and her correspondents: she is the European woman who turns danger, humiliation, and pain into vast wealth, independence, and female triumph. But the events, because they mimic the plots of contemporary fiction, are also controlled through emotional distance: the very real terror the Spanish woman surely felt is subsumed in a structure that—if fiction holds true—points to a happy ending.[39] One familiar moral objection to the romance is that, in uncovering the "hidden dreams of the world," it changes a reader's perception of reality so that the quotidian character of everyday life becomes dissatisfying and, more seriously, the genuine dangers of the world are muted and become even greater real-life threats. Lady Mary reads the Spanish woman's story through the power of this fictional construct: the violence is essentially erased, and a dangerous and powerful man is transformed into a means of female triumph.

Lady Mary does not end the narrative focused on a fantasy. Instead, she concludes with a moral lesson about female values illustrated by her heroine's motives: "I am afraid you'l think that my Freind fell in love with her Ravisher, but I am willing to take her word for it that she acted wholly on principles of Honnour, thô I think she might be reasonably touch'd at his Generosity, which is very often found amongst the Turks of Rank" (1:409). Lady Mary rejects the sentimentalizing of love and instead situates the Spanish woman's choice entirely in the aristocratic realm of honor that is rewarded with the generosity of Turkish rank. An avid reader of romances, Lady Mary is eager to see Turkey in just these positive terms: while women may be vulnerable, even murdered, they are finally saved by heroic virtue and acts of will that secure them moral independence. The events of this story have not been lifted from *The Arabian Nights* or seventeenth-century French fiction; Lady Mary claims an acquaintance with the Spanish woman and insists on the "truth" of the account. But life in Turkey, as Lady Mary interprets it, holds a mirror up to fiction, and this becomes the reality she sees most clearly.

At the conclusion of her journey, as she travels through Genoa on the way back to England, Lady Mary is again presented with a vision of a woman who endured violence but emerged in triumph. When visiting the Doria family palaces, she celebrates not only the perfection of the architecture and the magnificence of the furniture but also the extensive art collection: "I am charm'd with nothing so much as the Collection of Pictures by the Pencils of Raphael, Paulo Veronese, Titian, Carache [Carracci], Michael Angelo, Guido [Reni], and Corregio, which 2 I mention last as my particular favorites" (28 August 1718; 1:431). Her appreciation of these particular painters, however, depends less on the excellence of their artistic techniques than on the way they represent suffering:

> I own I can find no pleasure in objects of Horror, and in my Opinion the more naturaly a Crucifix is represented the more disagreable it is. These, my beloved Painters, shew nature and shew it in the most charming Light. I was particularly pleas'd with a Lucretia in the House of Balbi. The expressive Beauty of that Face and Bosome gives all the passion of Pity and admiration that could be rais'd in the Soul by the finest poem on that Subject. A Cleopatra of the same hand deserves to be mention'd, and I should say more of her if Lucretia had not first engag'd my Eyes. (1:431)

Lady Mary rejects the brutality of the "naturally" represented crucifix, preferring the "charming Light" of Reni's interpretation of Lucretia's suicide. This "charming Light" prohibits a direct response to a visceral physicality or a sympathetic identification with those emotions that are personally threatening—horror and powerlessness—and instead provides a means to transform pain into a more distant, controlled, shaped, and delimited aesthetic context.

This is precisely the veil of romance she brings to the embassy letters.

In Turkey, as in her response to this painting, Lady Mary views the body of a woman in an aesthetic context; uncovered and sensuous, it is an object worthy of painterly attention. Yet in the very act of uncovering, the body is exposed to danger, subject to violence, and vulnerable. The implicit threat in making visible what was once hidden must be muted, and so Lady Mary veils the danger with recourse to literature: Lucretia's story, like the Spanish woman's, "gives all the passion of Pity and admiration that could be rais'd in the Soul by the finest poem on that Subject." It does not result in horror because Lady Mary imposes on her observations the "charming Light" of fictive structures, romance narratives where women can be lifted out of danger and rewarded with a happy ending. This strategy allows her to argue for the autonomy and freedom the female heroic promises while glossing over the pain some women experience in Turkey. More important, it leads her to interpret her heroines as forever triumphant in moments of female transcendence.

As the embassy sails home, Lady Mary begins to play a new part: she becomes the world-weary traveler, longing for the familiar, made wise by her experience. She also begins to write the kinds of letters she will spend the next few years of her life composing—satiric portraits of the high life of the aristocracy. But in her final letter to the Abbé Conti, the empowered but weary traveler is particularly evident. The letter serves as a fitting conclusion to the embassy correspondence, for here Lady Mary flatters her own knowledge and experience while pretending to envy the uncomplicated life of an English milkmaid: "After having read all that is to be found in the Languages I am mistriss of, and having decaid my sight by midnight studys, I envy the easy peace of mind of a ruddy milk maid who, undisturb'd by doubts, hears the Sermon with humility every Sunday, having not confus'd the sentiments of Natural Duty in her head by the vain Enquirys of the Schools, who may be more Learned, yet after all must remain as ignorant" (September 1718; 1:444). Such disingenuous "envy" merely serves, of course, to emphasize just how far Lady Mary, now a cosmopolitan citizen of the world, has come. That her sensibilities have been radically modified is clear in her pronouncement about the differences between Turkish and Western customs: "[The Turkish people] are not so unpolish'd as we represent them. Tis true their Magnificence is of a different taste from ours, and perhaps of a better. I am allmost of the opinion that they have a right notion of Life; [for] they consume it in Music, Gardens, Wine, and delicate eating, while we are tormenting our brains with some Scheme of Politics or studying some Science which we can never attain. . . . I had rather be a rich Effendi with all his ignorance, than Sir Isaac Newton with all his knowledge" (19 May 1718; 1:414–15). Lady Mary laments the end of the journey that has brought her improved understanding and an expanded worldview; having undergone her own transformation, she hopes to recover the skills necessary to endure provincial English life and the ability to pretend that the plain fare of England is preferable to the sensuous delights of the East:

> After having seen part of Asia and Africa and allmost made the tour of Europe, I think the honest English Squire more happy who verily beleives the Greek wines less delicious than March beer, that the African fruits have not so fine a flavour as golden Pipins, and the Becá-figuas of Italy are not so well tasted as a rump of Beef, and that, in short, there is no perfect Enjoyment of this Life out of Old England. I pray God I may think so for the rest of my Life, and since I must be contented with our scanty allowance of Daylight, that I may forget the enlivening Sun of Constantinople. (September 1718; 1:444)

Chapter Four

※✖✖✖✖

The "Spectatress":
Satire and the Aristocrats

Upon her return to England, and without the "enlivening sun" of Constantinople, Lady Mary supplies her own brilliance in a series of satiric letters composed primarily during the 1720s and 1730s and sent to her sister and other aristocratic women friends. As in the Turkish Embassy Letters, she purports to be the detached observer of scenes before her: "As for my selfe, having nothing to say I say nothing. I insensibly dwindle into a Spectatress" (20 March 1725; 2:48). Yet her strategy in these letters is not to make the unknown familiar, as she did with the sensuous and exotic sights of a foreign culture, but to estrange the known. In this alternate form of journalistic reportage, Lady Mary turns her gaze to the customs of the English beau monde, and there she sees manners and customs, follies and foibles, equally remarkable: "I writ to you very lately (my dear Sister) but ridiculous things happening, I cannot help (as far as in me lies) sharing all my Pleasures with you. I own I enjoy vast delight in the Folly of Mankind, and God be prais'd that is an inexhaustible Source of Entertainment" (September 1725; 2:56).

Lady Mary assumes the right to comment on English society because she has a keen eye for the ridiculous and a certainty that her world is a stage full of absurdity. Yet her claim to "dwindle into a Spectatress" is as revealing as Millamant's "dwindling into a wife," for both women speak their desire for and their resistance to the assigned roles. In Turkey Lady Mary's womanhood and aristocracy functioned together relatively well: her discussions with Turkish men of rank led her to believe that aristocrats everywhere shared universal sentiments, while the romance allowed her to see women as free. In England, however, Lady Mary's womanhood and aristocracy form no such comfortable equation, and, through the course of the letters, these two important elements of her own self-definition are revealed to be a source of active conflict.

The "inexhaustible Source" of folly and "Entertainment" she cites above is the aristocracy. The frenetic energy of upper-class social life and its shifting personal alliances are a continual source of amusement for her and her sister: "All our Acquaintance are run mad; they do such things, such monstrous and stupendous things! Lady Harvey and Lady Bristol have quarrell'd in such a polite manner that they have given one another all the Titles so liberally bestow'd amongst the Ladys at Billingsgate. . . . Ned Thompson is as happy as the Money and charms of Belle Dunch can make him, and a miserable Dog for all that" (February 1725; 2:45–46). Yet for all her attention to the specific excesses of her acquaintances, she ends, contrary to the evidence in the letter itself, by insisting on the insignificance of her subject: "For my part, as it is my establish'd Opinion That this Globe of ours is no better than a Holland Cheese and the Walkers about in it Mites, I possess my Mind in patience, let what will happen, and should feel tolerably easy thô a great Rat came and eat halfe of it up."

It is this tension between the "stupendous" and the inconsequential that provides her with ample material for satire, primarily because she understands that the rules for polite behavior are subject to constant revision. The chief function of the courtly nobility, according to Norbert Elias, was "to distinguish themselves, to maintain themselves as a distinct formation, a social counterweight to the bourgeoisie." Yet once the middle class had the money and the power to mimic the behavior of the privileged, the aristocratic models of conduct became useless as a visible means of rank and distinction. Because "the embarrassment-threshold," as Elias calls it, constantly advanced, aristocrats asserted their control through "the intense vigilance with which [they] observe[d] and polish[ed] everything that distinguishe[d] them from people of lower rank: not only the external signs of status, but also their speech, their gestures, their social amusements and manners."[1] As aristocrats, Lady Mary and her friends perceive themselves as standard-bearers of the best in manners and conduct, and thus Lady Mary, sensitively attuned to this theatrical but shifting threshold, feels the pressure to maintain aristocratic class distinctions.

Yet her comments about life in English society are shaped not only by her rank but also by her gender; as a woman, she is controlled by a dominant culture that imposes very real restrictions on her behavior. Thus when she is invited, as an aristocrat, to set and maintain certain class standards, she must also face, as a member of a "privileged underclass," the constraints imposed upon her by a culture constructed according to male models. In a changing early-eighteenth-century culture, when wealth could be earned by men outside of court circles, aristocratic men still set the standards for the marks of individual male status. For women of privilege, however, the problem was made doubly difficult because the aristocratic imperatives often failed to match the changing demands of gender: on the one hand, aristocratic women had to display their difference in order to maintain it; on the other hand, they found that public display for *all* women had begun to be equated with sexual license. The tension in her remark about the notorious Lady Vane (whose "Memoirs of a Lady of Quality" are found in Smollett's *Peregrine Pickle*) comes from Lady Vane's public flaunting of her supposedly private sexual liaison, while the humor comes from Lady Mary's description of this "private" female behavior in terms of the "public" male prerogative of patriotism: "Lady Vane is returned hither in company with [her lover] Lord Berkeley, and went with him in publick to Cranford, where they remain as happy as love and youth can make them. I am told that though she does not pique herself upon fidelity to any one man (which is but a narrow way of thinking), she boasts that she has always been true to her nation, and, notwithstanding foreign attacks, has always reserved her charms for the use of her own countrymen" (January 1739; 2:133–34). In equating a woman's scandalous love affair with English nationalism, an equation that makes sexual fidelity "but a narrow way of thinking," Lady Mary turns illicit female sexuality into a necessary sacrifice in the "higher" cause of political solidarity. And the joke is funny precisely because such gender differences are there to be exploited.

Thus, for a noblewoman, class and gender form an unstable compound. Lady Mary had to devise a means by which a gentlewoman could "achieve effective public personification when the entire realm of public dignity had been defined in a specifically male way through the use of the male body-image." [2] While the subjects of these satiric letters concern almost exclusively the men and women of her own class, her treatment of questions of gender within the aristocratic imperatives highlights "difference" in a particularly visible way: it becomes a locus of anxiety as gentlewomen attempt to find a way to display their difference not just from nonaristocratic women but from all men as well. With neither political nor economic power at her disposal, Lady Mary exploits the considerable "cultural capital," to use Bourdieu's phrase, that she does have: to authorize and reject standards of conduct in the social world.

It is therefore not surprising, considering these competing, often contradictory pressures, that Lady Mary's letters are almost obsessively concerned with transgressions, for it is here, in their violation, that "correct" standards of conduct are particularly apparent. When an acquaintance, especially a woman, transgresses the code, Lady Mary is quick to cite and even to dwell on the infraction. But she is often surprisingly slow to censure. In fact, she is just as likely to celebrate the unauthorized behavior as condemn it. Such a contradictory construction of the limits of polite behavior indicates Lady Mary's resistance to the definitions of proper behavior in a culture whose standards were subject to revision, and the degree of this resistance is reflected in her language: the more extreme the transgression, the more extreme her discourse becomes as she crosses linguistic boundaries and mixes incompatible styles. This mixing, coming as it does from an aristocrat and a woman, complicates the categories of "high" and "low," "classical" and "grotesque," "institutionalized" and "unsanctioned." The Bakhtinian perspective on history—which produces a description of culture predicated on a "carnivalesque" of subversive "low" discourse that acts to put pressure on the monolithic social structure above—has been revised by Peter Stallybras and Allon White, who assert that the culture actually lurches between these two extremes. The high, they argue, is dependent on the low for the energy that conflict generates: "The primary site of contradiction, the site of conflicting desires and mutually incompatible representation, is undoubtedly the 'low.' . . . The 'top' attempts to reject and eliminate the 'bottom' for reasons of prestige and status, only to discover, not only that it is in some way frequently dependent upon that low-Other . . . but also that the top *includes* that low symbolically, as a primary eroticized constituent of its own fantasy life."[3] Lady Mary's always satiric, relentlessly evaluative, and very funny letters prove that, when viewed from within, the early-eighteenth-century aristocratic "upper" structure has no such singular monolithic status or internal coherence; conflict from within destabilizes and defines the "top."

Especially for aristocratic women, this conflict is largely generated by a strengthening demarcation of the boundary between public and private life. Throughout the eighteenth century, women increasingly lost their opportunities to display the "virtuous visibility" Mary Astell had once hoped they would signify and instead came to find that their virtue was defined primarily through their willingness to disappear into a bourgeois domestic invisibility. Thus the pressure on women generally and increasingly was to withdraw. Lady Mary's letters prove, however, that in reality this "boundary" between public and private is altogether permeable, for her narratives constantly disrupt the convenient binary in a form that itself mimics the problem. She re-creates instances of aristocratic public display through the reputedly "private" epistolary form, a sharing of her exaggerated descriptions of aristocratic performance. But she also circulates anecdotes concerning the private—often the sexual and thus supposedly "invisible"—lives of her female acquaintances in an epistolary form that makes such private behavior public. Thus the division between those two supposedly separate realms exists only as a creative fiction, one that is communally agreed upon but one that can be consciously manipulated when the circumstances demand it. For an aristocratic woman, such manipulation is essential, because a merely reputed division between public and private allows aristocratic women to display themselves in public, as one imperative of their status, in all their finery and with all the attendant dignity and respect due to their rank; simultaneously, however, the division allows them to act in private *as though* their behavior were not subject to the same scrutiny and the same potential public censure.

In the letters concerning the English beau monde, Lady Mary attempts to work through these competing demands of class and gender, to exploit the space for revision offered by the shifting "embarrassment-threshold," and to emphasize the impossibility of separating private from public behavior: from her privileged but female vantage point, she tries to negotiate a compromise that allows a woman to maintain both a visible and a respectable status in a world quick to seize upon instances of female misconduct. In the end, she fails to negotiate this compromise between display and decorum, but in the process she produces letters that sparkle with all the wit and verbal richness that the tension of competing imperatives can create.

I

Her revision of the social codes takes place within a relatively enclosed community of similarly privileged people. According to historian John Cannon, the "social elite" in 1720 was indeed a small group, and thus the opportunities for Lady Mary to learn the intimate details of all her acquaintances, both male and female, would have been many.[4] Even though she calls herself a "Spectatress," she is a "private" journalist in ways Addison and Steele cannot be. Unlike a newspaper reporter, she names names—citing specific individuals, telling their private stories, authorizing and criticizing as she pleases. She recounts, in one instance, the "freshest news in Town" concerning the near "Fatal Accident" that "happen'd 3 nights ago to a very pritty young Fellow, Brother to Lord Finch, who was drinking with a dearly beloved Drab whom you may have heard of, by the name of Sally Salisbury." The participants are named and the "accident" detailed: "In a jealous pique, she stabb'd him to the heart with a Knife. He fell down dead immediately, but a Surgeon being call'd for, and the Knife drawn out of his body, he open'd his Eyes, and his first words were to beg her to be freinds [*sic*] with him, and Kiss'd her" (25 December [1722]; 2:20). Lady Mary ridicules this young man of aristocratic lineage both for his stupidity in associating with a dangerous lower-class woman and more specifically for the sentimentalizing of his romantic attachment to this notorious prostitute.[5]

Moreover, unlike Addison and Steele, whose purpose was transparently didactic, Lady Mary and her aristocratic female epistolary friends participate in a subtler form of value definition. They desire, on the one hand, to share their sensibilities as a means of confirming their community, and, on the other hand, they participate in reworking the subtleties of that system. Lady Mary's assumption that her sister would appreciate the absurdity of the fracas recounted above confirms Patricia Meyer Spacks's claims, in her fascinating examination of gossip, that the sharing of such information grows out of a system of exchange, a partnership that pits "us" against "them": within what Spacks calls "the economics of gossip," there is a consistent sharing—of point of view, information, and reassurance.[6] This mutuality is essential because the information Lady Mary presents sometimes contains no overt judgment; the letters themselves create, as Bruce Redford asserts, both the text and context.[7] Take, for instance, the following comment Lady Mary sent to her sister concerning the Duchess of Montagu:

> Her Daughter Belle is at this instant in the Paradisal state of receiving visits every day from a passionate Lover who is her first Love, who she thinks the finest Gentleman in Europe, and is besides that Duke of Manchester. Her Mama and I often laugh and sigh refflecting on her Felicity, the Consummation of which will be in a fortnight. (2 April 1723; 2:22)

The seemingly innocent comment, that she laughs and sighs watching these young lovers, can also be read as the more barbed claim that the lovers' "Felicity"—not their marriage—will be shortly consummated. This kind of information, without an overt emotional context, elicits similar responses from epistolary partners once intimacy is generated and sustained. Lady Mary can send this letter to the Countess of Mar knowing that their shared identity—as sisters, as epistolary partners, and as aristocratic women—will evoke a mutual response: her sister, familiar with the participants, will laugh at Lady Mary's characterizations; also familiar with the less than satisfying marriage Lady Mary had made for herself, the Countess of Mar will appreciate the underlying lament. In fact, this mutual interpretation of events is as important as the events themselves; it is the shared epistolary system that creates significance, the set of normative behaviors, and the code of standards.

This sharing goes beyond similar emotional responses, for the fact of community creates the space for a redefinition of values. If, as Spacks has argued, gossip provides "a resource for the subordinated" and "a crucial means of self-expression, a crucial form of solidarity,"[8] such solidarity would seem to be predicated on knowledge, because "knowing the code"—and managing not to violate it—should determine whether one is included or excluded from community. However, the problems of ignorance and knowledge are more complicated than they initially appear. Two anecdotes, which reassess the value and function of marriage for both men and women, serve as paradigms for the ways Lady Mary treats ignorance and knowledge as she cites and then judges violations of the codes, judgments that function as opportunities for such redefinition and creation of community.

Tradition says that a honeymoon failure can be attributed to the bride's fear or ineptitude as well as to the groom's past debauchery. But here the situation is reversed and extraordinary enough for Lady Mary to retell:

> I am in hopes your King of France behaves better than our Duke of Bedford, who by the care of a pious Mother certainly preserv'd his Virginity to his marriage bed, where he was so much disapointed in his fair Bride (who thô his own Inclination could not bestow on him those expressless Raptures he had figur'd to himselfe) that he allready Pukes at the very name of her, and determines to let his Estate go to his Brother, rather than go through the filthy Drudgery of getting an Heir to it. N.B. This is true History and I think the most extrodinary has happen'd in this last age. This comes of living till sixteen without a competent knowledge either of practical or speculative Anatomy, and litterally thinking fine Ladys compos'd of Lillys and Roses. (August 1725; 2:55–56)

Lady Mary's complaint, directed at both the young man's distaste for his conjugal duties and those mothers who fail to teach their sons about "practical or speculative Anatomy," is couched in imagery almost Swiftian in its physicality: the groom, reminiscent of Stephron, "allready Pukes" at his beloved's name and considers sexual intercourse finally as "filthy Drudgery." In the last two sentences, however, this satirical tone shifts to a genuine lament about his "pious Mother" and her cultivation of a belief that women are indeed the "Lillys and Roses" found in a romance. Thus the young man's unrealized hopes about the bliss of the marriage bed are caused by both ignorance and exaggerated expectations.

The second anecdote presents a deviation resulting not from too much ignorance but from too much knowledge:

> As for news, the last Wedding is that of Peg Pelham, and I have, I think, never seen so comfortable a prospect of Happyness. According to all appearance she can not fail of being a Widow in 6 weeks at farthest, and

accordingly she has been so good a Huswife to line her wedding cloaths with black. (March 1727; 2:72)

The humor of the passage rests with Lady Mary's juxtaposing the generally satiric comment on the cause of marital bliss—widowhood—with the more specific comment on Peg Pelham's huswifery, an "oeconomy" always desirable in a new bride. Yet Lady Mary's ironic admiration also displays her fear that the condition of marriage generally is so unstable that she can subtly authorize this young bride not simply to line her trousseau with black but to marry only with widowhood in sight. This, of course, undermines a whole set of traditional values articulated in the larger culture. Thus, even though Lady Mary applauds Peg Pelham and ridicules the duke, both of her narratives serve as larger comments concerning the "correct" expectations one should bring to marriage, and through this process Lady Mary and her friends undercut and redefine the power of the standards they are told to honor.

The pressure generated when competing violations occur within a single incident—and Lady Mary's subsequent celebration of one and condemnation of the other—sheds light not only on the specific standards she brings to bear but also on her sense of the theatricality underlying fashionable behavior. An extended narrative, concerning the transgression of the sexual codes by a witty set of lovers who dupe an insensitive intruder, focuses on a young woman who fails to read the social signals (and whose ignorance is therefore punishable) and a couple who knowingly transgress the boundaries of sexual decorum with a style Lady Mary admires. The incident involves the daughter of a colonel whose self-absorption causes her to step over the "embarrassment-threshold" and whose insensitivity is ridiculed and ultimately exploded by the ploy of the clever lovers. Lady Mary calls the tale "the most diverting story about Town" and opens with an introduction to the major characters: "I can't tell whither you know a Tall, musical, silly, ugly thing, niece to Lady Essex Roberts, who is call'd Miss Leigh. She went a few day ago to visit Mrs. Betty Titchburne, Lady Sunderland's sister, who lives in the House with her, and was deny'd at the door; but with the true manners of a great Fool told the porter that if his Lady was at home she was very positive she would be very glad to see her" (23 June 1727; 2:78). Lady Mary's characterization of Miss Leigh, in the unpleasant adjectives "Tall, musical, silly, ugly," is expanded upon by Walpole, who in his correspondence describes her as "a virtuosa, a musician, a madwoman" apparently so in love with Handel that she wore his picture, along with the Pretender's, on her breast.[9] With the manners of "a great Fool," Miss Leigh ignores an important social convention: when one is politely refused entrance at the door, one turns with equal politeness and leaves.

Her unwelcome intrusion is a blunder so insensitive that it startles Mrs. Titchburne, who "was ready to drop down at the sight of her," but she tells the young woman, "in a grave way," that entry has been "deny'd to every mortal" because she intends "to pass the Evening in devout preparations." These preparations, however, turn out to have quite a secular purpose: Miss Leigh had not been there a quarter of an hour when there is a "violent rap" at the door, and somebody "vehemently" runs upstairs. Miss Titchburne, surprised again, says she "beleiv'd it was Mr. Edgcombe" and is "quite amaz'd how he took it into his Head to visit her." During these excuses, Lady Mary writes, "enter Edgcombe, who appear'd frighted at the sight of a third person." Miss Titchburne's seeming surprise and her disingenuous claim to be amazed by his presence is played off Edgcombe's very real shock upon seeing the musical Miss Leigh.

Although a scenario for instant embarrassment is set up, the lovers are quick to flatter Miss Leigh's vanity by asking her to play. When she sits down at the harpsichord, however, "her Audience decamp'd to the Bed Chamber, and left her to play over 3 or 4 lessons to her selfe." This scene, whose centerpiece is Miss Leigh's playing blithely to an empty house, could have been lifted from a comedy of manners: by enlivening her narrative with shifting entrances and exits, energy and confusion, Lady Mary creates a kind of dramatic irony complete with stage directions ("enter Edgcombe"). She invites her readers to share in the ridicule by aligning themselves with the witty lovers in the same way they would with a hero or heroine in comedy—for self-assurance and knowledge are the valued commodity in controlling this plot.

As Lady Mary continues to juxtapose the young woman's barging into a situation where she is obviously unwanted against her equally blind response to being abandoned and even shunned, the absurdity of the situation grows: "They return'd, and made what excuses they could, but said very frankly they had not heard her performance and begg'd her to begin again, which she comply'd with, and gave them the opertunity of a second retirement. Miss Leigh was by this time all Fire and Flame to see her heavenly Harmony thus slighted, and when they return'd told them she did not understand playing to an empty room. Mr. Edgecombe begg'd ten thousand pardons, and said if she would play Godi, it was a Tune he dy'd to hear, and it would be an Obligation he should never forget" (2:79). The couple's "frankly" claiming not to have heard a note and their retiring to the bedroom once again culminate in the wordplay of Mr. Edgcombe's request for the aria from Handel's *Ottone,* "a Tune he dy'd to hear" (2:79n). The pun on "dy'd" and its older meaning of sexual climax is doubly funny, for it is both a "frank" statement of his present intention and a description of the reason he had "not heard her performance" in the moments just past. Had Miss Leigh any self-awareness, she would have fled at that point, but not surprisingly she once again behaves inappropriately, this time in an act of retribution: "She made answer, she would do him a much greater Obligation by her Absence, which she suppos'd was all that was wanting at that Time, and run down stairs in a great Fury, to publish as fast as she could, and was so indefatigable in this pious design that in 4 and twenty hours all the people in Town had heard the story, and poor Edgcombe met with nothing where ever he went but complements about his third Tune, which is reckon'd very handsome in a Lover past forty" (2:79). Lady Mary's sympathies obviously lie with the clever lovers and their humiliation of an unwanted intruder who fails to see that rather than damaging Mr. Edgcombe's reputation she has made him and his "third Tune" objects of admiration. The lovers, fully aware of the absurdity of the situation, act with confident aggression, and thus Lady Mary empowers them to treat Miss Leigh with such contempt. Equally important, Lady Mary concentrates on exposing a doltish breach of decorum rather than the illicit love affair between two equally perceptive, intelligent, and clever people who are willing to carry a joke as far as it will go.[10]

II

Exposure, however, is a given for aristocrats, male and female. They maintained their status through the manipulation of the difference they could create between themselves and the "lower orders," a difference apparent in the rich and expensive fashions that artificially constructed the aristocratic body as well as in the class accents and mannered gestures of aristocratic "body management," as Dorinda Outram calls it.[11] Accordingly, public violations of the social codes provide a particularly rich opportunity for Lady Mary to push the boundaries of social and linguisitic decorum: when aristocratic exposure takes place within a legitimate and sanctioned form of public display—when aristocratic women necessarily invite the gaze of onlookers as one imperative of their status—Lady Mary delights in producing grotesque descriptions of an excessive, too insistent female presence.

In a letter addressed to Lady Pomfret and concerned with the events surrounding the October 1738 coronation of George III, Lady Mary refers to the "common" mob that rioted that day: "Our mobs grow very horrible; here are a vast number of legs and arms that only want a head to make a very formidable body" (2:125). This indistinguishable mass of fragmented body parts is typical of aristocratic representations of the "lower orders": the "grotesque body"—a multiple image that is "teeming, always already part of a throng" [12]—is opposed to the fully constituted and coherent classical body. The "want [of] a head" further emphasizes the disjunction between the contained and "managed" aristocratic body and the ungovernable, headless, "grotesque" mob, a group represented in the aristocratic imagination as lacking the unique individuality and singularity of the "upper" culture.

Lady Mary goes on, however, to make a double contrast by separating herself and Lady Pomfret from the equally frenetic aristocratic preparations for the day: "But while we readers of history are, perhaps, refining too much, the happier part of our sex are more usefully employed in preparation for the birth-day, where I hear Lady Pembroke is to shine in a particular manner, and Lady Cowper to exhibit some new devices worthy of her genius" (1:125). In this same role of "reader of history," Lady Mary had earlier created a brilliant series of grotesque portraits—emphasizing the vanity of the women present for the 1727 coronation ceremonies of George II—that highlights the comedy of female display. She does not employ images of a headless, fragmented mob teeming with scattered body parts but instead anatomizes individual aristocratic female bodies so that each takes on gigantic proportions.

Claiming that it was "very entertaining to Observe the variety of airs that all meant the same thing, the Business of every walker there being to conceal Vanity and gain Admiration" (October 1727; 2:85), Lady Mary emphasizes the visual power of the spectacle:

But she that drew the greatest Number of Eyes was indisputably the Countess of Orkney. She exposed behind a mixture of Fat and Wrinkles, and before a considerable pair of Bubbys a good deal withered, a great Belly that preceeded her; add to this the inimitable roll of her Eyes, and her Grey Hair which by good Fortune stood directly upright, and 'tis impossible to immagine a more Delightfull Spectacle. She had embellish'd all this with a great deal of Magnificence which made her as big again as usual, and I shou'd have thought her one of the largest things of God's making if my Lady St. John had not display'd all her Charms that day. (2:85–86)

The countess's body, displayed in a sanctioned public space and not simply visible but consciously adorned, invites and even demands onlookers, and thus Lady Mary relentlessly returns to the magnitude of her size, actually increasing her already too spectacular presence. Lady Mary then doubles the impact of her humor by claiming that the countess would have been "one of the largest things of God's making" were it not for the too substantial charms of Lady St. John—whom, delightfully, Lady Mary does not even bother to describe. This grotesquerie increases as Lady Mary's account itself multiplies: "The poor Dutchess of Montross Crep'd along with a Dozen of black Snakes playing round her Face; and my Lady Portland (who is fall'n away since her dismission from Court) represented very finely an Egyptian Mummy embroider'd over with Hieroglyphics" (2:86). The female body is a source of both humor and revulsion, as Lady Mary calls attention to its inherent "flaws"—the countess's fat and wrinkles—and as it is inappropriately constructed in a Medusan and mummified style complete with scripted hieroglyphics. In the end, however, Lady Mary ends up actively appreciating the aristocratic female display, taking delight in the shared vanity: "In General I could not perceive but the Old were as well pleas'd as the Young, and I (who dread growing Wise more than any thing in the World) was overjoy'd to observe one can never outlive one's Vanity" (2:86). She represents this group of aristocratic celebrants as very different from the "arms and legs" of the common mob. For all their aristocratic multiplicity and grotesqueness, they do not fall into the category of the indistinguishable mass; instead, Lady Mary endows them with a too visible aristocratic individuality.

This giddy, exclusively descriptive celebration of the public display of female "charms" differs from Lady Mary's account of a group of aristocratic women storming the House of Lords. She creates an image that indeed emphasizes and criticizes gender transgression by highlighting female display, but she makes her "teeming throng" of duchesses and ladies too apparent in an arena inappropriate to their status *and* their gender: the special aristocratic world of politics, a public space long held by the aristocracy to be an exclusively male province. She ridicules this violation in the "high" language of an epic discourse that itself had always been gendered; yet her exploitation of these conventions—as an attempt to deflate, diminish, and "feminize" the event in the mock epic form—actually results in her endowing her acquaintances with the genuine power that the heroic conventions confer.

Opening the letter by claiming that the whole town has been obsessed with politics, specifically a long and bitter debate on 1 March 1739, Lady Mary argues that "one ought to have some of the gifts of Lilly or Partridge" to discuss the matter and that only those mortals with "the talent of divination" should participate in politics. Having situated political intrigue in the realm of the supernatural, she laments that she is alone in this opinion:

> The ladies [have] shewn their zeal and appetite for knowledge in a most glorious manner. At the last warm debate in the House of Lords, it was unanimously resolved there should be no crowd of unnecessary auditors; consequently the fair sex were excluded, and the gallery destined to the sole use of the House of Commons. Notwithstanding which determination, a tribe of dames resolved to shew on this occasion, that neither men nor laws could resist them. These heroines were Lady Huntingdon, the Duchess of Queensbury, the Duchess of Ancaster, Lady Westmoreland, Lady Cobham, Lady Charlotte Edwin, Lady Archibald Hamilton and her daughter, Mrs. Scott, and Mrs. Pendarvis [*sic*], and Lady Frances Saunderson. I am thus particular in their names, since I look upon them to be the boldest assertors, and most resigned sufferers for liberty, I ever read of. (2:135–36)

Here Lady Mary exploits the language of revolution: this "tribe of dames," including "the boldest assertors" and the "most resigned sufferers for liberty," refuses to acknowledge the bounds of acceptable female behavior in allowing "neither men nor laws"—political power—to exclude them. Equally important is the fact that Lady Mary was a longtime friend and journalistic supporter of Walpole and his government, and these women favored the Opposition. Thus empowered by the spectacle they make of themselves and by her own political convictions, Lady Mary ridicules these women for their transgressions.

The conflict grows into confrontation as the women demand the right to enter:

> They presented themselves at the door at nine o'clock in the morning, where Sir William Saunderson respectfully informed them the [Lord] Chancellor had made an order against their admittance. The Duchess of Queensbury, as head of the squadron, pished at the ill-breeding of a mere lawyer, and desired him to let them up stairs privately. After some modest refusals he swore by G—— he would not let them in. Her grace, with a noble warmth, answered, by G—— they would come in, in spite of the Chancellor and the whole House. This being reported, the Peers resolved to starve them out; an order was made that the doors should not be opened till they had raised their siege. (2:136)

Lady Mary contrasts Sir William's initially respectful refusal to admit "the squadron" with the duchess's lack of respect in treating the Usher of the Black Rod as a "mere lawyer" and "pish[ing] at" his ill breeding. The duchess's own transgressions are highlighted when she provokes a shouting match, including the trading of the oath "by G—— ," on the steps of the House of Lords. This seeming impasse is finally resolved, however, through clever female "stratagems in war":

> These Amazons now shewed themselves qualified for the duty even of foot-soldiers; they stood there till five in the afternoon, without either sustenance or evacuation, every now and then playing vollies of thumps, kicks, and raps, against the door, with so much violence that the speakers in the House were scarce heard. When the Lords were not to be conquered by this, the two Duchesses (very well apprized of the use of stratagems in war) commanded a dead silence of half an hour; and the Chancellor, who thought this a certain proof of their absence, (the Commons also being very impatient to enter) gave order for the opening of the door; upon which they all rushed in, pushed aside their competitors, and placed themselves in the front rows of the gallery. (2:136–37)

Lady Mary exploits military language to emphasize further the discrepancy between a relatively trivial event and the epic language of battle. A "squadron" of "foot-soldiers" led by a duchess performs its "duty" by participating in a "siege," and, even though they cannot "conquer," when "commanded" by the "strategems in war" they manage to "rush in." The sacrifice the women make is not, of course, the risking of their lives; it is a sacrifice of the body, and Lady Mary does not hesitate to point to the biological functions of duchesses and ladies who stand "without either sustenance or evacuation." Ultimately, the women "win" not through continued violence or rebellion but through a "stratagem" of passive resistance—silence. Once the men are fooled into believing that the rebellion has been squashed, the women take their "rightful" places in the front of the gallery.

A revealing contrast to Lady Mary's narrative is the firsthand account by Mrs. Pendarves, a member of the "squadron," who opens her letter with a mildly ironic insistence on the value of public rather than private service: "Like a most noble patriot, I have given up all private advantages for the good of my country." Unfortunately, this promising beginning does not hold as Mrs. Pendarves settles into a more pedestrian recounting of the events:

> To tell you all the particulars of *our provocations,* the insults of the door-keepers, and our *unshaken intrepidity,* would flourish out more paper than a single frank would contain, but we bore the buffets of a stinking crowd from half an hour after ten till five in the afternoon, without moving an inch from our places, only see-sawing about as the motion of the multitude forced us. . . . [Finally] we generously gave [the members of the House of Commons] the liberty of taking their places. As soon as the door was opened they all rushed in, and we followed; some of them had the gallantry to *give us their places,* and with violent squeezing, and such a resolution as hardly was ever met with, we riggled ourselves into seats. I think that was the first time I wished to be a man—though nothing less than a peer. . . . Am I not a furious politician? But enough of these affairs, those of friendship suit my nature better, where the struggles that arise are from very different principles than what animate courtiers and politicians, whose selfish views, under the glare of the good of their country, so often fill their hearts with a train of evil thoughts.[13]

The differences between Lady Mary's epic retelling of the incident and this straightforward account reside in both the style and the narrative structure. Whereas Lady Mary packs her account with literary language, Mrs. Pendarves's narrative is sparse: her descriptive strategy is limited to calling the crowd "stinking" and citing their "see-sawing" motions.

She describes the women themselves simply as resolute, with their only real activity a "violent squeezing" that resulted in their "riggl[ing]" into their seats. This "riggl[ing]" stands in direct contrast to Lady Mary's "vollies of trumps, kicks, and raps" performed by a squadron of foot soldiers. Lady Mary also understands narrative form: her retelling invests the participants with energy—the women "rushed," "pushed," and "placed" themselves in the gallery—as opposed to Mrs. Pendarves's unembellished and anticlimactic "and we followed." [14]

While Lady Mary's mock-epic account highlights the disjunction between the classical body, always associated with the aristocracy and with high language, and the grotesque body that makes each woman indistinguishable from the other, she does name the "tribe of dames" individually. More than Lady Mary's, Mrs. Pendarves's nonironic account actually makes these aristocrats indistinguishable from a common mob. Moreover, while both women write about the trangression of the dictates of gender, Lady Mary's account complicates the problem of class. Mrs. Pendarves's wish to be a man, but "nothing less than a peer," overrides gender in preference of aristocratic status. Lady Mary's account, while it paints the duchesses as grotesque in their individualized multiplicity, simultaneously elevates them into the realm of the epic heroes. The result is the tension of incompatible iconography in both realms.

The conclusion of the letter points to Lady Mary's recognition of this tension as she, in an act of self-diminishment, sets up an uneasy dichotomy between the duchesses' "heroic" behavior and her own: "I beg your pardon, dear madam, for this long relation; but 'tis impossible to be short on so copious a subject; and you must own this action very well worthy of record, and I think not to be paralleled in any history, ancient or modern. I look so little in my own eyes (who was at that time ingloriously sitting over a tea-table), I hardly dare subscribe myself even, Yours" (2:137). Lady Mary presents an ironic image of herself that would initially insist that she, above such unladylike behavior, sat genteelly drinking tea. Without acknowledging her personal foray into political activism—her anonymous periodical *The Nonsense of Common-Sense* (1737–38)—she purports to live out of the public spotlight, choosing to violate literary, not social, conventions. However, her description of herself as "inglorious" is not altogether inaccurate. Her inactivity on this occasion stands in contrast to the tenacity that these women displayed in the face of powerful obstacles and that is indeed "not paralleled" and, as her letter itself proves, "worthy of record." Her epic treatment elevates the duchesses into larger-than-life Amazon warriors willing to endure hardships in order to achieve their ends. Like eighteenth-century poets, who longed to write real epic poetry but found themselves engaged in a mock epic (blaming the age for the reduction of heroic pretensions and for stifling epic urges), Lady Mary takes up the opposite strategy. Yet in writing a mock account of duchesses, ladies, and their seemingly trivial breaking of social decorums, Lady Mary also appreciates, if ironically, the courage these women displayed.

Acts of "heroism" such as these were particularly difficult for women to achieve, according to Dorinda Outram's study of the role of women during the French Revolution, because such acts required a "personification" based on the successful public display of physicality according to a male model. This physicality, while a "reservoir of authority" for men, was always a potential humiliation for women. Lady Mary's account of the duchesses proves that such a space for humiliation was there to be exploited. But Outram goes on to argue that, before the Revolution, Frenchwomen had a place in politics, even if their influence was always linked to sexuality: behind the scenes, they personalized politics, factionalized governments with a competition for favors, and destabilized potential alliances. Wielding such influence, women were powerful and despised. After the Revolution, women became respected only in consequence of being excluded from the public and banished to middle-class invisibility; a chaste woman could have no public authority, and if she aspired to such power she was automatically presumed to be sexually uncontrolled and politically threatening.[15]

In England, where the revolution occurred a century before, without bloodshed, and in a culture much less clearly divided between the aristocracy and the various levels of gentry, merchant, and middle class, this movement from female inclusion to exclusion was less readily discernible; yet it is clear that by the middle of the eighteenth century in England, women's public participation had lost its late-seventeenth-century connotation of "virtuous visibility." Citing John Brown's claim that "*Obscenity* itself is grown effeminate," Harriet Guest goes even further to argue that the middle class came increasingly to see female participation, female visibility, as equivalent to the obscene, a form of corruption. Brown's lament for the loss of the old days—when, in Guest's words, "men were manly, and women in public were prostitutes"—emphasizes the fact that female public participation had begun to confuse gender differences.[16] While aristocrats continued to stress class differences as their means of maintaining their status, the middle class worked to highlight gender distinctions. It did so, however, through the paradoxical process of placing and even coercing women into the silent invisibility of the domestic world. There, they became more obviously different from middle-class and aristocratic men who had a place and a voice in the world. This movement into the difference of the invisible domestic world presented problems for aristocratic women who had to be seen but who were beginning to be told that they had no sanctioned public place.

As aristocrats, Lady Mary and her acquaintances were comfortable being the objects of others' gazes. Such visibility was essential for the maintenance of class status. And even if these rites of observation allow her to ridicule her fellow aristocrats—as she does when she takes the role of "reader of history" to celebrate, exaggerate, and distort the visual spectacle of female bodies on public parade during the coronation ceremonies—such female display is both a traditional element of her class responsibilities and an occasion ripe for humor. As a woman, however, Lady Mary recognized the new cultural pressure urging women into the invisibility of the domestic world. Thus display, as a sign of aristocratic worth, competes with withdrawal, as a sign of proper womanliness.

III

Reputation presents one such sign. As a public phenomenon modified in private, it is a commodity whose value rises and falls according to the vicissitudes of fortune or the breaches in decorum that one is stupid enough, or unlucky enough, to have committed, and thus it occupies the liminal position of mediating between the two. The enactment or violation of polite standards—and its influence on one's reputation—would seem to be most apparent in public, as evidenced above in Lady Mary's exaggerations of the too visible displays staged by her aristocratic female acquaintances. However, reputations are more powerfully shaped by private, domestic relationships; as a result, anxiety about the interpenetration between the two supposedly separate spheres of public and private is particularly apparent in epistolary discourse: as

Homer Obed Brown puts it, "The letter gives answers (information); its emphasis is on *revelation*." [17]

Because reputation is linked, especially for women, with sex, Lady Mary's letters are almost obsessively concerned with others' sexual foibles. Yet absent from these same letters is any sermonizing. In fact, Lady Mary is more likely to judge an incident according to aesthetic rather than moral criteria. For instance, she calls the occasion of a married woman's being wooed by a lovesick gallant—a man whom the young woman ultimately humiliates by refusing the affair—not a sin but a "farce":

> I have so good an Opinion of your taste to beleive Arlequin in person will never make you laugh so much as the Earl of Stairs's furious passion for Lady Walpole, aged 14 and some months. Mrs. Murry undertook to bring the busyness to bear, and provided the oppertunity (a great Ingredient you'l say), but the young Lady prov'd skittish. She did not only turn this Heroic Flame into present ridicule, but expos'd all his generous Sentiments to divert her Husband and Father-in-law. His Lordship is gone to Scotland; and if there was any body wicked enough to write upon it, Here is a subject worthy the pen of the best Ballad maker in Grubstreet. ([June 1726]; 2:67)

It is not the immorality of Lord Stair's pursuit of Lady Walpole that piques Lady Mary's interest (nor does she complain about Mrs. Murray's "pimping" for the event). Instead it is Lady Walpole's volubility and the breach of social decorum that such a violation implies that fascinate Lady Mary: the young woman's act of retelling, of turning passion into narrative and thus "Heroic Flame" into ridicule, is the real source of amusement. Moreover, Lady Mary's remarks further reinforce the essentially public nature of such reputedly private sexual liaisons. Her suggestion that somebody "wicked enough" should commemorate the event acknowledges that the act of retelling transgresses the reputed boundary of privacy, but she does not call attention to the fact that such narratives constitute almost the singular subject of her own discourse, that her own act of "wickedness" is enacted there on the page. Instead, she locates the source of genuine public exposure in an institutionalized form of revelation, the Grub Street balladeers.

Lady Mary can produce her own collection of revelations because she possesses the necessary knowledge. Her witty treatment of marriage echoes the "sex intrigues" of Restoration comedy precisely because she *can* provide for public inspection information about private experience. Knowledge, and the Foucauldian power it confers, takes on a special resonance when applied to matters of sex, for it purports to bring to light the closest-kept secrets and thus creates the most unstable—potentially the most destructive and potentially the most comic—kind of power, a fact she fully recognizes. She recounts, for instance, one particularly theatrical incident where knowledge about the private use a woman has made of her body occasions a very public drawing-room scandal. The event occurred during the "Tunbridge battles" between Lady Townshend and Kitty Edwin: "The secret cause [of their feud] is variously guessed at; but it is certain Lady Townshend came into the great room gently behind her friend, and tapping her on the shoulder with her fan, said aloud, *I know where, how, and who.* These mysterious words drew the attention of all the company, and had such an effect upon poor Kitty, she was carried to her lodging in strong hystericks. However, by the intercession of prudent mediators peace was concluded" ([November 1738]; 2:131). Lady Townshend "wins" the battle precisely because she purports to have knowledge (whether or not she actually does) of the specifics of Kitty Edwin's private behavior: the *"where, how, and who."* Lady Mary acts in the same journalistic capacity—offering to her readers narratives concerning the secrets of her acquaintances and, in the process, accruing the same measure of power.

Marriage and the social rituals attendant upon it—courtship, contracts, scandals, and affairs—are sites of particular interest, and powerful tension, because Lady Mary does indeed have access to the *"where, how, and who."* She also knows that an aristocratic woman is expected to marry and to behave appropriately when "placed" in marriage, even as she fully acknowledges that unhappiness too often results from "misplacement": "Lady J. Wharton is to be marry'd to Mr. Holt, which I am sorry for, to see a young Woman that I realy think one of the agreablest Girls upon Earth so vilely misplac'd; but where are people match'd! I suppose we shall all come right in Heaven, as in a Country Dance, thô hands are strangly given and taken while they are in motion, at last all meet their partners when the Jig is done" ([ca. 11 August 1721]; 2:11). The disturbing suggestion that only through death and in the afterlife can one possibly find the appropriate partner is lightened by Lady Mary's metaphor equating marriage with the simple pleasures of a rustic dance, but the seeming impossibility of securing a happy marriage in this world underlies her lament.

Lady Mary has too much "real-world" evidence to support anything other than the conclusion that unhappiness in marriage is the lot of most women. In expressing her fears about the proliferation of messy, damaging, and very public parliamentary divorces, she offers a solution that will protect those most in need of it—women: "[Divorces] grow more fashionable every day, and in a little while won't be at all Scandalous. The best Expedient for the public and to prevent the Expence of private familys would be a genneral Act of Divorceing all the people in England. You know, those that pleas'd might marry over again, and it would save the Reputations of several Ladys that are now in peril of being expos'd every day" ([May 1725]; 2:51–52). Her general act of divorce would prevent women from the wrong kind of public exposure—from having to endure the genuinely public scandal that the recounting of their misconduct occasions in the parliamentary forum, scandal that permanently damages a woman's reputation without injuring her husband's.

Yet Lady Mary also rejects another possible "solution" to the problem of marital unhappiness: choosing a partner outside of one's class. The case of a privileged woman who, in desiring to marry a man "beneath her station," fails to value her aristocratic status presents a direct threat to Lady Mary's class identity. Although the subject had "furnished the tea-tables [at Bath] with fresh tattle for this last fortnight," Lady Gage informs Lady Mary of the completely inappropriate attempt of Lady Harriet Herbert to marry John Beard, a young actor "who sings in the farces at Drury-lane." As the daughter of the first Earl of Waldegrave, ambassador to France, and the widow of the son of the second Marquess of Powis, Lady Harriet was a woman of high social standing. When Lady Gage turns to Lady Mary for advice about how to prevent the unsuitable marriage, Lady Mary replies: "I told her honestly, that since the lady was capable of such amours, I did not doubt if this was broke off she would bestow her person and fortune on some hackney-coachman or chairman; and that I really saw no method of saving *her* from ruin, and her *family* from dishonour, but by poisoning her; and offered to be at the expence of the arsenic, and even to administer it with my own hands, if she would invite her to drink tea with her that evening" (November 1738; 2:127–28). The degree of the threat posed by this marriage is clear in the extremity of Lady Mary's solution: her comical remedy of "arsenic at tea" indicates that Lady Harriet's actions are potentially dangerous both to women (Lady Harriet's "ruin") and to the aristocracy (her family's "dishonour"). As J. V. Beckett puts it, "Most aristocrats regarded marital equality as part of the natural order of events, . . . [and] while marriage might be seen as an important financial transaction . . . it was even more crucial as a means of cementing the social fabric of the group."[18] The possibility of Lady Harriet's marrying so far beneath her station is a potential threat to this cohesive social fabric, for it would be weakened by the irrevocable loss of one of its female members, Lady Harriet herself.

The comedy in the letter takes on greater significance as Lady Mary leads up to a pronouncement about the damage such a misalliance can create. First, she claims the Lady Harriet's relations have "no reason to be amazed at her constitution" but instead are "violently surprized" by her desire for a legitimate marriage.[19] This snide comment comes from Lady Mary's knowledge of the history of scandal in Lady Harriet's family. The young woman follows in the footsteps of her grandmother, who was an illegitimate daughter of James II, and the subject of scandal in her widowhood when she became pregnant, refused to name her lover, and was forced into a convent (2:128n). Lady Mary concludes the letter with references to both women's "bad" behavior: "Such examples are very detrimental to our whole sex; and are apt to influence the other into a belief that we are unfit to manage either liberty or money." When women err, they become vulnerable and exposed to punishment "from above": men are provided with justifications for curtailing women's "liberty" (the "management" of their bodies) and for limiting women's freedom in the social world (withholding "money").

Thus questions of the body—especially questions about what women will or will not do with their bodies and what degree of exposure they are willing to risk—form the subject of many of Lady Mary's most intriguing letters. The body and its functions are such powerful sites of fascination precisely because they are considered the most exclusive and the most private property of the individual. In the early eighteenth century, a new and essentially bourgeois notion of a "body politic" was being redefined in such a way that women were excluded. In the political language of the Revolution, this new "body politic"—formed according to Locke's claims in the *Second Treatise* that the individual owns his body and the products of that body's labor and thus according to a male model of property and ownership—was also qualified by Locke's distinguishing a subject's voluntary submission to the artificial, constructed power of the magistrate from the "natural" forms of power: "that of a *father* over his children, a *master* over his servant, a *husband* over his wife, and a *lord* over his slave." [20] Thus the powerful public body was constituted by the property-owning male, who held a "natural" sway over the domestic as well as the political worlds.

When a female body, re-created in epistolary discourse, is exposed and circulated, it becomes particularly vulnerable and emblematic; the boundaries between public and private are revealed to be permeable, and the writer turns information into power. The female body, as Lady Mary learned in Turkey, is visible and substantial, capable of being viewed in an aesthetic context as an objet d'art. In England, because of its different rules of decorum and its different imperatives for female display, Lady Mary responds to the uncovered body with both fascination and ridicule. Her treatment of Mme de Broglio is a case in point. The revelation here exists on a variety of levels as Lady Mary exposes the woman's body as a means of "uncovering" it and conflating her behavior with bad judgment:

> Madam de Broglio makes a great Noise, but tis only from the frequency and Quantity of her pissing, which she does not fail to do at least ten times a day amongst a cloud of Wittnesses.
>
> > One would think her daughter of a River,
> > > As I heard Mr. Mirmont tell,
> > And the best Commendation that he could give her
> > > Was that she made Water excellent well.
> > > > With a fa la la etc.
> > > > > (December 1724; 2:43)

Because Mme de Broglio, as the wife of the French ambassador, could quite reasonably be expected to make a great "Noise" in society, Lady Mary can turn these expectations into the pun that describes the ambassadress in terms of the "noise" of her biological functions rather than her social power. Lady Mary feels empowered to ridicule her precisely because she has called attention to her body and revealed herself in this inappropriate way.

One final example of a woman who fails to manage her body appropriately and who thus makes a public spectacle of herself "for love" is the Duchess of Cleveland; she violates not only the dictates of gender but also the imperatives of age—and the dignity and wisdom that should accompany it—and thus provides a particularly personal threat to Lady Mary. The inseparability of the public from the private is also forcefully reinscribed in the narrative concerning the passion of the sixty-three-year-old duchess for the twenty-five-year-old illegitimate grandson of Charles II and Nell Gwynn, a love that makes the old woman an object of general scorn: "The Man in England that gives the greatest pleasure and the greatest pain is a Youth of Royal blood, with all his Grand-mother's beauty, Wit, and good Qualitys; in short, he is Nell Guin in person with the Sex alter'd, and occasions such fracas amongst the Ladys of Galantry that it passes [belief]. You'l stare to hear of her Grace of Cleveland at the Head of them" (April 1727; 2:74). The duchess's transgression is so severe that it provokes Lady Mary to poetry:

> The God of Love, enrag'd to see
> The Nymph despise his Flame,
> At Dice and cards mispend her Nights
> And slight a nobler Game;
>
> For the Neglect of offers past
> And Pride in days of yore,
> He kindles up a Fire at last
> That burns her at threescore.
>
> A polish'd white is smoothly spread
> Where whilom wrinkles lay,
> And glowing with an artfull red
> She ogles at the Play.
>
> Along the Mall she softly sails
> In White and Silver drest,
> Her neck expos'd to eastern Gales,
> And Jewells on her breast.
>
> Her children banish'd, Age forgot,
> Lord Sidney is her care,
> And, what is much a happier lot,
> Has hopes to be her Heir.

Lady Mary offers up a damning poetic portrait of a woman whose private passion spills over into a public display of its effects. Painted red and draped in virginal silver and white, the body of the duchess, reminiscent of Lady Wishfort's, becomes even more grotesque as Lady Mary focuses on the older woman's neck and breasts (two parts of female anatomy that age in quite visible ways) and describes them not only as exposed but bejewelled, calling attention to their "defects."

She concludes the letter in a very different tone, however, one that draws a particularly striking image from the duchess's private life and ends with an expression of Lady Mary's own fears: "This is all true History thô it is dogrell Rhime. In good earnest, [the duchess] has turn'd Lady Grace and Family out o' doors to make room for him, and there he lies like leafe Gold upon a pill. There never was so violent and so indiscreet a passion. Lady Stafford says, nothing was ever like it since Phedra and Hipolitus.—Lord ha' mercy upon us; see what we may all come to!" (April 1727; 2:74–75). The evocative image of the young Lord Sidney, lying "like leafe Gold upon a pill," satirically debases both lovers: the duchess's body becomes a pill that resonates not simply with medicinal implications and the sicknesses of old age but also with the threatening possibilities of poison. The youthful Lord Sidney, so comfortably languishing in all his gilt beauty, becomes the useless decoration of this potentially restorative but also potentially lethal cure.[21] Underlying Lady Mary's censure is her own fear that the duchess's "violent" and "indiscreet" passion may paint a picture of a future not unlike the one she and her friends may someday face, and thus she echoes Mrs. Fainall's lament about Lady Wishfort, one that emphasizes the "we" in the shared potential for humiliation that women face: "Lord ha' mercy upon us; see what we may all come to!" Her fears were not unjustified, of course, for her own midlife infatuation with Algarotti revealed that she, too, was capable of playing the fool for love.

III

The competing pressures of the public and private realms and Lady Mary's response to the supposed division between them often take the form of her mixing two supposedly "separate" languages: the political (an aristocratic discourse concerned with governmental forms of power) and the religious (a moral discourse often concerned with forms of private behavior). In two final letters, both extended descriptions of sexual excesses, Lady Mary forcefully reveals, through her use of these incompatible discourses, that the too easy dichotomy between public and private life is insupportable. The first letter recounts a public occasion, the birth-night celebration of 31 October 1723; here, she expresses real concern about women's staging a public display of their sexuality. The second brings to light a secret society of debauchery, a society she actively celebrates.

In a complex and relentlessly ironic letter, Lady Mary describes the birth-night party, another public and sanctioned aristocratic display. The letter provides an example not only of Lady Mary's mixing of incompatible, even competing styles but also of her anxieties about the loss of protection that a culturally sanctioned "hypocrisy"—an agreed-upon cultural division between the public and the private, a division that is also openly permeable—allows to women. She is both participant and spectator in the event, writing "piping hot" from the party and "warm'd with all the Agreable Ideas that fine Cloths, fine Gentlemen, brisk Tunes and lively dances can raise there," and she entertains Lady Mar with the "freshest Account" of the event by calling herself one of the best figures there: "To say truth, people are grown so extravagantly ugly that we old Beautys are force'd to come out on show days to keep the Court in Countenance" (2:31). Because she herself participates, a straightforward account of her own good showing would sound immodest and even false; thus she handles the occasion with amused self-deprecation by claiming a place even for the old beauties (she was thirty-four at the time). Such "modesty," however, barely masks her giddy delight in having cast such a fine figure amidst the general splendor.

The public display of aristocratic finery and gaiety leads her to remark about private sexual choices: "Mrs. West was [there], who is a great Prude, having but 2 lovers at a Time; I think those are Lord Haddingtoun and Mr. Lindsay, the one for use, the one for show" (2:31). The issues of "use" and "show" point directly to the seemingly double nature of existence: life in a community demands that one fulfill the social forms, hence one has, for "show," a publicly acceptable lover; but private life allows one an additional choice, a lover for "use."

There is, however, *no* real division between the realms of public and private: Lady Mary knows the identities of both lovers and names each for his specific role. Her epigrammatic remark reveals the fundamental tension of a social existence: she and her acquaintances act as though the public and private realms are separate, when obviously the slippage between them is undeniable, a fluidity that can result only in hypocrisy:

> The World improves in one virtue to a violent degree—I mean plain dealing. Hipocricy being (as the Scripture declares) a damnable Sin, I hope our publicans and Sinners will be sav'd by the open profession of a contrary virtue. I was told by a very good Author, who is deep in the secret, that at this very minute there is a bill cooking up at a Hunting Seat in Norfolk to have Not taken out of the Commandments and clap'd into the Creed the Ensuing session of Parliament. This bold attempt for the Liberty of the subject is wholly projected by Mr. Walpole, who pro-pos'd it to the Secret Committee in his Parlor. Will: Yonge seconded it, and answer'd for all his Acquaintance voteing right to a man. (2:31–32)

Lady Mary delights in a scheme whereby politicians take over the prov-ince of religion and legislate a "new morality," a world where "thou *shalt* commit adultery" and "I do *not* believe in God, the Father, Almighty" become the new commandments sanctioned for the "liberation" of citizens. No longer "oppressed" by the fictions of public and private separation, citizens loosen the restraints of traditionally moral sexual behavior; more important, they are apparently freed from hypocrisy.

But even this new morality is complicated by human contrariness: "Doddington very gravely objected that the obstinacy of Human Nature was such that he fear'd when they had possitive Commandments so to do, perhaps people would not commit adultery and bear False Wittness against their Neighbours with the readyness and Cheerfullness they do at present" (2:32). Such positive commandments point to the two "sins" that are most evident not only in Lady Mary's fashionable world but also in her letters: the sexual intrigues of her neighbors. And even though she predicts that the bill will be dropped, "tis certain it might be carry'd with great Ease, the world being intirely revenue du bagatelle, and Honnour, Virtue, Reputation etc., which we used to hear of in our Nursery, is as much laid aside and forgotten as crumple'd Riband" (2:32).

The metaphor of virtue discarded as one would a soiled fashion leads

her to abandon the political in order to focus on marriage and the consequences of the "new morality" for women. It also occasions an important
new tone as well:

> To speak plainly, I am very sorry for the forlorn state of Matrimony,
> which is as much ridicul'd by our Young Ladys as it us'd to be by young
> fellows; in short, both Sexes have found the Inconveniencys of it, and the
> Apellation of Rake is as genteel in a Woman as a Man of Quality. 'Tis no
> Scandal to say, Misse————the maid of Honnour looks very well now
> she's up again, and poor Biddy Noel has never been quite well since her
> last Flux. You may Imagine we marry'd Women look very silly; we have
> nothing to excuse our selves but that twas done a great while ago and we
> were very young when we did it. (2:32)

The threat present here is not a socially sanctioned hypocrisy but the
frank public acknowledgment of female sexuality. During the birth-
night celebration the exposure of women's bodies and their private
sexual behavior—the staple of the letters Lady Mary trades with her
epistolary partners—is not an item revealed through the "private" reading of epistolary discourse but a commodity too visible amid a glittering
and polite gathering. Here it is clear that Lady Mary does not lament the
"hypocrisy" of her society at all; rather, she laments the loss of the safety
and security produced by a culturally sanctioned and creative fiction
that defines a division between public and private life.

The danger presents itself in the seeming erasure of gender differences: young women, like young men of old, ridicule marriage as incon-
venient, consider "the Apellation of Rake as . . . genteel in a Woman as
a Man of Quality," and are not the least scandalized by a single woman's
pregnancy. Her use of the quotation ("Poor Biddy Noel has never been
quite well since her last Flux") reinforces the threat in such a widespread
acceptance of traditionally "immoral" behavior and the clear lack of
Astell's "virtuous visibility." In fact, in this new society it is Lady Mary
and her married friends who must apologize for their "indiscretion,"
that is, for having married, with the same excuse one used to hear for an
unplanned pregnancy: "Twas done a great while ago and we were very
young when we did it." Her lament predates John Brown's concerns
about almost the same phenomenon: "The Sexes have now little other
apparent Distinction, beyond that of Person and Dress: Their peculiar

and characteristic Manners are confounded and lost: The one Sex having advanced into *Boldness*, as the other have sunk into *Effeminacy*." [22] As Lady Mary understands, such a phenomenon is particularly threatening because it only *appears* to erase the double standard: in enacting the male model of sexual conduct, women forfeit the protection of a "hypocrisy" that allows them their visibility but keeps them from being vulnerable to charges of sexual license and irresponsibility, charges that men could overcome but women only rarely. Once female visibility becomes equated with the immoral, men have a justification for forcing women out of the spotlight; and, while Lady Mary cannot predict that men will impose upon women a bourgeois form of "domestic invisibility," she does perceive the threat in unprotected displays of female sexuality.

Thus in the birth-night letter, Lady Mary may claim to be amused and even delighted by the cleverness of the politican's scheme, but she is genuinely concerned about gentlewomen's loss of distinction and the protection that a culturally sanctioned hypocrisy provides. She expresses this concern in the only language that accurately reflects the "new" society: a consistent irony produced through the mixing of incompatible styles. Only such discourse can describe a world where aristocratic gender differences are lost and immorality is politically legislated, but not to women's benefit.

One final letter presents an example of Lady Mary's most extreme use of incompatible styles to communicate the tension, confusion, and resistance that female transgressions can generate. In examining the potential for chaos in her social circle, Lady Mary, as a "spectatress," differs significantly from Mr. Spectator and his program to facilitate stability. According to Michael Ketcham's groundbreaking study, *The Spectator* lacks incisive thinking and an ironic undermining of expectations because Addison and Steele hope to create a social structure out of a literary structure: "They do not test conventions or test language in order to examine their inadequacies or hidden potentials"; instead, they actually create conventions "in order to establish rather than question an idea of social order." [23] As evidenced above, Lady Mary's satire often pushes the limits of conventions—in mock epics or subverted political and religious discourse—because she *witnesses* the possibility for chaos in her aristocratic world. Her discourse, focused on incidents of social disorder, represents the inappropriateness of particular "polite" behaviors in a language and a literary structure incongruous to the occasion, an incompatibility that emphasizes the disjunctions in a world of shifting standards.

The letter begins with Lady Mary's acknowledgment that change and instability define social life; she cites a "metamorphosis" in her acquaintances "as wondrous to me as any in Ovid." First, she recounts the shocking second marriage of Lady Holderness, a woman communal gossip says is willing to renounce her children for the sake of the marriage.[24] Lady Mary finds the match altogether inexplicable for other reasons: the couple is "sunk in all the Joys of happy Love nothwithstanding she wants the use of her 2 hands by a Rheumatism, and he has an arm that he can't move. I wish I could send you the particulars of this Amour, which seems to me as curious as that between 2 Oysters, and as well worthy the serious Enquiry of the Naturalists" (2:37). Such private love among the gentry reminds her of a narrative whose "Heroine," as Lady Mary calls her, is Anastasia Robinson, the reigning prima donna for the decade following her 1714 performance in the opera *Creso*.[25] The social disturbance caused by Lady Holderness's bewildering engagement is mild compared to the political chaos produced when Mrs. Robinson's "honour" is publicly threatened. In this instance, Lady Mary illustrates an incident of aristocratic insult and challenge, not in a metaphor drawn from the sciences and demanding the "Enquiry of the Naturalists," but in the satirically reductive narrative form of the fairy tale, complete with giants, dwarfs, and threatened violence.[26] The form itself points not only to the absurdity of the fracas but also to the threat posed when the private becomes truly public, when the sexual becomes entangled in the political—not simply in literary style, but in reality.

On this occasion, Lord Peterborough, who just before his death claimed to have married Mrs. Robinson, becomes the champion of her "virtue." Lady Mary compares this activity to Don Quixote's mad quest, a knight errantry of the silliest order:

> [Anastasia Robinson] has engag'd halfe the Town in Arms from the Nicety of her virtue, which was not able to bear the too near approach of Senesino in the Opera, and her Condescention in accepting of Lord Peterborrough for a Champion, who has signaliz'd both his Love and Courage upon this occasion in as many instances as ever D[on] Quixote did for Dulcinea. Poor Senesino like a vanquish'd Giant was forc'd to confess

upon his knees that Anastasia was a non pareil of virtue and of Beauty.
Lord Stanhope, as dwarf to the said Giant, jok'd of his side, and was
challeng'd for his pains. Lord Delawar was Lord Peterborrough's second;
my Lady miscarry'd. (March 1724; 2:37–38)

At the center of the threatened violence is Senesino, a castrato of "majestic figure" brought to his knees "like a vanquish'd Giant." The image of
a giant Italian kneeling in submission at the feet of an English Quixote
is certainly amusing in its own right, but the problem of size, coupled
with the madness of violence in defense of a virtue already suspect,
is complicated by Lord Stanhope's interference. Stanhope, later Earl
of Chesterfield, was notably short in stature and, according to Lord
Hervey, had "a propensity to ridicule, in which he indulged himself
with infinite humour and no distinction, and with inexhaustible spirits
and no discretion" (2:38n). Such a lack of discretion is apparent when
this puny David baits a majestic Goliath and earns himself a challenge
as a result.

But this small, isolated incident takes on much larger dimensions
when the threatened violence ultimately spills over from the participants and into the highest echelons of power: "The Whole Town divided
into partys on this important point. Innumerable have been the disorders between the 2 sexes on so great an Account, besides halfe the
House of Peers being put under Arrest. By the Providence of Heaven
and the wise Cares of his Majesty no bloodshed ensu'd. However, things
are now tolerably accomodated, and the Fair Lady rides through the
Town in Triumph in the shineing Berlin of her Hero, not to reckon
the Essential advantage of £100 per month which (tis said) he allows
her" (2:38). Once the insignificant amours of the upper crust begin to
affect the larger world of politics, everyone, including even the House
of Lords, must choose sides. Peace reigns and the fairy tale concludes
only after the king proclaims, the giant is vanquished, and the fair
maiden lives happily ever after—in "Triumph" on one hundred pounds
a month.

The "gallantry" in the above anecdote, whose import is diminished
and whose absurdity is magnified through a whimsical literary form,
takes on greater power and greater threat in Lady Mary's final examination of the sexual high jinks of a group of young aristocrats. In what
might be the most daring piece of writing in all of her correspondence,

she again exploits political discourse and the language of religion to paint a picture not of public female transgression but of general, if supposedly private, sexual excess. She endows the group of young people, who call themselves the Schemers, with the weight of religious discourse, and they ascend into ethereal realms to become modern-day apostles. However, their means of ascension is suspect; masterminded and choreographed by the Schemers, sex becomes a secular rite of passage:

> In General, never was Galantry in so elevated a Figure as it is at present. 20 very pritty fellows (the Duke of Wharton being President and cheif [*sic*] director) have form'd themselves into a committee of Galantry. They call themselves Schemers, and meet regularly 3 times a week to consult on Galant Schemes for the advancement of that branch of Happyness which the vulgar call Whoring. (March 1724; 2:38)

This "branch of Happyness" was institutionalized by Viscount Hillsborrough, who opened his Hanover Square house "on Ash Wednesday" for the "best contriv'd Entertainment in the World, and the only remedy against spleen and vapours occasion'd by the Formality of that day, which still subsists amongst other rags of Popery not yet rooted out" (2:38). The plan, of course, contains a rank blasphemy: Ash Wednesday, the beginning of the Lenten fasts, was a High Church holiday for the Anglicans as well as the Catholics, and Lady Mary's calling this secular ceremony a "remedy" against the "spleen and vapours" of the day honored in a sacred ritual violates both the doctrines of the church and the demands of linguistic decorum.

Her examination of the house rules agreed upon by the Schemers is couched in the language of political probity: the rules are "several Articles absolutely necessary for the promotion of public good and the conservation of peace in private Familys." This ironic claim to "gallantry's" creation of better citizens and happier homes is dependent on one special element—secrecy. Each member must arrive "at the hour of 6 mask'd in a Domine," and all must swear not to attempt to discover the identity of "his brother's incognita": "If by Accident or the Lady's indiscretion her name should chance to be discover'd by one or more of the Schemers, that name should remain sacred and as unspeakable as the name of the Deity amongst the Jews" (2:39). The women's dressing in masks and dominoes, clothing Terry Castle calls a classic form of disguise and a traditional mark of intrigue, lends to the proceedings an ironic, sacramental air in keeping with the Schemers' subversion of the Lenten spirit.

Castle also argues that such robes are "cypherlike," a sign of negativity and an emblem of potential,[27] and such potential resonates in the "Solemnity" of the Schemers' ritual feasting:

> You may imagine such wholsome Laws brought all the best Company to this polite Assembly; add to these the Inducement of good Music, Fine Liquors, a splendid Supper, and the best punch you ever tasted. But you'l ask, how could they sup without shewing their faces? You must know the very Garrets were clean'd and lighted out at this Solemnity. The whole Company ⟨view'd the supper, which was large enough to⟩ suffer every fair one to point to what she thought most delightfull to be convey'd to her respective apartment.

The opening sentence of this section is a fine example of Lady Mary's ability to create comic impact: she moves from the high ("such wholsome Laws") to the low ("the best punch you ever tasted") so rapidly and smoothly that all the appetites of these men and women are brought into high relief. The focal point of the scene—the young women dressed in the secular equivalents of monk's habits and standing before a table, pointing wordlessly at the supper dishes—becomes a blasphemous imitation of the Mass translated into wholly secular terms.

Anonymity and secrecy are maintained by screens set up around individual tables: "Those who were yet in the state of probation, and scrupul'd too much happyness in this world for fear of its being deducted in the Next, had screens set round little neat Tables in the public rooms, which were as inviolate (but to the partners) as Walls of Adamant. You may imagine there were few of this latter Class, and tis to be hop'd that good Examples and the Indefatigable endeavors of the Schemers (who spare no pains in carrying on the good cause) will lessen them daily" (2:39). Lady Mary reverses the traditional language of religion in suggesting that those women who "scupl'd too much happyness in this world"—women who desire only flirtation, not lovemaking—exist in a "state of probation." Her remark has its real-life analogue in the three-part initiation process monks had to complete: a movement from the noviatiate, to probation, and then to final vows. Thus, like their religious counterparts, these young women await their final initiation—only theirs leads not to chastity but to sex.

In the final section, while donning the cloak of a "true patriot," Lady Mary raises her voice to proclaim the "new gospel":

> These Galantrys are continu'd every Wednesday during Lent, and I won't ask your pardon for this long Account of 'em since I consider the duty of a true English Woman is to do what Honnour she can to her native Country, and that it would be a Sin against the pious Love I bear the Land of my Nativity to confine the renown due to the Schemers within the small extent of this little Isleland, which ought to be spread where ever Men can sigh or Women wish. (2:39–40)

Employing this wonderfully overblown rhetoric of the patriotic nationalist and ironically aligning herself with Enlightenment philosophes such as Voltaire and Montesquieu, who were deeply impressed by the freedom and equality they saw coexisting in England,[28] Lady Mary makes use of her country's reputation for progress by praising the England celebrated as the most "progressive" nation on earth: a land of liberty, prosperity, science, and free inquiry. But she ends the letter with a complaint made even more powerful by its striking religious metaphor:

> Tis true they have the Envy and Curses of the old and ugly of both Sexes, and a general persecution from all old Women, but this is no more than all Reformations must expect in their beginning, and what the Christian Church suffer'd in a remarkable manner at its first blaze. You may easily beleive, The whole Generation of Fathers, Mothers, and Husbands raise as great a Clamour against this new institution as the pagan preists did of old against the light of the Gospel, and for the same reasons, since it strikes at the very foundation of their Authority, which Authority is built on grosse impositions upon Mankind. (2:40)

Calling the new sexual license the next Reformation, she is able to situate those unable to recognize both the light of this new gospel and the "first blaze" of this new church in the dark, unenlightened realm of the pagan.

The tension found in all the satiric letters is here at its most intense. The processes of "before and after" are completely reversed in

the Schemers' ritual: rather than participating in a Mardi Gras of sanctioned and legitimized revelry before the Lenten season, the Schemers
wantonly celebrate during the time of fasts and self-restraint. Their
"carnival" is indeed outside the law, beyond sanction, and without
legitimacy. Lady Mary obviously feels the pressure of the violation, but
as a writer she knows that the Schemers' devilry is too tempting to pass
up: stylistically complicitous with the Schemers, she exploits the opportunity to violate literary forms with the same aggression and style. The
freedom the Schemers enact in loosening the sexual bonds, Lady Mary
re-creates in the blasphemous and dangerous use of this sacred, "mock-
religious" language. But while her irony emphasizes the transgression,
she never points the moralist's finger of blame and indeed celebrates
the flamboyance of their transgressions: just as the Schemers have "out-
performed," "out-theatered" the church, Lady Mary creates a discourse
that allows her to circumvent the decorums and the "authorities" that
constrain her.

A very different public narrative concerning the Schemers' activities
appeared in the 6 June 1724 edition (no. 26) of the *Universal Journal*. The
editor of this weekly newspaper had earlier described the paper's purpose this way: "As to the Irregularities of the Beau Monde of both Sexes,
we shall visit them with our deceas'd Friend *Bickerstaff's* Ghost, whom
we have full Power to raise with all his former Authority and Dignity:
By him we shall chastise every growing Enormity, and reduce Dress
and Decorum to the just Standard of his Day" (no. 1). Such a "growing
Enormity" is to be found in the activities of the Schemers, who for all
their insistence on secrecy have not escaped public notice, as the *Journal*
acknowledges: "The Inhabitants of the polite Part of the Town are no
strangers to the Designs of these Bravadoes." The newspaper account,
unlike Lady Mary's, condemns the "bestial" nature of the Schemers'
pursuits: not only have they reportedly written to a member "of a Foreign Academy," desiring him "to get what knowledge he can of the
Statues made by the several Legislators of the Canibals . . . to serve them
as model for their own," they have supposedly planned to set the lions in
the Tower of London loose to roam free and terrorize the city. In direct
contrast to Lady Mary's discourse of patriots and apostles, the *Journal*
first likens the Schemers to the Roman triumvirate and then goes on to
point to the depth of their depravity: "Thus have our *Schemers* agreed,
that no Consideration whatsoever shall be a Check to their Pleasures,

when they are in Pursuit of 'em; nor shall any one refuse gratifying his
bestial Appetite, because the Person he has pitched upon is his Mother
or his Sister" (2). With these predictions of terror and incest, the only
"Reformation" the *Journal* can hope for is a genuinely religious one. The
editor, originally intending to publish the names of the Schemers "to see
whether a Knowledge of their being detected would not work the Reformation," reconsidered out of fear that their public identification might
only "harden their Hearts." The report therefore ends with the editor's
apology for having "terrify'd a great number of my Female Readers" but
with this offer of comfort: because the Schemers have "made free with
their Constitutions," they have often had to visit surgeons and apothecaries, and the *Journal* predicts that of the eighteen members "not Eight
will live to see the End of Autumn."

The differences in the accounts are significant: for Lady Mary, the
reputed secrecy of the society functions as a form of protection; for the
Journal, it is the source of the threat. Lady Mary's play with political and
religious language meets a straightforward condemnation of the bestial
nature of the Schemers' characters. Whereas the charges of cannibalism,
incest, and social regression form a topos of barbarism for the *Journal,*
Lady Mary's language draws on the imagery of theater and spectacle to
suggest an ironic theory of historical Enlightenment and progress. Yet
just as the Schemer's activities are here shown to be publicly available,
Lady Mary's own account turns out to be less than secret. Her letter
could never be "published" officially, for it is too scandalous in its blasphemy; yet the Schemers do become privy to and applaud her epistolary
performance. She insists that when they got their hands on the letter
she "had much ado to get it from 'em" (2:40), but her cavalier atti-
tude about the letter's having fallen into the wrong hands could indicate
that, even if she did not play an active part in actually transmitting
the letter to these young people, she is not altogether displeased by the
event. She rewards the Schemers with this scandalous narrative because
of their transgressive flamboyance, theatricality, and aggressive style,
and her delight in having her wit appreciated by the participants gives
her a chance to tout one final instance of the Schemers' violations of
convention.

As a "spectatress" and "reader of history," Lady Mary's satirical letters
treat, on the one hand, these private activities of her friends and ac-

quaintances. Through her "insider's" knowledge and through the epistolary form itself, she makes concrete the "invisible" elements of individual life—the bodies, the sexual liaisons, the absurd infatuations of her friends. On the other hand, she exaggerates and distorts the publicly available images of her aristocratic circle when she makes their often too visible presence loom large and even grotesque. Yet her letters also reveal the tension in a world split between the permeable boundaries of these reputedly public and private realms. She lives in a world where accounts of public events are shared in private epistolary discourse and where the private secrets of individual life become the public property of letter writers—a world where no absolute standards for "acceptable behavior" seem finally to apply. The women birth-night celebrants, following the roles provided by men, publicly flaunt their sexuality, much to Lady Mary's dismay; the Schemers, male and female, privately flaunt their debauchery and provoke Lady Mary's ironic celebration. Such transgressions, while the sources of her humor, also generate her desire to find some solution to the problem of an aristocratic woman's need to maintain a public visibility while simultaneously sustaining the "fiction" of privacy—as protection from charges of immorality but without a coercion into invisibility.

Horace Walpole recognized the source of the tension in these letters when in 1751 Lady Mary's niece lent him a collection of over fifty of these letters. Usually one of Lady Mary's strongest detractors, he was effusive in his praise: "They are charming! have more spirit and vivacity than you can conceive, and as much of the spirit of debauchery in them as you will conceive in her writing. . . . In most of them, the wit and style are superior to any letters I ever read but Madame Sévigné's. It is very remarkable how much better women write than men." [29] This very "wit and style," this "spirit of debauchery," are the results of the tension Lady Mary never successfully resolves. Her search for a less complicated and more secure place for a gentlewoman in a changing eighteenth-century world that appears to be dividing along gender, not class, lines—a division that insists that women choose invisible marks of domestic distinction and the exclusively private forms of authority that can only translate to Lady Mary as the erasure of difference and the complete loss of her status—must await her self-imposed exile from England.

She tells her sister in 1727, "I am so far from avoiding Company, I resolve never to live without; and when I am no longer an Actor upon this stage (by the way, I talk of twenty years hence at soonest), as a Spectator I may laugh at the farcical Actions that will doubtless be then represented, Nature being exceeding provident in providing Fools and Coxcombs in all Ages, who are the greatest preservatives against the Spleen that I ever could find out" ([July 1727]; 2:82). She leaves the stage sooner than she planned, however, when she abandons England in 1739. Only from the Italian countryside and only when she sends letters focused on three generations of aristocratic women—herself, her daughter, and her granddaughters—does she come to believe that female retirement is the only place that allows a gentlewoman to maintain her visible status as an aristocrat while avoiding the conflict, the violations and transgressions, inescapable in the social world.

Chapter Five

Reading, Writing, and the Novel

In 1739 Lady Mary abandoned her home and set out for the Continent on a journey that would last over twenty years. At the time she had few pressing family responsibilities to tie her to England: her marriage to Wortley had become less than satisfying for them both; her daughter had married happily and was settled in Scotland; and her profligate son was safely secured in Holland, out of the reach of his creditors. She herself, in the grip of a hopeless infatuation with Algarotti, chose to reside close to him in Italy. When she was finally forced to acknowledge the impossibility of such a relationship, she remained abroad for the next twenty-two years, often settling in rural retirement. Rarely visited by British friends and separated from the whole of English society for the last years of her life, she was never idle, using part of her time to improve the property where she lived and working equally hard to sustain a correspondence with her daughter, the Countess of Bute.

Separated from her daughter both geographically and, until 1746, emotionally, Lady Mary embarks on a program not only to maintain a newfound intimacy with her daughter but also to establish a relationship with her granddaughters.[1] The letters she composes from retirement provide an illuminating counterpart to the letters written when she struggled to create intimacy with Wortley: both collections are concerned with the proper place for gentlewomen—especially in relation to female happiness in marriage—but the correspondence with her daughter has less of the dramatic intensity, less of the resistance and effort, found in the Wortley correspondence. Instead the letters reveal the growth of an abiding affection between two women attempting to negotiate a relationship of mutuality and shared concern.

The singular tension arises when Lady Mary attempts to offer advice about the best ways to create secure futures for her granddaughters.[2] Her suggestions about the proper place for gentlewomen are drawn directly from the twofold passions of her later years: country living and novel reading. She describes herself as having "liv'd in a solitude not unlike that of Robinson Crusoe. Excepting my short trips to Louvere, my whole time is spent in my Closet and Garden" (3 June 1753; 3:32). She reiterates the description only a month later: "Gardening is certainly the next amusement to Reading" (26 July 1748; 2:408). The "worlds" of her garden and her books play an active part in shaping her arguments about the most appropriate station for a gentlewoman. She understands that most women of status enter the kind of society featured in the novel: they choose love, courtship, and marriage. At the same time, however, she insists that many such women, whether they marry or not, ultimately retire for a significant portion of their lives to the quiet retreat and the domestic pleasures of study and contemplation. These two destinies are exemplified in the choices Lady Mary and her daughter each made: "We are both plac'd properly in regard to our Different times of Life: you amidst the Fair, the Galant and the Gay, I in a retreat where I enjoy every amusement that Solitude can afford. I confess I sometimes wish for a little conversation, but I refflect that the commerce of the World gives more uneasyness than pleasure, and Quiet is all the Hope that can reasonably be indulg'd at my Age" (10 July 1748; 2:405).

Lady Mary offers, as the most comfortable and productive life for her granddaughters, the "world" of retirement that she herself chose. In the countryside, she cultivates a way of life that allows her to maintain the aristocratic "difference" lost in the bourgeois constructions of gender: in retirement, a gentlewoman is a visible presence in the world, celebrated for both her domesticity *and* her intellectual achievements. Lady Mary realizes that offering this same course of action to her granddaughters is a solution doomed to failure: it is unattractive both economically and psychologically to young girls who, about to make their public debuts in society and in the marriage market, would scarcely perceive such retreat as empowering. Thus in an attempt to overcome the resistance she will encounter—not just from the granddaughters but also from Lord and Lady Bute (whom Halsband describes as "a proto-Victorian of impeccable respectability")[3]—Lady Mary exploits the generic possibilities and rhetorical power of the familiar letter to offer two kinds of arguments intended to convince her recalcitrant family that retirement is the better, more satisfying destiny for most women. The first is a series of letters illustrating her own happiness in retirement, letters accompanied by "essays" that argue for an extensive female education. These letters, forming the subject of the next and final chapter, are bolstered by Lady Mary's voluminous literary criticism concerning the novel, the subject of this chapter.

The novel takes as its almost singular focus the social domain, the "world" Lady Mary has left behind. And even though the novels provide for her a concrete link with English culture, she is almost altogether resistant both to the standards of female behavior they advocate and to the values they articulate. Her passionate interest in the novel and her equally strong rejection of its models are evidence of the "fight to define the real" that Felicity Nussbaum has argued characterizes the mission of some eighteenth-century bourgeois autobiographers: the memoirists struggle to define a "real" that is not the sole possession of the ruling gender, race, or class but is defined through a new emphasis on "the published self as property in a money economy," a self created as autobiographers "stretch to 'represent' new kinds of consciousness and experience."[4] Many novels of the era, likewise written by bourgeois writers, present a similar "consumable interiority." As evidenced in Lady Mary's satirical letters, where she acts as the "Spectatress" of a social scene that is delightful, grotesque, excessive, and ridiculous, the "real" is perceptible for her in performance—in the visible, observable, empirically verifiable behavior of the individual. While the signals, gestures, and codes of behavior may indicate marks of an inner reality, one's public performance defines character. Novels, on the other hand, suggest the opposite premise: the real is constituted by an interiority, a reality that can be communicated in a prose style that, Lady Mary will argue, cultivates sympathy and indentification in the reader at the expense of exterior observation and judgment.

This chapter concentrates on Lady Mary's negative reactions to this "new" eighteenth-century genre and on her definitions of the insufficiencies of the moral values it presents to women living in the social world. Along with these arguments she also sends a series of her own short "novelistic" tales that tell the stories of her Italian women acquaintances. These embedded narratives function as "little histories," alternatives to the fantasy and unreality that Lady Mary charges underlie the novel. Lady Mary's criticism reveals the genre's powerful influence upon a reader as sophisticated as she was in letters that also highlight the strength of her aristocratic resistance to the new heroines of the age and the inappropriate, even dangerous, precedents she fears they set for women.

I

Lady Mary kept herself apprised of the literary scene in England by scouring newspapers such as the *Monthly Review* and requesting that her daughter send her boxes of books. She so cherishes the novels that her desire is almost an obsession, a fact she willingly confesses:

> I have at length receiv'd the Box with the Books enclos'd. . . . They amus'd me very much. I gave a very ridiculous proofe of it, fitter indeed for my Grand daughter than my selfe. I return'd from a party on Horseback and [having ridden] 20 mile[s], part of it by moon shine, it was ten at night when I found the Box arriv'd. I could not deny my selfe the pleasure of opening it, and falling upon Fielding's Works was fool enough to sit up all night reading. (1 October 1749; 2:443)

Her preference for the novel over other genres is clear in this request: "No more duplicates—as well as I love Nonsense, I do not desire to have it twice over in the same Words—no Translations, no Periodical papers, thô I confess some of the World entertain'd me very much" (13 May 1758; 3:146).[5] She rarely asks for poetry, history, or philosophy, and she actively forbids newspapers and translations. Yet she often compiles long lists of the titles of novels she desires: "I see in the news papers the names of the following Books: Fortunate Mistriss, Accomplish'd Rake, Mrs. Charke's Memoirs, Modern Lovers, History of 2 Orphans, Memoirs of David Ranger, Miss ⟨Mos⟩tyn, Dick Hazard, History of a Lady Platonist, Sophia Shakespear, Jasper Banks, Frank Hammond, Sir

Andrew Thompson, Van a Clergyman's Son, Cleanthes and Celemena" (3 April 1757; 3:125).

For all her insistence that these texts are mere "Nonsense," it is clear that reading functions as a substitute for the community she no longer has: "I yet retain, and carefully cherish, my taste for reading. If relais of Eyes were to be hir'd like post horses, I would never admit any but silent Companions. They afford a constant variety of Entertainment, and is allmost the only one pleasing in the Enjoiment and inoffensive in the Consequence" (April 1751; 2:480). In fact, she prefers her "silent Companions" to most human commerce: "I thank God my Taste still continues for the Gay part of reading; wiser people may think it trifling, but it serves to sweeten Life to me, and is, at worse, better than the Generallity of Conversation" (24 December 1750; 2:473).

After devouring each shipment of this "triffling" "Nonsense," she spends an inordinate amount of time writing about her reading, a compulsion to criticism she suspects her daughter might not understand: "I fancy you are now saying—'Tis a sad thing to grow old. What does my poor mama mean by troubling me with Criticisms on Books that no body but her selfe will ever read over?" (1 March 1752; 3:9). Yet in sending these responses, Lady Mary has the opportunity to play the parts of literary critic, moralist, and even novelist. Like many of her contemporaries, she searches for an adequate aesthetic for this new form, and her comments about the novel, beyond offering modern readers some of the first female literary criticism of the genre, indicate that she will not clear a space in the traditional literary canon for this new genre.

She writes without seeing any hierarchical relationship among the various texts. She speaks of Richardson's *Clarissa* (1747–48) in the same breath as *The Adventures of Mr. Loveill* (1750) and writes that she was "more entertain'd" by Sir John Hill's *Adventures of Mr. George Edwards, a Creole* (1751) than by Charlotte Lennox's *Female Quixote* (1752). Her refusal to endow the novel with any status is particularly evident when she relegates the texts to the world of mere material objects: "I do not doubt at least the greatest part of these are Trash, Lumber etc.; however, they will serve to pass away the Idle time" (3 April 1757; 3:126); "Daughter, Daughter, don't call names. You are allwaies abusing my Pleasures, which is what no mortal will bear. Trash, Lumber, sad stuff, are the Titles you give to my favorite Amusements. . . . We have all our Playthings; happy are they that can be contented with those they can obtain" (30 September 1757; 3:134). Unlike many of her contemporaries, she does not insist these "objects" should be shunned altogether, as does Sarah Pennington, who expresses the following sentiments to her daughters: "Novels and Romances never give yourself the Trouble of reading; though many of them contain some few good Morals, they are not worth picking out of the Rubbish intermixed. . . . They are so artfully managed as to excite idle Curiosity to see the Conclusion, . . . the common Catastrophe of a wedding, or sometimes a Funeral, from which useless Knowledge neither Pleasure or [sic] Profit accrues." [6] Instead, Lady Mary prefers to argue for the pleasures that come from the very simplicity of her "Playthings": "You will call all this Trash, Trumpery etc. . . . I see new story Books with the same pleasure your eldest Daughter does a new dress, or your youngest a new Baby" (22 September 1755; 3:88–89).

This recurring metaphor—equating the novel with children's toys—reveals her refusal to grant the novel any of the seriousness or philosophical import found in the traditional "high" forms of literature:

> As I approach a second childhood, I endeavor to enter into the Pleasures of it. Your youngest Son is, perhaps, at this very moment riding on a Poker with great Delight, not at all regretting that it is not a gold one, and much less wishing it an Arabian Horse, which he would not know how to manage; I am reading an Idle Tale, not expecting Wit or Truth in it, and am very glad it is not Metaphisics to puzzle my Judgment, or History to mislead my Opinion. He fortifys his Health by Exercise, I calm my Cares by Oblivion. The methods may appear low to busy people, but if he improves his strength, and I forget my Infirmitys, we attain very desirable ends. (30 September 1757; 3:134)

Lady Mary echoes modern claims about the instability of the novel's generic classification, but she does not suspect, as scholars such as John Bender have argued, that the novel will actively participate in the "disabling" of established genres. [7] Rather, she simply refuses them inclusion.

Even though she apologizes to her daughter for her interest in these nonstatus texts—"You will laugh at my making any [criticism] on a Work below Examination" (3:94)—her refusal to classify is undercut by her equally powerful interest in the form. She writes, "I think my time better employ'd in reading the Adventures of imaginary people, than the Dutchess of Marlbrô's, who pass'd the latter years of her Life in padling with her Will. . . . The active scenes are over at my Age. I indulge, with all the art I can, my taste for reading. If I would confine it to valuable Books, they are allmost rare as valuable Men. I must be content with what I can find" (30 September 1757; 3:134). Her negative responses grow in part out of her sense of the ephemerality of the form as it is linked with the problem of "consumption" in these eighteenth-century texts. This throwaway prose, unlike the best in literature, does not repay rereading; once consumed, Lady Mary insists, the novels hold no further fascination, as her remark about the scarcity of "valuable Books" attests. Yet while she might describe the texts of the novels as throwaways, the books themselves were not: even though there is no indication that she spent time rereading her novels, by the time of her death Lady Mary had amassed a significant collection.[8]

Moreover, there is a peculiar subconscious link in her mind between her continuous "consumption" of the novels and her literal consumption of food. In the middle of a long letter filled exclusively with literary criticism, Lady Mary invokes the character of Lady Qualmsick (from *The History of Pompey the Little*), a woman whose "Vapours" remind her that she herself has been persuaded into a "fancy'd loss of Appetite" by a local physician. This remark then prompts her into "a recollection of what I eat Yesterday," and she launches into a list of foods she literally consumed: breakfast and lunch consist of a half-pint of ass's milk, three cups of milk coffee, one large cup of milk chocolate, a dish of gravy soup with bread and roots, a wing and the body of a large fat capon, a veal sweetbread, custard and roasted chestnuts; for dinner she has more ass's milk, twelve chestnuts (equaling twenty-four of the English variety), an egg, and a "handsome Poringer of white Bread and milk" (16 February 1752; 3:5). This precise list and the equally detailed evaluation of her "consumption" of Lady Vane's "Memoirs," *Charlotte Summers, The History of Pompey the Little, Leonora,* and Mrs. Constantia Phillips's *Apology* together form one continuous "feast."

While she may claim the innocence and idleness of the pleasures of the novel, she is equally quick to judge: she applauds or criticizes a text primarily as it reinforces or undermines her own values. Lady Mary delights in many comic novels because she perceives no ideological threat in their representation of character. Such novels also share with her own satiric letters an appreciation of the social and theatrical nature of human conduct, an understanding that character is revealed in performance. Miss Smythies's *Stage-Coach,* a novel about a diverse group of travelers who pass their time telling stories, is an example of the innocent pleasures the comic novel generates. She appreciates the "Grotesque Figures that amuse" (22 September 1755; 3:89), such as the stereotypical, choleric Captain Cannon, who utters the oaths "No, powder her," or "Yes, sunburn her," a man bold enough to call another passenger "old square toes."[9] Her taste for this avowedly comic, even two-dimensional and inconsequential treatment finds additional satisfaction in *The History of Pompey the Little; or, The Life and Adventures of a Lap-Dog* (1751), a novel that initially held little promise:

> Candles came, and my Eyes grown weary I took up the next Book meerly because I suppos'd from the Title it could not engage me long. It was Pompey the Little, which has realy diverted me more than any of the others, and it was impossible to go to Bed till it was finish'd. It is a real and exact representation of Life as it is now acted in London, as it was in my time, and as it will be (I do not doubt) a Hundred years hence. . . . I found there many of my Acquaintance. Lady T[ownshend] and Lady O[rford] are so well painted, I fancy'd I heard them talk, and have heard them say the very things there repeated. (16 February 1752; 3:4)

As its name implies, the novel is an episodic and satiric ramble about the adventures of quite a dog-about-town as he attends masquerades, operas, and Garrick performances in the company of other dogs of quality. The method of this roman à clef is also similar to her own epistolary descriptions of the social world: a satiric treatment of the follies of her fashionable circle, including portraits of her friends and judgments about the absurdity of the English social scene.

The narrator justifies the "insignificance" of the subject by writing, "I cannot help promising myself some Encouragement, in this Life-writing Age especially, where no Character is thought too inconsiderable to engage the public Notice, or too abandoned to be set up as a Pattern of Imitation."[10] Lady Mary's appreciation of the satiric adventures of a lapdog confirms modern scholarly claims that the novel comes into existence only after readers are willing to take an interest in the "inconsiderable." The phenomenon permeates so deeply that Lady Mary gives herself license to record similar inconsiderable occurrences from her own life. Having read Fielding's *Journal of a Voyage to Lisbon* and claiming that the most edifying part concerned the history of the kitten, she feels free to share a personal, domestic detail with her daughter: "I was the more touch'd by [the *Journal*], having a few days before found [a kitten] in deplorable Circumstances in a neighbouring Vineyard. I did not only releive her present wants with some excellent milk, but had her put into a clean Basket and brought to my own House, where she has liv'd ever since very comfortably" (22 September 1755; 3:88). Lady Mary must also have realized that the very letters she pens are evidence of her own voluminous "Life-writing"—that she enacts, in real life, the novelist's prerogative, trusting that her daughter will appreciate this little narrative and counting on the interest others will take in her "inconsiderable" discourse.

Lady Mary is quick to express her outrage, however, when her aristocratic friends are unflatteringly represented. Charlotte Lennox provokes Lady Mary's ire by presenting a woman she presumes to be her friend, Isabella Finch. Lennox had dedicated her first book of poems (1747) to Finch, and when the expected patronage failed to materialize Lennox includes (in *The Life of Harriot Stuart* [1751]) a critical portrait of "Lady Cecilia," a woman described as having a "peculiar talent in procuring dependents, by her affected benevolence, whom she never designed to serve, and raising hopes she never intended to gratify," a woman "capable of meditating the blackest designs" and of "endeavoring to sacrifice [others'] fame, to give a sanction to her base desertion." [11] Lady Mary's aristocratic sensibilities are injured by this negative portrait, and her displeasure leads her haughtily to condemn Lennox as an ungrateful supplicant: "I was rouz'd into great surprize and Indignation by the monstrous abuse of one of the very, very few Women I have a real value for. . . . I did not think she had an Enemy upon Earth" (1 March 1752; 3:8). [12] Thus the novel's ability to present as "real" a distorted representation of this member of her class is also at work in Lady Mary's criticism of the genre. Peter Quennell calls her "a naturally ardent and demanding character" who "enjoyed the benefits and absorbed the prejudices that went with her exalted station," [13] and her literary responses are, as one might expect, rooted in this aristocratic bias and class privilege. Her familiar dismissal of Pope and Swift is only one such instance: "These two superior Beings were entitle'd by their Birth and hereditary Fortune to be only a couple of Link Boys. . . . [Their friendship] had a very strong Foundation: the Love of Flattery on one side and the Love of Money on the other" (23 June 1754; 3:57–58). Her delight in the novel is thus tempered by questions not only of "consumption" but of "production": she believes that too many such texts were written by nonstatus writers exclusively for profit, and her worst criticism is the label "sale work."

A letter about the "mean marriage" her half sister Lady Caroline made provides Lady Mary with an excuse to attack the nonaristocratic origins of most novelists and their pernicious representations of her class:

> It may be you will call this an old fashion'd way of thinking. The confounding of all Ranks and making a Jest of order has long been growing in England, and I perceive, by the Books you sent me, has made a very considerable progress. The Heros and Heroines of the age are Coblers and Kitchin Wenches. Perhaps you will say I should not take my Ideas of the manners of the times from such triffling Authors, but it is more truly to be found amongst them than any Historian. As they write meerly to get money, they allwaies fall into the notions that are most acceptable to the present Taste. It has long been the endeavor of our English Writers to represent people of Quality as the vilest and silliest part of the Nation. Being (generally) very low born themselves. (23 July 1753; 3:35–36)

Beyond revealing an especially keen awareness of changes in class sensibilities in England, her comments make a case for the novel as the best repository of these cultural shifts. As evidence she offers a familiar anti–Grub Street argument: novelists write for money, a substance that permeates all class barriers; because novels sell the most when they appeal to the most common tastes, novelists can generate increased sales by writing only what is pleasing, thus enhancing their purses and ensuring the continuance of this fully self-sustaining system. Aristocrats, who once owned the province of writing generally, are novelistically represented as vile (morally bankrupt) and silly (superfluous and ignorant). Replacing them as the contemporary cultural representations of the hero and heroine are "Coblers and Kitchin Wenches." The "confounding of all Ranks" and the "Jest of order" are the result of the common status of money-grubbing scribblers who now control the arena of social and moral instruction. Predating similar claims from modern scholars such as Bender, she even goes so far as to suggest that the fictions themselves, rather than mirroring reality, actually generate cultural change: "I am much mistaken if this Levelling Principle does not one day or other break out in fatal consequences to the public, as it has allready done in many private Families."

She charges that even her second cousin, Henry Fielding, a writer of some social status, has been infected by the new money-novel nexus, and she will allow him only a small measure of her compassion because he "has realy a fund of true Humour, and was to be pity'd at his first entrance into the World, having no choice (as he said himselfe) but to be a Hackney Writer or a Hackney Coachman" (23 July 1754; 3:66). Though she will recommend his novels, faults and all—recognizing that his writing is indeed a "new species"—she keenly feels the conflict between status and money, between talent and expediency, in Fielding's situation, and she takes him to task for his efforts:

> Since I was born, no original has appear'd excepting Congreve, and Fielding, who would I beleive have approach'd nearer to his excellencies if not forc'd by necessity to publish without correction, and throw many productions into the World he would have thrown into the Fire if meat could have been got without money, or money without Scribbling. The Greatest Virtue, Justice, and the most distinguishing prerogative of Mankind, writeing, when duly executed do Honor to Human nature, but when degenerated into Trades are the most contemptible ways of getting Bread.(3:67–68) [14]

The especially revealing comment, "If meat could have been got without money, or money without Scribbling," points to the new literary reality of 1754, when writing had indeed become a trade and when "Scribbling" could generate significant reward. Thus her implied criticism of the novel—that it does not do "Honor to Human nature"—grows out of both an aesthetic and a class complaint: life, as it is represented in the novel, is not idealized and aristocratic, "honoring" human nature by presenting models better than life, but is merely the bourgeois representation of "Coblers and Kitchin Wenches" living their bourgeois lives. For all her dismissal of Pope's money grubbing, she shares his loathing of the new literary marketplace and the ephemeral, unstable products it generates. [15]

II

In this context, the accounts called "memoirs" or "apologies" are of compelling interest to Lady Mary. She is both fascinated and repelled by the scandalous *amours* of her countrywomen. Like her own satiric letters about the English aristocracy, these texts bring to light the sexual misconduct of women, but, unlike her letters, the memoirists' portrayals are fraught with uncertainty. That the scandalous memoirs offer a "consumable interiority" important in the bourgeois construction of a gendered identity, as Felicity Nussbaum has argued, is the source of Lady Mary's displeasure. As the subjects of published prose "histories," the comic adventures of lapdogs and other truly "inconsiderable" creatures cause Lady Mary little anxiety; when her real-life female acquaintances represent themselves in print and reveal their secrets, defining for the literate population at large the "real" behavior of women, Lady Mary perceives a potential threat. Moreover, unlike the male spiritual autobiographers, the female memoirists translate a female fall into public notoriety: "The fall from chastity and familial favor becomes the pattern of a public declaration of identity." By the middle of the eighteenth century, Nussbaum argues, such declarations had "cleared a *public* space for writers and readers of documents about the private 'self,'" a "self" that became a "desirable commodity" by the end of the century.[16] It is this public, female commodification that generates Lady Mary's unease. Her remarks about the "Memoirs" of Lady Vane, a woman with whom Lady Mary was acquainted (Lady Vane married two of Lady Mary's relatives, Lord William Hamilton and William Vane) and Mrs. Phillips's *Apology* are paradigmatic of the ways she judges public declarations of female "interiority" and the potential danger such confessions present (16 February 1752; 3:2). Her complaints cluster around the questions of truth telling and self-justification, uncertainties arising from the complications of publication and self-interest.

Lady Mary begins her critique of Lady Vane's memoirs by judging that they "contain more Truth and less malice than any I ever read in my Life. When she speaks of her own being disinterested, I am apt to beleive she really thinks her selfe so, as many highway men, after having no possibillity of retreiving the character of Honesty, please themselves with that of being Generous, because whatever they get on the road they allways spend at the next ale House, and are still as beggarly as ever" (3:2). Lady Mary is willing to allow Lady Vane a measure of sincerity, but only that degree of self-delusion demanded by public self-justification. In likening Lady Vane to a highwayman, "generous" only to those who share the pleasures and only after the irretrievable loss of the character of honesty, she emphasizes the inherent self-interest in such public declarations of identity. She voices a similar suspicion about the content of *An Apology for the Conduct of Mrs. Constantia Phillips* (1748–49): "I expected to find at least probable, if not true, facts, and was not disapointed" (3:5–6). The conjunction of "true" and "probable" as modifiers for "fact" jars modern readers, but Lady Mary is fully aware that the methods of fiction create a forum for special pleading.

Not only was she acquainted with the ostensible authors of these texts, but also they moved occasionally in her social circle. So while she might not be able, finally, to judge the degree of sincerity in their apologies or the truthfulness of their repentance—because she has no "real" access to these writers' consciousnesses—she is fully familiar with her own responses to the beauty or character of each writer and each writer's lover. Lady Mary uses her own private "history" to suggest the fictonalized nature of the published representations, a fiction at odds with her reality. Positioning herself as the repository of "truth," she feels justified in providing an alternative account drawn from her own lived experience. Of Lady Vane's lover, Sewallis Shirley, Lady Mary says, "He appear'd to me gentile, well bred, well shap'd and sensible." But she is unmoved by the particular beauties that prompt Lady Vane's praise: "But the charms of his Face and Eyes, which Lady V[ane] describes with so much warmth, were, I confess, allwaies invisible to me, and the artificial part of his character very glareing, which I think her story shows in a strong light" (3:3–4). Lady Mary even more forcefully rejects Mrs. Phillips's celebratory descriptions of her lover, "Mr. S——te," by claiming that he was "one of the most disagreable Fellows about Town, as odious in his outside as stupid in his conversation, and I should as soon have expected to hear of his Conquests at the Head of an Army as amongst Women; yet he has been (it seems) the darling favourite of the most experienc'd of the Sex" (3:6). Immune to the charms of both men and fully aware of the serious flaws in their characters, Lady Mary attempts to cast doubt generally on the truth of the whole of both narratives and specifically on the authenticity of the products of individual consciousness and their claims to a truth in interiority. She argues that such narratives of self-revelation are at odds with the "empirical evidence" she possesses and with the performances she trusts, both in life and in letters.

Her resistance to published and profitable declarations of a novelistic identity also makes explicit an aristocratic woman's different definitions of these terms. The very fact of publication offends Lady Mary's aristocratic sensibilities, and thus she holds fast to her strong injunctions against publication. Although she was a prolific writer—penning romances in her youth, authoring anonymously the periodical *The Nonsense of Common-Sense,* generating an impressive lifelong collection of poetry, and even writing during her exile a history of her times (which she assured her daughter she burned installment by installment)—she steadfastly refused to publish under her name.[17] In 1753, when visited by one of the chief chaplains to Cardinal Querini, she was asked to donate her "Works" to the public library that joined the episcopal palace. Her reaction was characteristically severe: "I was struck dumb for some time with this astonishing request. When I recover'd my vexatious surprize (foreseeing the Consequence) I made answer, I was highly sensible of the Honor design'd me, but upon my word I had never printed a single line in my Life" (10 October 1753; 3:38–39). Her antipathy to publication was strong because she was always "foreseeing the Consequence"; yet she claims to be willing to lose a good friend rather than to contribute to a collection that the chaplain assures her "admitted none but the most Eminent Authors."

This self-censoring in the public arena was not without its price for an aristocratic woman with a reputation as a writer. Lady Mary had been willing to share her literary endeavors, but only in exclusive private company. This attempt to limit her audience was, of course, doomed to failure. One paradigmatic example of the ways Lady Mary's reputation as a writer and her production of "private" verse could result in suspicion and bad feeling among her acquaintances occurred after the attempted rape of Lady Mary's friend Griselda Murray and Lady Mary's poetic response to the incident. Robert Halsband reports the salient events: at 4:00 A.M. on the morning of 14 October 1721, Arthur Gray, a footman employed in the household, burst into Mrs. Murray's room, pistol in hand, saying (according to newspaper accounts), "I have been in love with you since the first Moment I saw you, and am now come to gratify my Desires. I risque my Life in this Attempt if I don't enjoy you; but if I'm so happy, I know you to be a Lady of so much Prudence, that you won't expose your Character to an ill-judging World, in prosecuting me."[18] Mrs. Murray eventually fought off his attempts, striking the pistol out of his hand and summoning help. Gray was later imprisoned and ultimately transported, but while awaiting trial he reportedly sent to Mrs. Murray a letter blaming his behavior on love.

The incident immediately became a town scandal. Newspapers printed ballads likening Mrs. Murray to Lucrece, and Mrs. Murray herself sent to the Countess of Mar a copy of an anonymous ballad, "Virtue in Danger," that contains these bawdy stanzas, punning on the meaning of the pistol:

> A Sword he had and it hard by
> A thing appear'd with all
> Which we for very Modesty
> A Pistol chuse to call.
> This Pistol in one hand he took
> And thus began to woo her,
> Oh how this tender Creature shooke
> When he presented to her!
>
> (ll. 25–32)

By the summer of 1722 Mrs. Murray had begun to attribute the verse to Lady Mary and publicly assailed her for writing the ballad, even though she had earlier presented the poem to Lady Mary's sister without complaint. Lady Mary claims by 1726 that Mrs. Murray had declared "open Wars" against her and was "pleas'd to attack me in very Billingsgate language at a Masquerade" (22 April 1726; 2:64). The enmity became so intense that it spilled over into the legal arena: Mrs. Murray went so far as to assist in the kidnapping of Lady Mar, out of Lady Mary's custody, and a lengthy custody battle ensued. Even after Lady Mar was returned to Lady Mary's care, Mrs. Murray is reported to have said in court that "it was a shame to keep [Lady Mar] in the custody of her sister, who was less sane" (699).

Lady Mary never admitted writing "Virtue in Danger" (although she never denied writing it either), but she did own a poem that was in many ways even more scandalous, "Epistle From Arthur G[ray] to Mrs M[urra]y," which offers a sympathetic treatment of the footman's passion and his hopes for her final forgiveness:

> Yet when you see me waver in the Wind,
> My Guilty Flame extinct, my Soul resign'd
> Sure you may pity, what you can't approve,
> The cruel Consequence of Furious Love.
>
> (ll. 91–94)

The dangers of "private" publication are painfully obvious in this incident, and Lady Mary laments such ill consequences to her daughter: "Sure no body ever had such various provocations to print as my selfe. I have seen things I have wrote so mangle'd and falsify'd I have scarce known them. I have seen Poems I never read publish'd with my Name at length, and others that were truly and singly wrote by me, printed under the names of others. I have made my selfe easy under all these mortifications by the refflection I did not deserve them, having never aim'd at the Vanity of popular Applause" (10 October 1753; 3:39). Even though she is angry at being misrepresented in print, her aristocratic sense of self-containment will not allow her to correct the public misconception, nor will she publicly own her literary endeavors for fear that others will charge her with aiming "at the Vanity of popular Applause."

Constrained by the decorums of her sex and class, Lady Mary instead chooses the genre that indeed allows her a declaration of an identity, but one that does not place her in the jeopardy inherent in publication: she writes a supposedly "private" letter, which she presumes will then be shared "publicly" among a circle of family and friends limited in its scope. Moreover, she hopes that the performative nature of the epistolary identity she intentionally cultivates—one visible in her play with literary styles, forms, and genres—will distance her from the necessity of "suspect" confessions, self-justifications, and titillation as the means to define a "real" female identity. The nature of epistolary exchange also allows her to remain outside the genuine money economy that publication makes explicit while generating literary artifacts that produce identity, but one not necessarily deformed by profit.[19]

Lady Mary mildly suggests that the female memoirists' "apologies" can provide positive moral lessons: "[Lady Vane's] History, rightly consider'd, would be more instructive to young Women than any Sermon I know. They may see there what mortifications and variety of misery are the unavoidable consequences of Gallant[r]ys. I think there is no rational Creature than [sic] would not prefer the life of the strictest Carmelite to the round of Hurry and misfortune she has gone through" (3:2). Yet she also implies that such careful consideration, overcome by the power of sympathy, is too often lacking, and that women's truth telling, their public declarations of "bad" behavior, will instead create a printed model for female misconduct.

Such "bad" models are equally present in the novel, Lady Mary argues, for these fictionalized narratives similarly cultivate a reader's belief that heightened sentiments, which find their authority in the transparency and immediacy of interiority and not in wise behavior, will produce happy endings. John Bender puts it this way: "From the eighteenth century onward, the realist novel has attempted the appearance of having removed all distance between itself and the processes of daily life: it pretends to be a transparent, unmediated form of knowledge about that life. . . . The master fiction of the realist novel lies in the pretense that it shows the actual processes whereby material things and consciousness are all produced simultaneously through sensory experience." [20] This conflict for Lady Mary is configured as a schism between consciousness and performance: on the one hand, Lady Mary is drawn to declarations of individual identity and feels the power of their emotional sway; on the other, when she judges characters according to what they *do* rather than the quality of their sentiments, she finds only lamentable models of conduct. [21]

She recalls for her daughter the powerful and dangerous emotional impact of a narrative that had a lifelong influence on her, Prior's "Henry and Emma":

> I was so much charm'd at fourteen with the Dialogue of Henry and Emma, I can say it by heart to this Day, without refflecting on the monstrous folly of the story in plain prose, where a young Heiress to a fond Father is represented falling in love with a Fellow she had only seen as a Huntsman, a Faulkner, and a Beggar, and who confesses, without any circumstances of excuse, that he is oblig'd to run his country, having newly committed a Murder. She ought reasonably to have suppos'd him (at best) a Highway man, yet the Virtuous Virgin resolves to run away with him to live amongst the Banditti, and wait upon his Trollop if she had no other Way of enjoying his Company. This senseless Tale is, however, so well varnish'd with melody of Words and pomp of Sentiments, I am convince'd it has hurt more Girls than ever were injur'd by the lewdest Poems extant. (23 July 1754; 3:68)

This fantastic romance narrative of love and potential betrayal, Lady Mary argues, is far more corrupting than lewd literature, and she herself still feels the impact of a story that she can recite "by heart to this day," having committed this "monstrous folly" to memory. [22]

Even Henry Fielding earns her wrath for presenting examples of "bad" behavior because he exploits fiction's potentially dangerous power to promote unrealistic expectations. Calling Tom Jones and Mr. Booth "Sorry Scoundrels," she refuses to pardon the novels for being "very mischeivous": "They place a merit in extravagant Passions, and encourrage young people to hope for impossible events to draw them out of the misery they chuse to plunge themselves into, expecting legacys from unknown Relations, and generous Benefactors to distress'd Virtue, as much out of Nature as Fairy Treasures" (23 July 1754; 3:66). She objects to the foundation of fantasy on which these novels are built, especially as they reward characters who fail to take responsibility for their actions. Because they trust in fantastic rewards for virtue, young readers will be encouraged to cultivate "extravagant Passions," put their faith in "distress'd Virtue," and trust that "impossible events" will solve their problems rather than concentrating on good sense and wise management, the qualities she advocates because she believes that one's actions, not one's hopes, produce results.

The combination of fantasy infused with the passionate emotions produced by heightened sentiments is particularly powerful in *The History of Charlotte Summers, the Fortunate Parish Girl* (1749), a novel that provides for Lady Mary an especially good example of a woman's poor judgment being rewarded with love and status. Charlotte's story begins when she is rescued from poverty by Lady Bountiful and soon falls in love with Lady Bountiful's son, Thomas, even though she knows her patroness will disapprove. She is forced to flee Lady Bountiful's residence after an attempted rape by the villainous Mr. Crofts (the man whom Lady Bountiful hopes Charlotte will marry) and after a dream that urged her to "fly, Miss Summers, or you are undone."[23] Heading for London, she meets misfortunes along the way, although she always maintains her inherent goodness and generosity of spirit. At the conclusion, when she rediscovers her father and is revealed to be an heiress, she happily marries Sir Thomas. Lady Mary, however, finds little to admire in the novel: "The author has fallen into the common mistake of Romance writers, intending a virtuous character and not knowing how to draw it, the first step of his Heroine (leaving her Patronesse's House) being alltogether absurd and ridiculous, justly entitleing her to all the misfortunes she met with" (16 February 1752; 3:4).

Lady Mary refuses to enter into the ideological framework set up by the novel itself, a framework that rests on Charlotte's sensibilities rather than on her behavior. As John Bender puts it, the realist novel pretends that character is autonomous, even though there is an invisible authority organizing the mode of representation; the novel presents the illusion that consciousness is as free to shape circumstance as it is to be shaped by it.[24] For the average reader, it is Charlotte's extraordinarily keen awareness of the conflicting demands upon her that elevates her to the position of heroine: her love for Sir Thomas is juxtaposed with the debt of gratitude she owes his mother; her desire to please Lady Bountiful conflicts with the terrifying prospect of a would-be rapist presented as an acceptable suitor. Superbly sensitive to her plight as a dependent woman, she is unable to extricate herself from such competing pressures and thus abandons the only home she has ever known. Yet rather than sympathizing with the helpless woman's dilemma, Lady Mary seizes on her dangerous behavior and calls her flight "absurd and ridiculous."

It is apparent that the novel asks Lady Mary to reorder her familiar responses to experience: to abandon her observance of social life in England as though it were the stage and to experience instead the supposedly unmediated access to another's consciousness. She clings, however, to her familiar point of view:

> I am not of Cowley's mind that his World is
>
> > a Dull ill acted Comedy,
>
> nor of Mrs. Philips's that it is
>
> > a too well acted Tragedy.
>
> I look upon it as a very pretty Farce for those that can see it in that Light. I confess a severe Critic that would examine by ancient Rules might find many deffects, but tis ridiculous to judge seriously of a puppet show. Those that can laugh and be diverted with absurditys are the wisest Spectators, be it of writeings, action, or people. (22 September 1755; 3:89)

Lady Mary will thus acknowledge the power of the novelist's method, but she refuses its transparency and continues to *read* these texts as if she were witnessing the *drama* of their unfolding, "be it of writeings, action, or people." She does not surrender the fundamental principle by which she had always ordered experience: she remains a "Spectatress," judging characters by their actions. Pointing to these difficulties of dramatizing inner worth when sentimentality is revealed in performance, Robert Markley cites Steele as an example of a writer "trapped" in the mystification of a rhetoric that simultaneously celebrates innate virtue and demands that performance seem genuine, not calculated. Such writing must "sustain the fiction" that it is a "natural" expression of a "true" self.[25] It is just this claim to the "natural" access to "truth" that Lady Mary, as an aristocrat trained to value the visible, suspects.

The conclusion of the narrative—Charlotte's being rewarded with the status of heiress—also displeases Lady Mary. The narrator of Charlotte's story, who purports to be "the first Begotten, of the poetical issue, of the much celebrated Biographer of *Joseph Andrews,* and *Tom Jones, . . .* a natural Brat of that facetious Gentleman," self-consciously points to the conventions of the happy ending for such fiction and, as part of a continuous dialogue with posited readers, pretends to submit to the force of readers' desire for a marriage—in this case, the Widow Lackit's protests: "Sure you won't give over without marrying her? It is impossible that she can be happy without a Husband. Besides, it is contrary to all Rule to end a History of this Kind, without marrying the Hero and Heroine."[26] It is just this "Rule" for the endings of female histories that provokes Lady Mary's loudest protests in her criticism about the author's "intending a virtuous character and not knowing how to draw it." Rendered powerless through the course of the narrative, Charlotte is nevertheless rewarded in the end, metamorphosing from a poverty-stricken waif into a kinder, more sensitive Lady Bountiful because of the fineness of her sensibilities. When the novel implies that her inner virtues rescue her and prompt her rehabilitation at the end, Lady Mary balks. As it works to cultivate sentiment, the fictional method itself erases the real agent of the heroine's rescue—money. Lady Mary responds to the middle-class strategy of equation that, as Markley points out, allows sentimentality to stake a middle-class claim to "the role of England's moral conscience"[27] by fully resisting that equation of sensibility with moral excellence and, more important, aristocratic worth—even though she makes no mention of the fact that the text actually confirms the very class values that it seems to reject and that Lady Mary herself embraces.

Moreover, she seems unaware of the reality of her own reading and writing experience. She sits alone, reading, writing, and judging as though she *were* a spectator in the theater; she will then send these judgments to a woman who will read and respond to the evaluations Lady Mary offers but not to events she has observed. John Paul Hunter, in an essay concerning the "decline" of eighteenth-century theater and the paradoxes of Cibber's *Apology,* cites the manager's preference for performance over print: Cibber praises the uniform and communal response to drama rather than the singular and isolated responses of individual readers. However, as Hunter points out, Cibber chooses print, the autobiography, as the form for his expression, a genre written from the privacy of his closet to other readers in their closets; he does not stage his "life" in a real theatrical performance.[28] The responses from both Cibber and Lady Mary reveal for modern readers the blurred boundaries separating late-seventeenth-century notions of character as visible in performance from the late-eighteenth-century preference for interiority. Both artists resist and exploit the possibilities of textual representation while refusing to shift the epistemological grounds of their judgment and observations from the theater and performance to the novel and consciousness.

III

That such agreement not only exists but has taken on active power in the world is evident in Lady Mary's attacks on her favorite target, Samuel Richardson. The combination of heightened emotions and "fantasy" found in his novels—the supposedly unmediated reality, the potential manipulation and even failure of empirical observation, and the presentation of bad female models of bourgeois behavior—produces her most extensive comments about the dangers of this new fiction. His powerful and potentially destructive messages lead Lady Mary to predict that he will do "much harm in the Boarding Schools," and she insists that he must "have his Absurditys detected" (20 October 1755; 3:94).

Toward that end, she sends her daughter "cameo-narratives"—small, dramatic, and especially well-constructed novelistic histories of events in the lives of her Italian acquaintances, tales she hopes will function as antidotes to Richardson's fiction. While her own narrative abilities are impressive, more important is her concentration on the failure or weakness of women characters. Rejecting Richardson's methods, she sets up a dialogue between her interpretations of demonstrable female error and the dangers of invisible virtue as it is articulated in his fiction. In speculating about Richardson's "real" profession, she imagines that he must have some self-interest in promoting marriage: "It is certain there are as many marriages as ever. Richardson is so eager for the multiplication of them, I suppose he is some parish Curate, whose cheife profit depends on Weddings and christenings" (20 October 1755; 3:95). Thus all three of her narratives focus on female value as the novel depicts it: in women's choices about sex and marriage. Lady Mary's third-person retelling of incidents and behaviors, stripped of the novel's reputed access to the heroine's consciousness, emphasizes her refusal, perhaps even her inability, to abandon her belief that only visible performance defines character.

Her strongest attacks depend on Richardson's lower-class status. From her own aristocratic and well-traveled perspective, Lady Mary freely criticizes his ignorance of Italian customs in allowing Sir Charles Grandison and Clementina to meet in her father's home, for it would be "as repugnant to Custom as it would be in London for a young Lady of Quality to dance on the Ropes at Bartholomew Fair" (3:91). Richardson's low status accounts for his lack of understanding about the speech and behavior of people of quality ("He has no Idea of the manners of high Life. His old Lord M. talks in the style of a Country Justice, and his virtuous young Ladies romp like the Wenches round a May pole" [3.97]), and she takes him to task for failing to respect the expensive pleasures of old china, since he "never had (probably) money enough to purchase any, or even a Ticket for a Masquerade" (3:97). Lady Mary recommends that he "confine his Pen to the Amours of Housemaids and the conversation at the Steward's Table, where I imagine he has sometimes intruded, thô oftner in the Servants' Hall" (3:96).

For all this class snobbery and aristocratic hauteur, Lady Mary cites Richardson's portraits of women as the source of her greatest displeasure. For many, the most powerful mid-eighteenth-century story of "Virtue rewarded" was *Pamela;* for others, *Pamela* was the most powerful story of virtue falsified. As a means of detecting Richardson's absurdities, eliciting the potential harm he will cause, and uncovering the "realities" of social life, Lady Mary relates a real-life case of one disastrous consequence of *Pamela* in a striking bit of local history involving a servant girl who marries her master (8 December 1754; 3:70–76). The tale confirms her worst fears: that lower-class women will use Richardson's novel as a primer and that, as a result, life will imitate art in ways she finds entirely unsuitable. Having earlier claimed that *Pamela* "has met with very extrordinary (and I think undeserv'd) success. . . . It was all the Fashion at Paris and Versailles, and is still the Joy of the Chambermaids of all Nations" (17 October 1750; 2:470), she claims in her letter that she does not know "under what constellation that Foolish stuff was wrote, but it has been translated into more Languages than any modern performance I ever heard of" (3:70).

Lady Mary recounts the adventures of Octavia, a beggar child taken in and raised by Signora Diana. After nine years of quiet living, the young woman began to make "a great noise" in the community, because "Beauty is as difficult to conceal as Light." Rejecting marriage proposals from "honest thriving Tradmen," Octavia took a post with an elderly countess. There she met the young heir, Count Jeronimo Soci, who "during the six months that she had serv'd in the House had try'd every Art of a fine Gentleman accustom'd to Victorys of that sort, to vanquish the virtue of this fair virgin." After the countess's death, Octavia took a post with an elderly judge, where she was again besieged, but this time with marriage proposals from the old gentleman. She chose to escape back to the safety of Signora Diana's house, and when asked why she refused a respectable judge, she replied that "she scrupul'd entering into the Holy Bands of Matrimony where her Heart did not sincerely accompany all the words of the Ceremony." Two weeks later, a large equipage with four well-armed servants arrived and transported "the Young Damsel," wearing the gifts of "lac'd Linnen and fine Nightgown," to her wedding to Count Soci. A priest, called "Parson Williams" by the town, reported that the count remarked that "the Lovely Octavia has brought him an inestimable Portion, since he owes to her the Salvation of his Soul," and after returning to the palace Octavia immediately dismissed the "superfluous Servants" and "put his Family into an exact method of Oeconomy." Even though the count invited Octavia's mother to live with them, the new countess advised the old woman to stay at Louvere, "promising to take care she shall want nothing, accompany'd with a Token of 20 sequins, which is at least 19 more than ever she saw in her Life."

That Lady Mary intends her own narrative to function as criticism is clear in her remarks about her daughter's likely interpretation of the story:

> I am afraid you are heartily tir'd with this tedious Tale. I will not lengthen it with Refflections; I fancy yours will be [the] same with mine.

All these adventures proceed from Artifice on one side and weakness
on the other. An Honest, open, tender mind is betraid to Ruin by the
charms that make the Fortune of a designing Head, which when join'd
with a Beautifull Face can never fail of advancement, except barr'd by a
Wise Mother who locks up her Daughters from view till no body cares to
look on 'em.

Lady Mary trusts that her daughter will share her responses and find
no one to admire in this narrative: Octavia, driven by "Artifice" and a
"designing Head," succeeds in achieving a status inappropriate for her.
Yet Lady Mary's suggestion that locking a beautiful woman away from
view is the only way to prevent the betrayal of an "Honest, open, tender
mind" is obviously unreasonable, and she draws a comparison from the
example of one of her acquaintances to illustrate:

My poor Freind the D[uche]ss of Bolton was educated in Solitude, with
some choice Books, by a Saint-like Governess. Cramm'd with virtue and
good Qualitys, she thought it impossible not to find Gratitude, thô she
fail'd to give Passion, and upon this plan threw away her Estate, was
despis'd by her Husband, and laugh'd at by the Public. Polly, bred in an
Alehouse and produce'd on the stage, has obtain'd Wealth and Title and
found the way to be esteem'd. So usefull is early Experience; without it
halfe of Life is disipated in correcting the Errors that we have been taught
to receive as indisputable Truths.

Lady Mary's reference to "Polly" is a specific one: Lavinia Fenton, who
originally played the part of Polly Peachum in *The Beggar's Opera,* married her longtime lover, the Duke of Bolton, the husband of the duchess
in Lady Mary's example, a month after the duchess died.[29] Lady Mary
intimates that women of the lower classes, seeing the possibility of ac-
quiring fortune and position through marriage, have acquired a "useful"
early experience that facilitates their programs to raise their status.
Aristocratic women, however, are made vulnerable in their marriage
choices by their improper educations. The Duchess of Bolton, for example, naively trusted that her genuine virtues and good qualities, not
the "artificial" virtues of lower-class women, would earn her a husband's gratitude. The very foundation of the class system, as Lady Mary
understands it, suffers irreparable damage as a result of inappropriate
education and too little experience—and, one might add, the "wrong"

kind of novel reading—for aristocrats who must be taught to suspect the lower- and middle-class appearance of a virtue that is easily feigned and that brings only destructive consequences.

Lady Mary's attacks on *Pamela* are not altogether surprising, since she, like many of her contemporaries, saw more of Shamela in the events of Richardson's text than Pamela. Her attacks on *Clarissa,* however, are stronger still, and her criticism is founded in her strong emotional response to a novel that presents a particularly threatening instance of female misconduct softened by the sympathetic identification the epistolary form itself generates. Her most succinct statement about *Clarissa*—"On the whole 'tis most miserable stuff" (3:9)—emphasizes the emotional power that produces its pernicious effects. While she may be moved by Richardson's works when they touch her personal history ("The 2 first Tomes of Clarissa touch'd me as being very ressembling to my Maiden Days. I find in the pictures of Sir Thomas Grandison and his Lady what I have heard of my Mother and seen of my Father" [3:90]), she strongly distrusts the emotional manipulation: "This Richardson is a strange Fellow. I heartily despise him and eagerly read him, nay, sob over his works in a most scandalous manner" (3:90). Her claim that she wept over *Clarissa* "like any milk maid of sixteen over the Ballad of the Ladie's Fall" (3:9) gives concrete shape to the class issue provoking her judgment: the comparison of Richardson's novel to a cheap broadside ballad and herself to a common servant is a perfect example of the "confounding of all Ranks" and the "jest of Order" that she predicts such fiction will encourage.

Most important, Lady Mary links this issue of emotional response with the more serious questions of Clarissa's violations of epistolary decorum, her immorality, and even her madness. She begins by censuring Anna Howe, who, even though she "is call'd a young Lady of sense and Honor, is not only extreme silly, but a more vicious character than Sally Martin, whose Crimes are owing at first to Seduction and afterwards to necesssity, while this virtuous Damsel, without any reason insults her mother at home and ridicules her abroad, abuses the man she marrys, and is impertinent and Impudent with great applause" (3:9). Anna's "crimes" of impertinence and impudence, which Lady Mary labels as more vicious than those of the woman who encouraged Lovelace to seduce Clarissa, are matched by the heroine's own: "Even that model of Perfection, Clarissa, is so faulty in her behaviour as to deserve little Compassion. Any Girl that runs away with a young Fellow without intending to marry him should be carry'd to Bridewell or Bedlam the next day" (1 March 1752; 3:9). John Richetti argues that readers of Clarissa become spectators of a drama unfolding through the epistolary form. If this is true, then Lady Mary might be expected to appreciate a novel employing her own method and her own source of judgments. However, she always evaluates behavior shorn of any appreciation for consciousness, motive, or sentiment. Thus she resists what Richetti calls one of Richardson's most "novelistic" strategies: Clarissa's attempts to equate "understanding" with "action."[30] For Lady Mary, therefore, Clarissa's madness is first of all a matter of behavior, and she speculates that Richardson's "real" profession cannot be that of the physician: "He is not a Man Midwife, for he would be better skill'd in Physic than to think Fits and Madness any Ornament to the Characters of his Heroines" (3:95–96).

Clarissa's "madness" is most evident, however, in what Lady Mary calls her failures of epistolary decorum, an arena where Lady Mary feels herself particularly empowered to judge: "[Clarissa declares] all she thinks to all the people she sees, without refflecting that in this Mortal state of Imperfection Fig leaves are as necessary for our Minds as our Bodies, and tis as indecent to shew all we think as all we have" (20 October 1755; 3:97). Modern scholars, of course, celebrate Clarissa's ability to write without self-censoring, citing it as one of Richardson's finest achievements. But Lady Mary takes the position that control and restraint—the shaped, performative prose of her own letters—characterize proper behavior, both in life and in epistolary style. Richardson's novels present, in Richetti's words, "an internalizing revision of any literary means for imagining and presenting character"; Lady Mary can respond to such seemingly unmediated "internalizing" only by calling it actively obscene, for it violates not only custom but also her definition of the "subject" and the means by which a woman should fashion her identity. She resists what Richetti also describes as the character's "attempts to locate [a] self and to establish a stable relationship between the self and the stylistic and generic means by which it dramatizes or externalizes itself."[31] For Lady Mary, such stability is either flat or dangerously disingenuous, for it is precisely the fluidity of performance, the multiplicities of human identity, that the epistolary form and she herself cultivate.

Moreover, unlike the scandalous memoirs of her countrywomen who write after their private loss of chastity and public reputation, the events in *Clarissa* unfold as they happen. For all his claims on the title page that his text is a "history," Richardson's present tense, "writing to the moment," purports to be reality in process. The power of this sequential reality, combined with Clarissa's seemingly unmediated epistolary discourse—a presentation of a female subjectivity supposedly transparently available—Lady Mary more severely criticizes as a moral failing: the "indecency" of "showing all we have." Such lewdness, Lady Mary argues, is actually a symptom of the heroine's madness: "The Divine Clarissa never acted prudently till she [had lost her wits], and then very wisely desir'd to be carry'd to Bedlam, which is realy all that is to be done in that Case" (3:96).

Lady Mary addresses these same problems of morality and madness when she links one of her own narratives, concerning the Marchioness Lyscinnia, with the Richardsonian heroines. Lady Mary's story is a potentially tragic fable, a cautionary tale about an aristocratic woman who chooses the solitary life but ends up universally despised (22 March 1756; 3:100–103). The marchioness, a great heiress, married into a prominent and wealthy family. The conflict arose from the heroine's character: "She brought with her such a Diabolical temper and such Luciferan Pride tha[t] neither Husband, Relations or Servants had ever a moment's Peace with her." After eight years of "Warfare," she abandoned her husband and two daughters (the oldest barely six) to take refuge at her father's home. Even though she was exhorted to return to her family by the pope, who "found it harder to reduce one Woman than ten Heretics," she continued to live at her father's estate "in the Enjoyment of her ill humour, living in great Splendor, thô almost Solitary, having by some Impertinence or other disgusted all her Acquaintance." The events turn toward the macabre when she becomes ill after tasting a bowl of poisoned broth. Her maids, ignoring her complaints, drink the broth and die. Though the marchioness "loudly accus'd" her husband as the murderer, Lady Mary describes him as having "a cloud of Wittnesses that he never gave her the least reason of complaint, and even since her leaving him has allways spoke of her with kindness and courted her Return. He is said to be remarkably sweet temper'd, and has the best character of any Man of Quality in this Country." Elements of the Gothic infuse the conclusion of the narrative, where Lady Mary describes the marchioness as so fearful of assassination that she has imprisoned herself in her chamber and will eat only what is first tasted by servants.

Lady Mary likens the events to those in Richardson's fiction:

> I decide nothing; but such is the Destiny of a Lady who would have been one of Richardson's Heroines, having never been suspected of the least Galantry, hateing and being hated universally, of a most noble Spirit, it being proverbial,—as Proud as the Marchioness Lyscinnia.

Lady Mary's feelings are difficult to sort out. On the one hand, her emphasis on this woman's tenacity in holding out against the powerful men in her life, including the pope himself, expresses some genuine admiration. She also implies some sympathy for the marchioness's terror and her present condition—like Clarissa, she is shut away in a claustrophobic chamber and endures pain as a result of the coercion that the powerful can bring to bear. Yet a much less sympathetic case can be made for Lady Mary's perceiving parallels between the pride and obstinancy of the marchioness and both Richardsonian heroines. None was ever "suspected of the least Galantry," but the marchioness is guilty of "hateing and being hated," of allowing a display of arrogance and self-satisfaction to overshadow all other obligations. Lady Mary may argue for a link between the marchioness's paranoia and the madness she sees in Richardson's Clarissa: Lady Mary's suggestion that Clarissa "never acted prudently" until she had lost her wits could just as easily describe the presently chastened marchioness.

Yet this story also has all the markings of tragedy for Lady Mary: a woman of high position falls low. But unlike the powerful attraction of Richardson's portrait of *Clarissa,* Lady Mary's treatment of her "heroine" resonates entirely differently, primarily because her narrative inspires none of the tenderness Richardson's creation of Clarissa evokes. Her story does not represent the heroine as a victim whose heightened sensibilities and fine sentiments generate admiration and sympathy. In stripping the tale of what she had earlier called "the melody of Words and the pomp of Sentiments" and in refusing even to point toward the possibility of a fantasy happy ending, Lady Mary creates a narrative without the power to generate "tribes of Clarissas" (3:106) willing to follow a bad example simply because it masquerades as an unmediated entry into sensibility, an emotionally compelling but morally suspect tale offered as an exemplar. She, like her cousin Fielding, understands that Richardson's fiction presents no moral authority other than the consciousness of its heroine. As Fielding demonstrated in *Shamela,* such consciousness—detached from the kind of narrative authority he creates in *Tom Jones* and the kind that Lady Mary purports to have in her obviously constructed and clearly mediated discourse—can be false. Ronald Paulson puts it succinctly: "By reality Fielding means moral or factual truth apprehended by the reader, whereas he sees in Richardson a reality that means the true workings of a character's mind, without any concern for the truth or falseness of apprehension in relation to the external world."[32]

Lady Mary's offering of real moral exempla can be found in her descriptions of Italian men. She generally couches her sketches in the "aristocratic" form of the panegyric in contrast to the "bourgeois" narrative structure of the novel she uses to examine women's lives. In writing about men, Lady Mary concentrates on their deeds, especially their service to others, as they cultivate and refine the health of both the body and the soul. Her tribute to the Marquis Maffei upon his death is an example of the way she celebrates the beneficence of a fellow aristocrat. The marquis erected "a little Empire from the general esteem, and a Conversation (so they call an Assembly) which he establish'd in his Palace" (24 July [1755]; 3:84). This little empire consisted of piazzas where coffee, tea, chocolate, and "all sort of cool and sweet meats" were available as he welcomed visitors into galleries displaying fine collections of antiquities, medals, and cameos. He also provided suites for dancing, card playing (but not gambling), and conversation, "which allways turn'd upon some point of Learning, either Historical or Poetical, Controversie and Politics being utterly prohibited" (3:85). Beyond praising these "civilized" pleasures, Lady Mary reserves her most succinct tribute for his benign influence: "Thus at very little expence (his fortune not permitting a large one) he had the happiness of giving his Countrimen a Tast of Polite Pleasure and shewing the youth how to pass their Time agreably without Debauchery" (3:85).

She applauds a man of lower social status, a local physician, for his benign influence when he displays extraordinary skill and moral integrity. Her tribute opens with what must have been a startling sentence for her daughter to read: "Soon after I wrote my last letter to my Dear child, I was seiz'd with so violent a Fever, accompany'd with so many bad Symptoms, my Life was despair'd of by the Physician of Gottolengo, I prepar'd my selfe for Death with as much resignation as that Circumstance admits" (23 June 1754; 3:52–53). The neighbors, without her knowledge, sent for Dr. Baglioni, and on his advice and with this airy statement of bravado, Lady Mary agreed to be taken to Louvere: "It has allways been my opinion that it is a matter of the utmost Indifference where we expire, and I consented to be remov'd." After recovering so completely that she "appear'd almost a Miracle to all" that saw her, she celebrates the doctor, universally called "the Miraculous Man," for the singularity of his character and his demonstrable skills. Modern readers, understanding the primitive state of eighteenth-century medicine, see just why he was successful: he refuses to allow his patients to see either apothecaries or surgeons, preferring to operate himself ("with great dexterity"), and he medicates exclusively with juices, herbs, and Louvere waters. As "the 7th Doctor of his Family in a direct line," he draws all his knowledge from experience and from the journals left by his forefathers. Yet it is finally his selflessness that singles him out:

> He is as regular in his attendance on the poorest peasant, from whom he never can receive one farthing, as on the richest of the Nobility, and when ever he is wanted will climb 3 or 4 mile in the mountains, in the hottest Sun or heaviest rain, where a Horse cannot go, to arrive at a Cottage where, if their condition requires it, he does not only give them advice and med'cines Gratis, but Bread, Wine, and whatever is needfull. . . . I often see him as dirty and tir'd as a foot post, having eat nothing all day but a roll or two that he carrys in his pocket, yet blest with such a perpetual flow of Spirits, he is allwaies Gay to a degree above chearfullness. (3:53)

Lady Mary's celebration of Dr. Baglioni's virtues of dedication and a cheerfulness free from avarice and complaint echoes Pope's panegyric to the Man of Ross:

> But clear and artless, pouring thro' the plain
> Health to the sick, and solace to the swain.
>
> . . . .
>
> Is any sick? THE MAN OF ROSS relieves,
> Prescribes, attends, the med'cine makes, and gives.

While certainly personally grateful to the man who saved her life, Lady Mary praises a good country doctor, "dirty and tir'd as a foot post," in the same gentle tones she appreciated the preeminent marquis.

These tributes provide a startling contrast to Lady Mary's treatment of Italian women, whose "bad"—that is, novelistic—behavior Lady Mary protests. In criticizing *Clarissa,* Lady Mary powerfully reiterates that there is greater potential danger in sentimental fiction than in the straightforwardly lewd: "The circumstances are so laid as to inspire tenderness, notwithstanding the low style and absurd incidents, and I look upon this and Pamela to be two Books that will do more general mischeif than the Works of Lord Rochester" (3:9). Libertine sexual excess—events that take place in an external, visible reality—may be less damaging than the bourgeois promises of reward for an undemonstrable chastity and inner worth. Lady Mary reinforces her claim that the dangers of this fantasy of virtue, especially when invested with such emotional power, far outweigh those of realistic depictions of simple debauchery in a final narrative about a woman of quality who chooses an affair with a lower-class man (30 November 1753; 3:42–47). Whereas Octavia schemes and is rewarded and the marchioness alienates through her pride and madness, the "heroine" in this final narrative most clearly attempts to hide her immorality while cultivating a public virtue, a virtue that is revealed to be feigned because Lady Mary does indeed gain access to the "truth" of her behavior. In a narrative combining a mixture of deadly melodrama and farce, Lady Mary herself takes the role of the real heroine, acting with the proper intelligence, composure, and courage required of the best of female performance.

The story opens when Lady Mary recalls that, as she was quietly reading one day, the chambermaid of her neighbor burst into the closet, sobbing and begging Lady Mary to come to the master's house, where two brothers were about to murder each other. Lady Mary, hurrying away "without staying for hoods or attendance," quickly raced next door and upstairs to the bedroom where she found quite a different scene: "Signora Laura [lay] prostrate on the Ground, melting in Tears, and her Husband [stood] with a drawn stilleto in his Hand, swearing she should never see to morrow's Sun." Leaving the action frozen in tableau at this murderous point, Lady Mary backtracks to relate the cause. While her husband was away for the day, Signora Bono was to take a local farmer's rent; when "a Handsome Lad of eighteen" arrived, she asked him to dine with her, produced the best wines in the cellar, and "resolv'd to give him chere entiere." When her husband returned home more quickly than expected, he "found his beloved Spouse asleep on the bed with her Galant." This emotionally charged, even potentially deadly situation Lady Mary recounts as farce:

The young Fellow immediately leap'd out of the Window, which look'd into the Garden and was open (it being summer), and escap'd over the Fields, leaving his Breeches on a chair by the Bed side, a very striking circumstance. In short, the Case was such I do not think the Queen of Fairies her selfe could have found an excuse, thô Chaucer tells us she has made a solemn promise to leave none of her Sex unfurnish'd with one, to all eternity. As to the poor Criminal, she had nothing to say for her selfe but what I dare swear you will hear from your youngest daughter if ever you catch her stealing of sweetmeats: Pray, pray, she would do so no more, and indeed it was the first time.

Lady Mary's whimsical allusion to Chaucer's *Merchant's Tale,* which insists that not even supernatural intervention can erase the fact of this adultery, is further deflated by her comparison of the signora's "crime" to a child's stealing of sweetmeats, a childishness supported by the signora's unconvincing claim that this act of adultery was "the first time" and that she would "do so no more."[33]

The narrative concludes when Lady Mary plunges back into the action she left suspended at the beginning of the letter. She asked Signor Carlo to put away the knife, "not being pleas'd with its glittering," and this concrete image intensifies the drama by emphasizing the potential violence. Yet armed herself with real courage and an extraordinary presence of mind, Lady Mary offers this man, with "the Countenance and Gesture of a Man distracted," a reasonable argument about the consequences of murder: "[I] represented to him as well as I could the Crime of a Murder which, if he could justify before Men, was still a crying Sin before God, the disgrace he would bring on himselfe and posterity, and irreparable injury he would do his eldest Daughter (a pretty Girl of 15, that I knew he was extreme fond of)." Rushing in, seemingly without thought of the possible danger to herself, and proceeding to lay a most reasonable claim before the enraged husband, Lady Mary places herself in the center of the action. Admirable in her quick-wittedness and intrepid in the face of danger, she becomes the unworthy signora's salvation. The final image is that of Lady Mary sitting patiently for hours in the company of warring spouses, the only one that stands between them and scandal and perhaps even murder: "[I] was forc'd to stay there near 5 hours (almost from 5 to ten at night) before I durst leave them together, which I would not do till he had sworn in the most serious

manner he would make no future attempt on her Life. I was content
with his Oath, knowing him to be very devout, and found I was not
mistaken." The difficulties women faced in becoming heroines in their
own real lives is examined by Dorinda Outram, who writes that Mme
Roland's solution to the problem "was through identification with the
heroines of fiction, heroines of novels which had greater currency, and
more power and vigour, than in any preceding century."[34] Lady Mary
chooses a different way out, not through sympathizing with the novel's
heroines but by presenting an alternative: real "action" for a "subject"
whose behavior is "heroic."

At the conclusion, Lady Mary reveals the most surprising fact of all:
even though the suspense, detail, and deft handling of the narrative
all conspire to make it seem immediate, as if Lady Mary had rushed
home to commit the incident to paper, the events actually occurred two
years before the telling—and still remain a secret: "The Lady retains
the satisfaction of insulting all her acquaintance on the foundation of a
spotless Character that only She can boast in the Parish, where she is
most heartily hated, from these airs of impertinent virtue, and another
very essential reason, being the best dress'd Woman amongst them, thô
one of the plainest in her figure." Like the marchioness, and as Lady
Mary's implied criticism links her with the Richardsonian heroines, the
signora is "heartily hated" because of her "airs of impertinent virtue"
and her fashionable clothing, a virtue Lady Mary knows she wears and
discards as easily as her dresses. Unable to believe that "any Woman who
had liv'd virtuous till forty (for such was her age) could suddenly be
endow'd with such consummate Impudence to solicite a youth at first
sight, there being no probabillity, his age and station consider'd, that
he would have made any attempt of that kind," Lady Mary argues that
the signora's virtuous reputation is in fact a result of years of deceit:

> I must confess I was wicked enough to think the unblemish'd reputation
> she had hitherto maintain'd, and did not fail to put us in mind of, was
> owing to a series of such Frolicks; and to say truth, they are the only
> Amours that can reasonably hope to remain undiscover'd. Ladies that can
> resolve to make Love thus ex tempore may pass unobserv'd, especially if
> they can content themselves with Low Life, where fear may oblige their
> Favourites to Secrecy. There wants only a very Lewd Constitution, a very
> bad Heart, and a moderate understanding, to make this conduct easy,

and I do not doubt it has been practis'd by many prudes beside her I am now speaking of.

Because they have no visible, performative test of "proof," the inner and undemonstrable virtues can mask a "Lewd Constitution" and "a very bad Heart." Thus the novelistic standard of female "virtue" can be easily falsified. Only deeds—such as Lady Mary's own courage, composure, and compassion—are the appropriate standards one should apply in judging the quality of human character.

Lady Mary's remarks about the novels she both loves and resists provide modern readers with an instance of genuine "reader-response" criticism from an intelligent, sophisticated, and articulate eighteenth-century reader. Her remarks are not altogether representative of "average" eighteenth-century readers, of course, for her criticism is dependent on her class status: as an aristocrat, she insists on her right to define the "real" and the "best" in human behavior—qualities dependent on one's deeds, not expressions of interiority—as opposed to those bourgeois novelists who write only for money and hence fail to honor human nature. More important, however, Lady Mary's gender shapes her resistance to the models of female behavior presented as "appropriate" in the novel. She argues that such sensibilities train young readers, especially women, to believe in the power of an invisible and undemonstrable virtue, to believe that sentiment and not performance will produce rewards and happiness.

Because she herself responds to the powerful emotional sway of such fiction, she fears that those without adequate training—those without the opportunities she herself had to struggle to achieve—will come to future harm. Thus her literary criticism functions in part to bolster and reinforce her more forthright and aggressive remarks about the necessity for an extensive female education. The next and final chapter concerns Lady Mary's roles as retired gentlewoman and educator; both parts work together to create and illustrate her program to empower her granddaughters with the education necessary to combat the pernicious effects of the fiction she herself feels drawn to and to enliven and enrich the retirement she foresees as their final destiny. In describing to her daughter the joys of her own retirement in the country, Lady Mary also demonstrates that a life of female autonomy, happiness, and productivity can be achieved when women are protected by the proper education from the errors committed by the heroines of eighteenth-century fiction.

Chapter Six

Retirement

At the end of a long harangue about the deficiencies of Richardson's fiction, Lady Mary closes a letter to her daughter by saying: "With all my Contempt [for his works], I will take notice of one good thing, I mean his project of an English Monastary. It was a favorite Scheme of mine when I as fiveteen, and had I then been mistriss of an Independant fortune, would certainly have executed it and elected my selfe Lady Abbess" (20 October 1755; 3:97). She is quick to lament the altered future that would have produced—"There would you and your 10 children have been lost for ever" (3:25)—but she claims that the retired life "has allwaies been my Inclination" and that Lady Stafford "us'd to tell me my true vocation was a monastery" (6 March 1753; 3:27). Toward that end, she offers advice to her granddaughters from this perspective: "I look upon my Grand daughters as a sort of Lay Nuns. Destiny may have laid up other things for them, but they have no reason to expect to pass their time otherwise than their Aunts do [in retirement] at present, and I know by Experience it is in the power of Study not only to make solitude tolerable but agreable" (3:25).[1]

The eighteenth-century fascination with the meaning and value of retirement was perhaps nowhere more apparent than in *The Spectator*. Addison and Steele advocate, according to Michael Ketcham, a "modified ideal of retirement" derived from classical morality and filtered through the seventeenth-century essays of Cowley. Steele in particular writes of the common man "whose retirement is not a removal from the world but a disinterestedness sustained within it." *The Spectator* advocated this Horation ideal based on the presumption that one could isolate oneself from the demands of the public world and then *return* to society an improved person. Ketcham writes that "the psychology of retirement returns to the social world; the true values of the mind afford social graces; judgment and reflection are manifested in manner and discourse. In [the figure of the retired man] we find a merger of several patterns: the retired man and the agreeable man coalesce; the public and the private come together in an ideal form of beauty." [2] Thus Mr. Spectator is able to generate for himself "a public sort of Obscurity" (*Spectator* No. 4).

Lady Mary herself experiences such "public obscurity" during her last twenty years on the Continent, but she never achieves that optimistic coalescing of public and private, that "ideal form of beauty," that Mr. Spectator advocates. Her letters indeed suggest that the worlds between which she alternated, rural retirement and the public company of Englishmen and -women abroad, could not be more different. From the countryside, she describes her life as purposeful: luxuriating in the natural beauty of the land she tends, she feels empowered to cultivate and shape both it and the lives of her neighbors. She situates herself in the role of the female squire, one whose presence contributes to the general health and happiness of those around her. What she does not send to her daughter, however, are descriptions of the darker, more disturbing aspects of her life alone: her fears of growing old, her loneliness, her vulnerability to being duped by the feigned friendships of her Italian acquaintances, and the difficulties of being an aristocratic woman whose reputation as a writer is often ridiculed by the English community abroad. She does not mention the pressures she must endure when she leaves the security of her retirement to participate, if only temporarily, in a familiar but alienating social world.

The varied nature of the letters she sends from retirement is the subject of this chapter. From her own life as a "Lay Nun," Lady Mary offers two kinds of letters to her daughter and family: "essays" insisting on the value of education for gentlewomen whose destiny lies in retirement, and self-representations of the pleasures and productivity of the retired state. The letters function together as they alternate between abstract advice and concrete illustrations drawn from her own experiences. Letters detailing the pains of old age and her feelings of isolation she sends to Sir James and Lady Frances Stueart, two English ex-patriots who provide her most important late-in-life friendship. In both correspondences, Lady Mary is concerned with the issue of power. Playing the country squire, Lady Mary seeks to control her daughter's image of female retirement by assuming a role that suggests such retreat generates a satisfying and even powerful influence for a woman equipped to face its challenges. As an aging social outcast from the fashionable English community abroad, she reshapes the role of outsider to endow it with the power of wisdom and occasionally even humility. That she feels free to create such divergent and contradictory images of herself is a testament not only to the affection she feels for these particular epistolary partners but also the power of the letter to dramatize the variousness of the self. Lady Mary's letters to her daughter, written from the Italian countryside, and her correspondence with Sir James and Lady Frances Steuart, written during the years shortly before she returned to England, reveal the most sustained and contradictory examples of her performance of a self. From one setting, Lady Mary tells competing stories of herself as spectator and actor, one who defines her own identity through performance and one who must suffer and respond to others' definitions of the meaning of those performances.

I

About marriage, especially as the singular goal and exclusive form of identity for women as it was articulated in eighteenth-century fiction and in the culture at large, Lady Mary offers a warning: "If [men] have any Merit there are so many roads for them to meet good Fortune, they can no way fail of it but by not deserving it. We have but one of establishing Ours, and that surrounded with precipices, and perhaps, after all, better miss'd than found" (15 April 1755; 3:83). Thus for her "Lay Nuns" Lady Mary offers a way to "miss" the hazards of marriage while cultivating the pleasures of female autonomy through education.

Recognizing that daughters of privilege are groomed solely for marriage, their singular "good Fortune," Lady Mary takes up a calculated rhetorical strategy: working from the premise that the Bute daughters will find their destiny in retirement, whether they marry or not, Lady

Mary sends "advice" intended to ensure that her granddaughters will receive an extensive and systematic education that not only will prepare them for a life out of the social spotlight but also will generate for them an active and an abiding personal pleasure. Her remarks in the "education essays" often echo Bathsua Makin's arguments in *An Essay to Revive the Antient Education of Gentlewomen:* "Unmarried Persons, who are able to subsist without a dependance, have a fairer opportunity than Men, to improve their principles and to ripen the Seed of Learning from early years. Besides, this will be an honest and profitable diversion to possess their minds, to keep out worse thought."[3] Thus hoping to "ripen the Seed[s]" of her own granddaughters' learning and with Richardson's singular "good" idea underlying her discourse, she writes essays in the mode of the *Spectator,* knowing that it is the form most conducive to persuading all her family members that only a sound education that prepares a woman for retirement will produce the best and happiest lives.

An equally compelling concern for her grandsons and their upbringing is palpably absent in this correspondence. In expressing her happiness about the birth of one of her daughter's sons, Lady Mary writes, "I am never in pain for any of that Sex" (15 April 1755; 3:83), and effectively abandons the subject.[4] Only one letter takes up the subject of proper male behavior, and Lady Mary opens by referring to her friend Sir Charles Williams, whose present unhappiness might have been avoided "if he had known how to distinguish between false and true Felicity, and instead of seeking to encrease an Estate already too large, and hunting after Pleasures that have made him rotten and ridiculous, he had bounded his desires of Wealth and follow'd the Dictates of his Conscience!" (7 July 1757; 3:131). Lady Mary offers this portrait of the "rotten" aristocrat, whose venereal disease and too great love of pleasure causes his unhappiness and excessive greed, "for the use of your growing Sons, who I hope no Golden Temptations will induce to marry Women they cannot love, or comply with Measures they do not approve" (3:131).

But this comment leads to a larger, national, anti-imperialist argument. After urging each grandson to strive to be a "Wise and Honest Man" rather than one who cultivates "silly Splendor" and after complimenting Lord Bute's "Oeconomy" and good example in that regard, she expresses the wish that such frugality would become an English trait, for

it would limit her country's participation in expensive and futile wars
and would produce these additional benefits:

> We shall see we are an Island, and endeavor to extend our Commerce
> rather than the Quixote Reputation of redressing wrongs and placeing
> Diadems on Heads that should be equally indifferent to us. When Time
> has ripen'd Mankind into common Sense, the Name of Conqueror will be
> an odious Title. I could easily prove that had the Spainyards establish'd a
> Trade with the Americans, they would have enrich'd their Country more
> than by the addition [of] 22 Kingdoms and all the Mines they now work;
> I don't say possess, since thô they are the proprietors, others enjoy the
> Profit. (7 July 1757; 3:132)

The imperialism of her nation, more interested in securing political
hegemony in foreign lands than in the productive results of trade, can
be easily reduced to the family, a strategy for which Locke himself set
the precedent. Lady Mary implies that husbands interfere where they
"should be equally indifferent," and her protest against the "odious
Title" of "Conqueror" paints a portrait of the coercive patriarchal family
power brought to bear by husbands, who fail to understand that they,
too, are "islands" and that civilized "commerce" with women would
produce happier and more productive results.

Such "commerce" between the sexes, Lady Mary suggests, need not
require marriage for women, only education—a systematic, extensive,
and comprehensive "male" variety of learning. About the insufficiency
of gentlewomen's training Lady Mary was fully aware. She herself was
allowed no formal training, and the "instruction" she did receive was
entirely unsuitable: "My own [education] was one of the worst in the
World, being exactly the same as Clarissa Harlow's, her pious Mrs. Norton so perfectly ressembling my Governess (who had been Nurse to my
Mother) I could almost fancy the Author was acquainted with her. She
took so much pains from my Infancy to fill my Head with supersti-
tious Tales and false notions, it was none of her Fault I am not at this
day afraid of Witches and Hobgoblins, or turn'd Methodist" (6 March
1753; 3:25–26). On her own, Lady Mary read voraciously and taught
herself languages, without assistance or applause from her family. Her
commitment to the life of the mind was later reinforced by the Italian
intellectual climate, where "the character of a learned Woman is far
from being ridiculous, . . . the greatest Familys being proud of having

produce'd female Writers, and a Milanese Lady being now proffessor of Mathematics in the University of Bologna" (10 October 1753; 3:39).[5] The reality of the female academic especially pleases her when she considers the status of women in her own nation: "To say Truth, there is no part of the World where our Sex is treated with so much contempt as in England" (3:40).

As her first step in combatting this English contempt, Lady Mary offers advice about the education of her granddaughters by expressing her desire to join in the parenting of the eldest granddaughter: "I receiv'd your agreable Letter of Sept. 24 yesterday, Nov. 29, and am very glad our Daughter (for I think she belongs to us both) turns out so much to your satisfaction" (30 November 1753; 3:42). Her interest in "our Daughter" and the appropriation of a measure of influence in the young woman's future happiness lead to an extraordinary set of companion letters (28 June 1753, 6 March 1753; 3:20–27), which together constitute Lady Mary's program for the granddaughters' proper education. Aware that her advice runs counter to traditional practices, she acknowledges that both her daughter and Lord Bute will be scandalized by her remarks. She opens the second letter with "a sort of Apology" for having "extremely shock'd" Lord Bute in suggesting "a learned Education for Daughters," and she uses a metaphor that points to the exclusivity, even the aura of sacred mystery, surrounding traditional practices: "The generality of Men beleive [education for women] as great a prophanation as the Clergy would do if the Laity should presume to exercise the functions of the priesthood" (3:25). Unlike Mary, Lady Chudleigh, she does not urge women to "to put in for a Share, to enter their Claims, and not permit the Men any longer to monopolize the Perfections of Mind, to engross the Goods of the Understanding."[6] Rather than speaking this militant language, Lady Mary concentrates on logic as her primary rhetorical strategy—a device that Bute, a man allowed a university education, would recognize and respect.[7]

She opens the first letter with a ploy that lays the groundwork for an argument about the equal power of the female mind. She expresses satisfaction that the eldest granddaughter is a "good Arithmetician," for it is "the best proofe of understanding" and "one of the cheif distinctions between us and Brutes" (3:20). But Lady Mary is also wise enough to know that capacity is not enough, that there must also be motivation and desire. The stumbling blocks include the young women themselves, parents, and a society that sees education for them as unnecessary. She must therefore articulate persuasive arguments for the positive results of female education, and she writes clearly in the argument mode: "I will therefore speak to you as supposing [the eldest granddaughter] not only capable but desirous of Learning" (3:21).

Beginning with a seemingly contradictory revelation, Lady Mary confesses that Lady Bute's youth did not include extensive academic training: "You had no deffect either in mind or person to hinder, and much in your circumstances to attract, the highest offers. It seem'd your business to learn how to live in the World, as it is [the eldest granddaughter's] to know how to be easy out of it" (3:21). Lady Mary never forgets the cultural imperative aimed at the daughters of privilege—they should marry and marry well—nor does she appear to offer any radical restructuring of this imperative: "I am not now endeavoring to remove the prejudices of Mankind" (3:27). Instead, she lays the groundwork for her argument that the ultimate female destiny is often retirement by cautioning against the Butes' excessive ambitions for all the granddaughters in the marriage market:

> It is the common Error of Builders and Parents to follow some Plan they think beautifull (and perhaps is so) without considering that nothing is beautifull that is misplac'd. Hence we see so many Edifices rais'd that the raisers can never inhabit, being too large for their Fortunes. Vistos are laid open over barren heaths, and apartments contriv'd for a coolness very agreable in Italy but killing in the North of Brittain. Thus every Woman endeavors to breed her Daughter a fine Lady, qualifying her for a station in which she will never appear, and at the same time incapacitateing her for that retirement to which she is destin'd. Learning (if she has a real taste for it) will not only make her contented but happy in it. (3:21)

Useless graces and a taste for luxury—a house too large for those without equal fortune—result in an empty life for women who *count* on elevated status as their future. The issue of "place" emphasizes the equation: a woman brought up to expect grandeur is like an Italian villa transported to the killing cold of England. Such women become positively incapacitated for the retirement Lady Mary foresees as their ultimate condition. This advice, too, echoes Makin's, who chooses as her rhetorical strategy to redefine the nature of the "Portion": "I hope I shall by this Discourse perswade some Parents to be more careful for the future of the Breeding of their Daughters. You cark and care to get great Portions for them, which sometimes occasions their ruine. Here is a sure Portion, an easie way to make them excellent. How many born to good Fortunes, when their Wealth hath been wasted, have supported themselves and Families too by their Wisdom?"[8]

To illustrate such disablement, Lady Mary points to the deficiencies of the traditional education for gentlewomen by equating women with princes, both of whom are handicapped by the debilitating effects of their improper training:

> There is nothing so like the Education of a Woman of Quality as that of a Prince. They are taught to dance and the exterior part of what is call'd good breeding. . . . The same characters are form'd by the same Lessons, which inclines me to think (if I dare say it) that Nature has not plac'd us in an inferior Rank to Men, no more than the Females of other Animals, where we see no distinction of capacity, thô I am persuaded if there was a Common-wealth of rational Horses (as Doctor Swift has suppos'd) it would be an establish'd maxim amongst them that a mare could not be taught to pace. (3:26–27)

Unlike Makin, who argues that lack of education injures the soul— "Meerly to teach Gentlewomen to Frisk and Dance, to paint their Faces, to curl their Hair, to put on a Whisk, to wear gay Clothes, is not truly to adorn but to adulterate their Bodies; yea (what is worse) to defile their Souls"[9]—Lady Mary creates a dual and contradictory resonance by locating the paradox in status. She confirms the elevated, even "royal" quality of female intellectual capacity while simultaneously deflating the "aristocratic" treatment (lessons in dancing and good breeding) that cripples both princes and women for any other life. She later elaborates on the subject by citing another paradox in contemporary arguments and lamenting the results of inequitable treatment: "But I think it the highest Injustice to be debarr'd the Entertainment of my Closet, and that the same Studies which raise the character of a Man should hurt that of a Woman. We are educated in the grossest ignorance, and no art omitted to stiffle our natural reason; if some few get above their Nurses' instructions, our knowledge must rest conceal'd and be as useless to the World as Gold in the Mine" (10 October 1753; 3:40). And she herself provides the best example not only of the inherent injustice in deny-ing women equal access to education but of the wealth that remains necessarily concealed in a woman's mind.

In the most important premise of her argument, Lady Mary predicts that the futures of her granddaughters will not inevitably include marriage and high "place": "The ultimate end of your Education was to make you a good Wife (and I have the comfort to hear that you are one); [the eldest granddaughter's] ought to be, to make her Happy in a Virgin state. I will not say it is happier, but it is undoubtedly safer than any Marriage. In a Lottery where there is (at the lowest computation) ten thousand blanks to a prize, it is the most prudent choice not to venture" (3:24). The underlying framework of the argument, couched in the metaphor of a lottery illustrating the dissatisfactions of marriage, rests on the husbandless future Lady Mary posits for her granddaughters. In economic terms, the number of marriageable daughters compared to the number of eldest sons was certainly not ten thousand to one, but the odds of marrying all the daughters to wealth and position were very low.[10] More powerfully, Lady Mary cites the "blank" to describe unsuitable and unsatisfying husbands, and here the ten thousand-to-one odds are particularly disturbing, especially in reference to Lady Mary's claims about virginity. Considering the chances of a woman's contracting a venereal disease from her husband or of dying in childbirth, her claim to the safety of the virgin state, while obviously exaggerated, is true. Thus in the marriage lottery, where chance plays as large a part as planning, the Bute daughters were not certain "winners."

Moreover, Lady Mary implies that, even were a woman not to draw a "blank"—were she to marry and maintain her social position—such a woman often discovers that her destiny, too, lies in retirement. Lady Mary writes to Wortley expressing some surprise that her daughter's marriage has remained so obviously satisfying for her and Lord Bute: "What I think extrodinary is my Daughter's continuing so many years agreable to Lord Bute, Mr. Mackensie telling me the last time I saw him that his Brother frequently said amongst his companions that he was still as much in Love with his Wife as before he marry'd her" (17 July 1748; 2:406). Such a comment reveals her certainty that few gentlewomen marry as happily, a premise so deep and pervasive that she assumes it almost unconsciously. The "natural" destiny of most gentlewomen is rarely as fortunate—and Lady Mary is herself again the best example. Therefore, her primary complaint is directed at the long-standing justifications concerning female education as it is based on the inevitablility of marriage: valuing the bodies of women of status while appreciating the minds of privileged men, the powerful in the culture insist that marriage is the exclusive role for gentlewomen, and parents accordingly train their daughters to develop skills necessary solely for that event. Thus it "naturally" becomes common wisdom that women's education is superfluous.

Against this decision, Lady Mary joyfully celebrates not just the contentment but the active happiness education can produce. She offers a "syllabus" to her daughter, a plan similar to the training offered to men of privilege, while reminding the Butes again that intellectual achievement is not a task but a pleasure. In a clever rhetorical play that would appeal to her daughter's sensibilities, Lady Mary recommends that the granddaughter read English poetry, not simply for the quality of the verse or the fineness of the sentiment but also as a way to avoid being duped by unscrupulous young men in a dangerous marriage market:

> Many a young Damsel has been ruin'd by a fine copy of Verses, which she would have laugh'd at if she had known it had been stoln from Mr. Waller. I remember when I was a Girl I sav'd one of my Companions from Destruction, who communicated to me an epistle she was quite charm'd with. As she had a natural good taste, she observ'd the Lines were not so smooth as Prior's or Pope's, but had more thought and spirit than any of theirs. . . . In the midst of this Triumph, I shew'd her they were taken from Randolph's Poems, and the unfortunate Transcriber was dismiss'd with the scorn he deserv'd. To say Truth, the poor Plagiary was very unlucky to fall into my Hands; that Author, being no longer in Fashion, would have escap'd any one of less universal reading than my selfe. (3:22)

The embedded narrative becomes a cautionary tale that ends happily, thanks to the very study she advocates, and once again she represents a most successful model for such intellectual empowerment. More threatening still to the status quo, she recommends that the granddaughters be taught Latin and Greek but urges Lady Bute to convince her children that languages are only "Vehicles of Learning" and that "true knowledge consists in knowing things, not words" (3:21); thus "History, Geography, and Philosophy will furnish her with materials to pass away chearfully a longer Life than is alloted to mortals" (3:23), because "Whoever will cultivate their own mind will find full employment. . . . Add to this the search after knowledge (every branch of which is entertaining), and the longest Life is too short for the persuit of it" (3:25).

Yet two of her comments about the value of women's time and the display of a woman's learning strike modern readers as reactionary. The first, a remark about the pleasures of reading, contains an aside that points to the value hierarchy Lady Mary presumes her daughter embraces:

> [The eldest granddaughter] will not want new Fashions nor regret the loss of expensive Diversions or variety of company if she can be amus'd with an Author in her closet. To render this amusement extensive, she should be permitted to learn the Languages. I have heard it lamented that Boys lose so many years in meer learning of Words. This is no Objection to a Girl, whose time is not so precious. She cannot advance her selfe in any proffession, and has therefore more hours to spare; and as you say her memory is good, she will be very agreably employ'd this way. (3:21)

Because young Englishwomen were in fact barred from the professions and because all avenues except marriage seemed closed to them, Lady Mary's comment functions primarily as a complaint about the lack of imagination brought to bear on the question of female vocation. In her endeavor to persuade the Bute family, however, these statements serve an important rhetorical purpose: they acknowledge the traditional assessment of the value of female time but replace traditional practice with a vigorous new program for study. More strongly, she cloaks an essentially subversive strategy concerning the display of female learning in the language of respectability: "The second caution to be given her (and which is most absolutely necessary) is to conceal whatever Learning she attains, with as much solicitude as she would hide crookedness or lameness. The parade of it can only serve to draw on her the envy, and consequently the most inveterate Hatred, of all he and she Fools, which will certainly be at least three parts in four of all her Acquaintance" (3:22). Lady Mary's directive to conceal a woman's learning differs little in substance from that given by Chesterfield to his son: "Wear your learning, like your watch, in a private pocket: and do not pull it out and strike it; merely to show that you have one. If you are asked what o'clock it is, tell it; but do not proclaim it hourly and unasked, like the watchman." [11] The two pieces of advice certainly have a different metaphorical resonance: his metaphor equates learning with a man's possession, a commonplace tool, while Lady Mary's metaphor posits a handicap, a particularly disturbing assessment of the ridicule a learned woman may encounter. Still, Chesterfield suggests that learning not be displayed but worn "in a private pocket," and thus both injunctions serve as strategies for success: Chesterfield calls for display on demand, while Lady Mary offers her granddaughters a way in the world that acknowledges the status quo without surrendering to its oppression. Katherine Rogers complains that Lady Mary undercuts her feminism by camouflaging her ideas in flippancy or apology, but Patricia Meyer Spacks provides a more insightful interpretation: "Behind Lady Mary's irony . . . one hears a single note of complaint and feels the bitter tensions of passivity, . . . the concealment rather than the absence of force."[12] Such strategies, however, also serve a larger rhetorical purpose: they provide a means by which she can circumvent some of the resistance from her unsympathetic audience, even as they allow her to "prove" that learning itself is the valuable commodity. If her granddaughters sacrifice the public fame that men "will not suffer us to share," it is a meaningless mark of value in retirement, where self-determination and control are the rewards.

Lady Mary closes the first letter by reminding her daughter of their discussion of the hazards of matrimony, a warning that she issued "in the strongest manner." Then, in a most curious sentence structure, full of negatives and backtrackings, Lady Mary expresses her "happiness" about her daughter's decision to marry: "I was not sorry to see you not determin'd on a single Life, knowing it was not your Father's Intention" (3:24). In contrast, the second letter initially points to the reality not factored into the cultural justifications against female education: "My only Design is to point out to my Grand Daughters the method of being contented with that retreat to which probably their circumstances will oblige them, and which is perhaps preferable to all the show of public Life. It has allwaies been my Inclination" (3:27). Lady Mary then reiterates the power of education by citing a family example, one she hopes her daughter will allow her the privilege to imitate: "I was in the most regular commerce with my Grand mother, thô the difference of our time of Life was much greater, she being past 45 when she marry'd my Grand Father. She dy'd at 96, retaining to the last the vivacity and clearness of her understanding, which was very uncommon" (3:27). Thus the two powerful underlying premises close each argument: whether they marry or not, most women discover that the retired life is their destiny, and they ought, therefore, to be empowered with an education that not only protects and delights but also actually lengthens and improves the quality of a woman's life.

II

Unlike the many autobiographies, diaries, and memoirs in which women define themselves through their social, sexual, and psychic vulnerabilities, the retirement letters Lady Mary sends from the countryside stress her independence and active life. As she describes the deep satisfaction she takes in her domestic activities, Lady Mary uses the details of this retired life to construct the most contented image of herself found anywhere in the correspondence. Whereas the novels, her "silent companions," provide "passive" pleasures, country living produces more active joys. Shorn of critical content and always overidealized, her descriptions of such pleasurable activity insist on the happiness to be found in isolation and serve to illustrate the arguments she makes: taking the role of the landowning squire, she describes not only her productivity but also the resulting autonomy generated for a woman, alone and contented, out of the bustle of society.

She writes that she is more often out of humor in town "than amongst my plants and Poultry in the Country. . . . You should consider ⟨I have lived almost⟩ a Hermit ten years, and the world is as new ⟨to me as to a co⟩untry Girl transported from Wales to Cove⟨nt Garden⟩" (22 May 1759; 3:211–12). She reinforces the image of herself as a contented rustic hermit, removed from the color and energy of the Italian version of Covent Garden, in a remarkable descriptive letter sent from her country home outside Gottolengo, a bit of land that she occupied and lovingly tended. Suffused with sensory detail, the letter only partially emphasizes the sensual pleasures of her environment; underlying the evocative descriptions is her performance as a powerful landowning presence.[13]

At the dairy house, which lies "a long mile" from her house in town, she fashioned a comfortable living space for herself, "that is to say, strewd the floor with Rushes, cover'd the chimney with moss and branches, and adorn'd the Room with Basons of earthern ware (which is made here to great perfection) fill'd with Flowers, and put in some straw chairs and a Couch Bed, which is my whole Furniture" (10 July 1748; 2:403). In this rustic setting, one hardly fitting for the daughter of a duke and the wife of one of England's wealthiest citizens, she positions herself as though she were Squire Allworthy surveying the prospect and viewing her little kingdom: "This Spot of Ground is so Beautifull I am afraid you will scarce credit the Description, which, however, I can assure you shall be very litteral, without any embellishment from Imagination." Giving primacy to the visual, she re-creates not only immediacy but a sense of spatial expansiveness: "It is on a Bank forming a kind of Peninsula rais'd from the River Oglio 50 foot, to which you may descend by easy stairs cut in the Turf, and either take the air on the River, which is as large as the Thames at Richmond, or by walking an avenu two hundred yards on the side of it you find a Wood of a hundred acres, which was allready cut into walks and rideings when I took it." More important, she emphasizes not only the beauty of the landscape but also her ability to modify nature to suit her needs: "I have only added 15 Bowers in different views, with seats of Turf." At the conclusion, when Lady Mary unexpectedly enters the scene, what was once mere verbal landscape painting becomes a personal narrative that closes with an image of her, secure in her mastery, scribbling away in the cool noon: "I am now writeing to you in one of these arbours, which is so thick shaded the Sun is not troublesome even at Noon" (2:403).

Beyond the descriptive beauties, she includes details of her own activities fashioned, in their immediate sensory impact, to emphasize the pleasures of "rustic" life: "Another [bower] is on the side of the River, where I have made a camp Kitchin, that I may take the Fish, dress and eat it immediately, and at the same time see the Barks which ascend or Descend every day, to or from Mantua, Guastalla or Pont de vic, all considerable Towns. This little Wood is carpetted (in their succeeding seasons) with violets and strawberrys, inhabited by a nation of Nightingales, and fill'd with Game of all kinds excepting Deer and wild Boar, the first being unknown here, and not being large enough for the other" (2:403). These images—the aroma of fresh strawberries, the song of the nightingales, the vision of herself cooking freshly caught fish, and the movements of the barges sailing just on the periphery—combine to freeze her momentarily, in the midst of the color, noise, and movement of the scene, as if she were framed in a portrait. But the details of this picture are consciously set against the dictates of traditional portraiture. This is no set piece of a fine lady with her lapdog, nor is this at all reminiscent of Jervas's mannered and romanticized painting of her as a shepherdess. Lady Mary constructs an image of herself that implicitly rejects contemporary English culture as it harks back to an even more powerful and aristocratic precedent: the conventions of Horatian retirement. The portrait she presents is one of a woman who has rejected the debilitating effects of the city in favor of the life of the sophisticated country squire, one who luxuriates in the abundance of natural splendor while bringing to it the civilities of cultured sensibility. There is, however, no hint of a return to the complexities of fashionable company.

Perhaps it is this letter that Gamaliel Bradford remembers when she writes, "[Lady Mary] was too full of resources to need people, too critical to love people, too little sympathetic to pity people." [14] In criticizing Lady Mary for these reasons, Bradford recognizes the lack of what Patricia Meyer Spacks has argued is central in many women's autobiographies: emotional dependence. Spacks claims that such dependence lies at the center of women's lives because society approves identity for women through relationships, not accomplishments. [15] Lady Mary's description of her role in the country suggests an active rejection of such an identity as she sets a stage where there are no demands on her: the wildlife is wholly unthreatening, for no wild boar exist to present a danger; the nightingales, indifferent to wit or learning, perform for her.

The images insist that she alone is in control of her life; she is the agent, the initiator of change:

> My Garden was a plain Vineyard when it came into my hands not two years ago, and it is with a small expence turn'd into a Garden that (apart from the advantage of the climate) I like better than that of Kensington. . . . I have turn'd [the Italian vineyard] into cover'd Gallerys of shade, that I can walk in the heat without being incommoded by it. I have made a dineing room of Verdure, capable of holding a Table of 20 Covers. The whole ground is 317 feet in length and 200 in Breadth. You see it is far from large, but so prettily dispos'd (thô I say it) that I never saw a more agreable rustic Garden, abounding with all sort of Fruit, and produces a variety of Wines. (2:403–4)

Her delight in her garden, which she calls "my greatest amusement" and which she elevates into the status of cultural artifact by likening it to the fondness of "a young Author of his first play when it has been well receiv'd by the Town" (26 July 1748; 2:407), is generated by this power to effect change. The verbs themselves point to her active agency ("I have turn'd" and "I have made") as she transforms the natural, a "plain vineyard," into the human, a habitable space more satisfying than the magnificence and splendor of Kensington gardens. She implies that this power of metamorphosis, a phenomenon that she applauded in Turkey and easily transports to Italy, allows her to conquer even the heat of the sun without sacrificing the abundance of the harvest.

The life she describes is not entirely devoid of other human beings, however, and she provides an account of her day that is "as regular as that of any Monastery." After rising at six and breakfasting, she joins the weeder women to work with them for two hours, after which she inspects both the dairy and the poultry, where her pride in the stock is apparent: "I have at present 200 chicken, besides Turkys, Geese, Ducks, and Peacocks. All things have hitherto prosper'd under my Care. My Bees and silk worms are double'd, and I am told that, without accidents, my Capital will be so in two years time" (2:404). This statement serves to promote her role as the more-than-capable manager: her care and nurturing have resulted in doubled growth, and her skillful production results in the increased security of capital. Such productivity is matched by the small human pleasures of rural life. In the afternoons she reads for an hour, dines, and sleeps until three o'clock, after which she summons "some of my old Priests" for cards. When it is cool enough to go out, she walks in the woods or takes the air on horseback. Even more significant to her is that these pleasures can be had at very little expense: "The Fishery of this part of the River belongs to me, and my Fisherman's little boat (where I have a green Lutestring Awning) serves me for a Barge. He and his Son are my Rowers, without any expence, he being very well paid by the profit of the Fish, which I give him on condition of having every day one dish for my Table" (2:404).

This lovely account of her day, packed with domestic details conveying the extraordinary satisfaction she feels in this life, is also accompanied by an insistent, almost relentless use of the first-person possessive pronoun: "my Dairy," "my Poultry," "my Care," "my Bees and silk worms," "my Capital," "my Books," "my old Priests," "my Wood," "my Fisherman's little boat," "my Rowers," and "my Table." Having previously lived according to someone else's dictates, she describes this work—performed according to her directions and coupled with the resulting prosperity due to her care—as endowing her with a rightful sense of ownership. And through this straightforward assumption of the land and a desire to work for its improvement, she describes the transformation of this small, natural space into a pastoral paradise.

Her paradise is not, however, without its amusements and the pleasures of "culture" that can be purchased at very little expense. Unable to attend the opera because of bad weather, the people of the village ask to erect a theater in her "Saloon": "I easily comply'd with their request, and was surpriz'd at the Beauty of their scenes, which thô painted by a country painter are better colour'd and the perspective better manag'd than in any of the second rate Theatres in London. I lik'd it so well, it is not yet pull'd down." Better still, the music, costumes, and lighting were paid for by the parish, so the whole three days of entertainment cost her only one barrel of wine. At the conclusion of this little narrative, with a kind of giddy abandon, she "sings" of her country amusements:

> ————all my whole care
> Is my farming affair,
> To make my Corn grow, and my apples Trees bear.

And she ends by reiterating her pleasure and her productivity: "My improvements give me great pleasure, and so much profit that if I could live a hundred years longer I should certainly provide for all my Grand children" (10 May 1748; 2:401–2).

It is also apparent that descriptions such as these are overly romantic, too perfect, and without critical content. In its very literariness, such an idealized representation of herself and the country functions as a rhetorical strategy of persuasion intended to combat the negative mythology implicit in the image of a single woman's retreat. To counter the Bute family's pity and even active condescension about the "plight" of the retired woman, Lady Mary paints herself as a sophisticated rustic, emphasizing the civilized nature of her pleasures, the aristocratic nature of her management, and more powerfully, the aggressive nature of her productive self-determination. Thus Lady Mary makes the Butes' own aristocratic values work to support female autonomy.

Most important, such productivity does not go unnoticed by her Italian neighbors. In a later remark, she contrasts life in the world of show with her own seclusion, arguing that the life of public vanity is a vain, futile, and fleeting pleasure: "I have had this morning as much delight in a Walk in the Sun as ever I felt formerly in the crouded Mall even when I imagin'd I had my share of the admiration of the place, which was generally sour'd before I slept by the Informations of my female Freinds, who seldom fail'd to tell me it was observ'd I had shew'd an inch above my shoe heels, or some other criticism of equal weight, which was construe'd affectation, and utterly destoy'd all the Satisfaction my vanity had given me" (27 November 1749; 2:446–47). In the country, she is equally vain about being admired, but this time for entirely different reasons: "I have now no other but in my little Huswifery, which is easily gratify'd in this Country, where (by the help of my receipt Book) I make a very shineing Figure amongst my Neighbours by the Introduction of Custards, Cheesecakes and mince'd Pies, which were entirely unknown in these Parts, and are receiv'd with universal applause, and I have reason to beleive will preserve my Memory even to Future ages, particularly by the art of Butter makeing, in which I have so improv'd them that they now make as good as in any part of England" (2:447). The retired life, she argues, allows a woman the same opportunity to make "a very shineing Figure," but in a very different context. Rural retreat does not mean Gothic isolation, nor does it prohibit human community. Her description posits that a contribution to the general happiness of the community, rather than the personal and ephemeral vanity of public life, brings her not only greater satisfaction but equal applause. In retirement, a woman can cultivate domestic pleasures and autonomy without disappearing into an anonymous invisibility. Later she puts it more strongly: "I now find by experience more sincere pleasures with my Books and Garden than all the Flutter of a Court could give me" (6 March 1753; 3:27).

III

Lady Mary's correspondence with Sir James and Lady Frances Stueart, written primarily during her time in Venice and Padua (1758–62), reveals a striking counterpoint to the idealized and celebratory letters she sends to her daughter.[16] James Steuart, a Scottish lawyer, was exiled after being implicated in the Jacobite rebellion of 1745. He, his wife, and his son eventually settled at Tübingen, where he devoted himself to his learned studies, including the writing of books on Newton's chronology and German coins (his magnum opus on political economy would be published in 1767).[17] Lady Mary first met the Steuarts in 1758, when they traveled from the Tyrol to Venice in an effort to improve Sir James's health. Lady Mary tells her daughter: "Here arriv'd a few days ago Sir

James Stuart with his Lady. That name was sufficient to make me fly to wait on her. I was charm'd to find a Man of uncommon Sense and Learning, and a Lady that without Beauty is more Aimable than the fairest of her Sex. I offer'd them all the little good offices in my power, and invited them to Supper" (13 May 1758; 3:145–46).

The Steuarts provide for Lady Mary a warm and abiding late-in-life friendship. She expresses her affection for each of them more straight-forwardly than with any other nonfamily correspondent: "Dear Fanny, this letter is to you both, designed to make you smile, laugh if you will; but be so just to believe me, with warm affection and sincere esteem, ever yours, M.W.M. *N.B.* You are obliged to me for the shortness of this epistle. When I write to you, I could write all day with pleasure, but I will not indulge even a pleasure at the expence of giving you trouble" (27 November 1758; 3:192). During one of their separations, she writes, equally affectionately, of the pain of their absence: "A propos of toast-ing, upon my honour I have not tasted a drop of punch since we parted. I cannot bear the sight of it; it would recall too tender ideas, and I should be quarrelling with Fortune for our separation, which I ought to thank her divinity for having brought us together" (5 September 1758; 3:172).

The Steuarts are especially appealing correspondents for Lady Mary because they, too, were exiles. The sanctioned political powers within the English community suspected them of harboring treasonous inten-tions, and they chose to live out of the social spotlight. Thus the Steuarts provide a "safe" outlet for Lady Mary's frustrations concerning her own precarious place in the fashionable public world of the displaced English. Moreover, the Steuarts felt little affection for the man Lady Mary per-ceived as perhaps her most powerful enemy on the Continent: John Murray, British Resident in Venice, appointed in July 1754. She writes to her daughter that "the Brittish Minister here [is] such a scandalous Fellow in every Sense of that word, he is not [to] be trusted to change a Sequin, despis'd by this Government for his smuggling, which was his original proffession, and always surrounded with Pimps and Brokers, who are his Privy Councellors" (30 May 1757; 3:127). Halsband suspects that, beyond the discourtesies she perceived in Murray's actions (his failure to send her the English newspapers she requested and to pay her, an English citizen, the expected courtesy visit), the problem may have stemmed from their political differences: Murray accused her of favoring

William Pitt, coleader of the new coalition government, while he supported the opposition. In the letter to her daughter cited above, Lady Mary confirms the political differences in a reference to the Steuarts' politics and her ostracism: "I offer'd [them] all the little good offices in my power, and invited them to Supper, upon which our wise Minister has discover'd that I am in the Interest of Popery and Slavery. . . . It is very remarkable that after having suffer'd all the rage of that Party at Avignon for my attachment to the present reigning Family, I should be accus'd here of favouring Rebellion, when I hop'd all our Odious Divisions were forgotten" (3:145–46). Even General Graeme, one of Lord Bute's kinsmen, recognizes Murray's ill-treatment of Lady Mary: "I do think the resident ought to show some more respect than he has done of late to a woman of her birth and country" (3:206n).

Precisely because the English community in Venice criticizes her for her friendship with the Steuarts, her correspondence provides important emotional and intellectual outlets. In letters to them, she expresses her vulnerabilities quite openly. After Wortley's death, for instance, when she needs to return home and complications arise, Lady Mary confesses her fear in bleak imagery and the language of superstition: "I am grown timorous and suspicious; . . . I retain, how[ever], such a degree of that uncommon thing called Common Sense not to trouble the felicity of my children with my foreboding dreams, which I hope will prove as idle as the croaking of ravens or the noise of that harmless animal distinguished by the odious name of screech-owl. You will say, why then do I trouble you with my old wives' prophecies? Need I tell you that it is one of the privileges of friendship to talk of our own follies and infirmities?" (12 April 1761; 3:269). She is also confessional in expressing the "negative" emotions that she hides from her daughter in the descriptions of her idealized rustic retreat. The limitations created by her old age, and particularly her feelings of impotence and imprisonment as her body continues to decay, remind her of a machine in the process of disintegration: she closes a letter to the Steuarts with the signature "the machine called M.W. Montagu" (13 January 1759; 3:199) and uses the metaphor to argue for the value of study, which serves "at least to lull asleep those corroding reflections that embitter life, and wear out the frail machine in which we inhabit" (4 May 1759; 3:209).

That "frail machine" is the source of her fears about a proposed visit to the Steuarts in Germany. In the world of older age, possibilities seem to have contracted, and obstacles take on greater proportions. She hears "such frightful stories of precipices and hovels during the whole journey, I begin to fear there is no such pleasure allotted me in the book of fate. The Alps were once mole-hills in my sight when they interposed between me and the slightest inclination; now age begins to freeze, and brings with it the usual train of melancholy apprehensions" (13 January 1759; 3:198). Unlike the expansive vistas she recounts from her home in Brescia, life in old age, as she describes it to the Steuarts, has only boundaries: "I am very unwilling, but am afraid I must submit to the confinement of my boat and my easy chair, and go no farther than they can carry me. Why are our views so extensive and our power so miserably limited? This is among the mysteries which (as you justly say) will remain ever unfolded to our shallow capacities" (3:198).

For all the melancholy in these reflections, Lady Mary is also freed to send to the Steuarts, an appreciative audience, letters sparkling with the same satirical energy and wit she brought to her earlier descriptions of the absurdities of the English social world. She writes, "Let us then (which is the only true philosophy) be contented with our chance, and make the best of that very bad bargain of being born in this vile planet, where we may find however (God be thanked!) much to laugh at, tho' little to approve" (13 January 1759; 3:198). Throughout her lifelong correspondence with women friends, Lady Mary finds "little to approve" in the behavior of men, yet she is comfortable writing in the same satirical vein not only to Lady Fanny but also to Sir James. In one instance, as a means of comforting Steuart about his wife's "disorder"— her "hysterical complaints"—Lady Mary writes, "I own I am charmed with [Dr. Thomas Sydenham's] taking off the reproach which you men so saucily throw on our sex, as if we alone were subject to vapours. He clearly proves that your wise honourable spleen is the same disorder and arises from the same cause" (5 September 1758; 3:171). As she levels gender differences through biology, insisting that men and women both suffer from the "vapours" (even if men refuse the description), her remarks serve to comment on a larger issue: men have the power to assign cultural value, and they accordingly label their own disease "wise" and "honourable" while women's illness is described as a deficit in character. Lady Mary might have longed to write to her daughter in a similiar comic vein about male tyranny, the double standard, and the cultural limitations on female capacity, but her need to persuade rather than to entertain her daughter results in the measured discourse of rational argument, not wit.

With the Steuarts, Lady Mary can point to the male power to define cultural value in a tirade, only half mocking, on the tyranny of the other sex: "But you vile usurpers do not only engross learning, power, and authority to yourselves, but will be our superiors even in constitution of mind, and fancy you are incapable of the woman's weakness of fear and tenderness. Ignorance!" (3:171–72). Later, she continues in an even stronger vein to develop her complaint about male misuse of power, this time pointing more specifically to the absurdity of the double standard: "That tyrannical sex, . . . with absurd cruelty first put the invaluable deposite of their precious honor in our hands, and then oblige us to prove a negative for the preservation of it. I hate Mankind with all the fury of an old maid (indeed most women of my age do), and have no real esteem but for those heroines who give them as good as they bring" (27 November 1758; 3:191–92).

Sir James, in particular, becomes a correspondent with whom Lady Mary can vent her anger, express her sadnesses, and speak of the frustrations of age. She can also perform with all the artistry and literary skill at her disposal.[18] Using her favorite theatrical metaphor, she had earlier written to Steuart to define "the comic scenes that are daily exhibited on the great stage of the world for my entertainment" (18 October 1758; 3:183). His powerful intellect, combined with his affection for her, were conducive to some of her most daring late-in-life epistolary performances. That she perceives writing to be one category of performance is clear in her remarks about Sir James's *Political Economy*. After receiving a copy he sent, she thanks him for his "valuable and magnificent present" by expressing the wish that it had a larger audience: "It is pity the world should be deprived of the advantage of so useful a performance" (1 March 1760; 3:237). She cites a kinship of performance between herself and Sir James as she ends one letter with this reference to the mutuality of their endeavors: "As to you, Sir, I make no excuses; you are bound to have indulgence for me, as for a sister of the quill. I have heard Mr. Addison say he always listened to poets with patience, to keep up the dignity of the fraternity" (5 September 1758; 3:173).

As a "sister of the quill," Lady Mary composes two long and very different letters bringing to bear all her literary and satirical skill. Whether developing an extensive metaphor or re-creating dialogue in fully dramatic form, Lady Mary composes both letters as complaints about Murray and his misuse of social and political power, a coercion that results in the powerful degree of alienation she feels, lost in a world of expatriate English, exiled from real political power, trapped in an aging body but living with a mind teeming with energy and frustration. Most important, both letters are fundamentally concerned with questions of authorship, literary productivity, and Lady Mary's contradictory feelings about writing and publication. Isobel Grundy argues that, although Lady Mary's ambitions about her poetry played "a large but mostly secret part" in her life, by 1758 in Venice she suffered humiliation and mockery from Murray and his social circle as a result of her reputation as a writer. Grundy elicits the terms of the paradox constraining Lady Mary: "To be known as an authoress was still a liability," even though "[Lady Mary's] birth and country, precisely the things which forbade her to be a published female writer, were her only possible hope for enforcing respect in the face of sneers about her excessive reading and writing." [19]

The first letter is certainly the most cryptic of all the letters in the last half of her correspondence. Full of blasphemous energy and striking metaphors, Lady Mary spins out in dense and oblique prose a complaint about the behavior of Murray and his party, and she chooses for herself the most powerful and fearsome female role: the witch. The letter has its genesis in one written less than a week earlier to her daughter; in it, Lady Mary expresses her extreme displeasure with Robert Dodsley's having published, under the authorship of the detestable William Yonge, a poem that Lady Mary herself actually wrote. The circumstances were these. Lady Frances Hertford, an older woman pursuing the younger and resistant Lord William Hamilton, composed a verse appeal to her lover: "Dear Colin, prevent my warm blushes." On behalf of Lord William, Lady Mary composed a "burlesque rejection" for him, a poem that includes these wounding verses:

> That you are in a terrible takeing
> By all these sweet Oglings I see,
> But the Fruit that can fall without shakeing
> Indeed is too mellow for me.
> (ll. 9–12, "Answer'd by Me. M. W. M.")

Dodsley, however, mistakenly assigns the authorship of Lady Mary's reply to the detestable William Yonge. The result is that Lady Mary appears *in print* to speak a lover's lament to Yonge, while he is given the upper hand in a satirical reply actually written by Lady Mary herself.[20] She sighs to her daughter, "I do not beleive either Job or Socrates ever had such a provocation," but she is mortified by the misapplication of authorship because it provides "an excellent piece of Scandal for the same sort of people [Murray and his party] that propagate with Success that your Nurse left her estate, Husband, and Family to go with me to England, and then I turn'd her to starve after defrauding her of God knows what" (8 November 1758; 3:187–88). That Lady Mary places the responsibility for such rumors with Murray is confirmed in her closing: "I thank God Witches are out of Fashion, or I should expect to have it depos'd by several credible wittnesses that I had been seen flying through the Air on a broomstick etc." The problems of rumor, scandal, witches, and writing initially take shape in the letter to her daughter.

She picks up the image of the witch and develops it in the letter sent a week later to Sir James, who was interested in the supernatural (14 November 1758; 3:188–90). Her hatred of the minister and the frustrations and impotence of old age are the sources of her anger, yet rather than merely complaining about the loss of her standing and social influence, she appropriates the dangers of the diabolical. She begins by asking that only Sir James, and not his wife, see the letter: "[Lady Fanny] is the best woman in the world, and I would by no means make her uneasy; but there will be such strange things in [the letter] that the Talmud or the Revelations are not half so mysterious." Lady Mary claims not to know what "these prodigys portend"—as she likens her letter to sacred texts demanding hermeneutical investigation—but she insists that strange and inexplicable occurrences are afoot in the social world:

> But I never should have suspected halfe the wonders I see before my eyes, and am convinced of the necessity of the repeal of the Witch-act (as it is commonly called), I mean, to speak correctly, the tacit permission given to Witches, so scandalous to all good Christians, tho' I tremble to think of it for my own interests. It is certain the British islands have allwaies been strangely addicted to this diabolical intercourse, of which I dare swear you know many instances; but since this public encouragement given to it, I am afraid there will not be an old woman in the nation intirely free from suspicion. The Devil rages more powerfully than ever.

Such "wonders" include Lady Mary's having been "seen flying in the air in the figure of Julian Cox, whose history is related with so much candour and truth by the pious pen of Joseph Glanville, chaplain to King Charles. . . . She was about 70 years old (very near my age), and the whole sworn to before Judge Archer, 1663." She insists that only witchcraft and transformations can define the extraordinary perverseness of life in the Venetian enclave reserved for English men and women.

The argument deepens according to a mock-philosophical principle as Lady Mary points to the only power left to an old woman: " 'Tis one of my wicked maxims to make the best of a bad bargain; and I have said publicly that every period of life has its privileges, and that even the most despicable creatures alive may find some pleasures. Now observe this comment: who are the most despicable creatures? Certainly, Old women. What pleasure can an old woman take?—Only Witchcraft." Having acknowledged the "pleasure" she takes in the diabolical, she goes on to implicate Steuart himself in the nefarious discourse: "I own all the facts, as many witches have done before me, and go every night in a public manner astride upon a black cat to a meeting where you are suspected to appear. This last article is not sworn to, it being doubtfull in what manner our clandestine midnight correspondance is carried on. Some think it treasonable, others lewd (don't tell Lady Fanny), but all agree there was something very odd and unaccountable in such sudden likings. I confess, as I said before, it is witchcraft." Her positioning of Steuart as a partner in this "midnight correspondance" powerfully declares her scorn for Murray and his party—a community of petty-minded English perplexed by a friendship founded on intellectual compatibility rather than on sex or politics, a community that can see such affection only in terms of dangerous and even treasonable motives. This "confession" of sorcery to Steuart, a man often privy to the inner recesses of her heart, is also an extravagant, if somewhat grotesque, compliment to their mutual trust and their shared good judgment.

The letter closes without her usual signature: "You won't wonder I do not sign (notwithstanding all my impudence) such dangerous truths. Who knows the consequence? The Devil is said to desert his votaries." Yet she ends with this unexpected nota bene: "You have dispossessed me of the real Devils who haunted me; I mean the 9 Muses." Having earlier called herself "haunted . . . by the Daemon of Poesie" (18 October 1758; 3:183), she refuses to publish in her own name, yet the result is the public infamy of continuously misapplied authorship and undeserved humiliation, an event so perverse as to seem an act of diabolical sorcery.

Thus the multiple resonances of the meaning of the word *witch* serve startling yet appropriate contradictory purposes for her. The word can be traced through its Middle English root, *wicche,* and its Old English form of *wicce* to mean magic and power, cunning and trickery. Lady Mary's reputation as a writer, coupled with her old age and a friendship inexplicable to the English community abroad, serve to empower this diabolical discourse. However, the word is also intimately related to the Latin *weik* and *wiktime,* or "victim," the animal sacrificed in religious ritual. The discourtesy to Lady Mary personally and the outright ridicule aimed at her literary endeavors place her in the vulnerable position of the victim. The tension inherent in the relationship between the witch and the victim thus describes both Lady Mary's joy in the Steuart friendship and her unhappiness among the powerful of the Venetian English community. She does not, however, indulge in an act of simple self-pity but instead appropriates the image of the witch to refashion for herself the intriguing parts of sorceress and victim, even as she compliments Steuart and the delight she takes in their mutual exclusion, a fact she uses as evidence for their superior moral and intellectual judgment.

A second letter, also concerning the hostility between Lady Mary and Murray, lacks the manic gaiety and clever playfulness of satirical devilry and instead presents a sadder version of Lady Mary's isolation (19 July 1759; 3:215–21). It takes as its subject the question of "worldly glory" in the fashionable public society. It, too, concerns Lady Mary's writing and is one of the most dramatic letters in the whole collection, often couched in dialogue and drawing on elements from the theater to describe human behavior. The letter opens with her acknowledgment that, to preserve her eyesight, she had dictated the first part of the letter to a secretary. The results were altogether unsatisfying, because correcting the errors fatigued her eyes more than "scribbling two sheets of paper" would have done. She confesses, "The evil [of blindness] is of so horrid a nature, I own I feel no philosophy that could support me under it, and no mountain-girl ever trembled more at one of Whitfield's pathetic lectures than I do at the word Blindness." The terrors of blindness lead her to re-create a dialogue that took place at the home of her enemy, Murray:

"Why then (say my wise monitors) will you persist in reading or writing seven hours in a day?"—I am happy while I read and write.—"Indeed one would suffer a great deal to be happy," say the men sneering; and the ladies wink at each other and hold up their fans. A fine lady of three-score had the goodness to add—"At least, Madam, you should use spectacles; I have used them my selfe these twenty years. I was advised to it by a famous oculist when I was fifteen. I am really of opinion they have preserved my sight, notwithstanding the passion I always had both for reading and drawing."—This good woman, you must know, is halfe blind, and never read a larger volume than a newspaper. I will not trouble you with the whole conversation, tho' it would make an excellent scene in a farce. (3:216–17)

Those at the gathering go on, in "the best-bred way in the world," to accuse Lady Mary of lying when she insists that she reads without glasses, and the aforementioned matron further suggests that she would "be very proud to see the writing" Lady Mary talked of, having heard her say that she had no correspondents but her daughter and Wortley. The matron's sister interrupts to say, "simpering," "You forget Sir J[ames] S[teuart]."

Lady Mary responds with anger to the remark: "I took her up something short, I confess, and said in a dry stern tone—'Madam, I do write to Sir J[ames] S[teuart], and will do it as long as he will permit that honor'" (3:217). The exchange angers Lady Mary for two reasons. First, the company implies that she is engaged in writing other than familiar correspondence; when one remembers Lady Mary's dismay concerning the Dodsley incident eight months before, it is not surprising that she still feels the sting of that public humiliation. Moreover, an attack on her friends the Steuarts brings out her most aggressive and protective instincts: to counter their disapprobation, she describes her correspondence with the Steuarts as an "honor" they bestow on her. Her rude response, however, "occasioned a profound silence for some minutes," until the company fell into more a good-natured discourse about the ill health that results from too much study. With some disingenuousness, Lady Mary insists, "I never studied any thing in my life, and have always (at least from 15) thought the reputation of learning a misfortune to a woman," and thus "was resolve[d] to believe these stories were not meant at me," even though it is clear that the company thinks she spends her time in written performances that are too literary and too intellectual for mere correspondence.

In a sad dramatization of her exclusion from polite company, she confesses that, as she "grew silent in [her] turn" and began to smoke a card over a candle, the dialogue continued around her:

> When it was observed I entered into none of these topics, I was addressed by an obliging lady who pitied my stupidity. —"Indeed, Madam, you should buy horses to that fine machine you have at Padoua; of what use is it standing in the portico?"—"Perhaps," said another wittily, "of as much use as a standing dish."—A gaping school-boy added with still more wit, —"I have seen at a country-gentleman's table a venison-pastry made of wood."—I was not at all vexed by said school-boy, not because he was (in more senses than one) the highest of the company, but knowing he did not mean to offend me. I confess (to my shame be it spoken), I was grieved at the triumph that appeared in the eyes of the King and Queen of the company [Murray and his wife], the court being tolerably full. (3:217)

Here, she uses gesture—her smoking of the card over the flame—to suggest mood and her role in the discourse: she plays the part of the distracted, contemplative outsider who, in her silence and her idle activity, listens attentively for remarks intended as personal attacks.

Once Murray departs, followed by a train of admirers who chuckle at Lady Mary's expense, she is left in the company of the women, who "renewed their generous endeavors to set me right." In a particularly aggressive move, she takes the opportunity to enact under their very noses the suspicions leveled against her:

> I (graceless beast that I am) take up the smoked card which lay before me, and with the corner of another write—
>
> > If ever I one thought bestow
> > On what such fools advise,
> > May I be dull enough to grow
> > Most miserably wise—
>
> and flung down the card on the table, and myselfe out of the room in the most indecent fury. A few minutes on the cold water convinced me of my folly, and I went home as much mortified as my Lord E[dgecumbe] when he has lost his last stake at Hazard. (3:218)

When inspired by injury and humiliation, she produces spontaneously and publicly exactly the kind of verse they charge her with producing in secret, thus ultimately reinforcing the legitimacy of their attacks. Yet she disparages the value of her poetry by likening it to those "celebrated beauties [who] often talk of the charms of good sense, having some reason to fear their mental qualities are not quite so conspicuous as their outside lovely form," even though this letter itself is evidence of the care she has taken to reproduce not only this piece of verse but also a stanza attacking Mrs. Wright, Lord Brudenelle, and Colonel Hamilton, three of the company in attendance that night:

> I know not why, but heaven has sent this way
> A nymph fair, kind, poetical and gay;
> And what is more (tho' I express it dully),
> A noble, wise, right honorable cully;
> A soldier worthy of the name he bears,
> As brave and senseless as the sword he wears.

Her extended and dramatic re-creation of this entire "scene"—one which she herself provoked—ends with a familiar and debasing theatrical metaphor: "You will not doubt I am talking of a puppet-shew, and indeed so I am, but the figures (some of them) bigger than the life, and not stuffed with straw like those commonly shewn at fairs. I will allow you to think me madder than Don Quixote when I confess I am governed by the Que dira-t-on of these things, tho' I remember whereof they are made and know they are but dust. Nothing vexes me so much as that they are below satyre." The theatrical nature of public existence is doubly disturbing because, although she attempts to contain her anger by satirizing her acquaintances as mere puppets at the fair, her impotence—as a woman and as a writer—leaves her no recourse: "I think there are but two pleasures permitted to mortal man, Love and Vengeance, both which are, in a peculiar manner, forbidden to us wretches who are condemned to petticoats" (3:219).

Being denied inclusion in this social world and criticized for the literary endeavors that were the passion of her life lead her to speculate on the nature of the most productive kind of work. She begins by claiming that Algarotti is in Bologna "composing panegyrics on whoever is victor in this uncertain war," while their friend Antonio Vallisniere (who held the chair of natural history at Padua University) is touring in an attempt to add to his collection. She then asks:

Which do you think the best employed? I confess I am woman enough to think the naturalist who searches after variegated butterflies, or even the lady who adorns her grotto with shades of shells, nay, even the devout people who spend 20 years in making a magnificent presepia [models of Christ's navitity] at Naples, throw away time in a more rational manner than any hero, ancient or modern. The lofty Pindar who celebrated the Newmarket of those days, or the divine Homer who recorded the bloody battles the most in fashion, appear to me either to have been extremely mistaken or extremely mercenary. (3:220)

A letter concerned with love and vengeance, politics and gallantry—the passions of the polite world—culminates in this final distinction between public and private glory. With particular clarity and poignancy, the letter indicates the degree to which the social world has become just such a battleground for Lady Mary; it also indicates that she is willing to give up her triumphs and victories for the more important and, she indicates, less "public" work of the artist. Like the scientist who collects natural beauties in the form of butterflies, the private woman who constructs her own artistic grotto, or the devout worshiper who fashions religious iconography, Lady Mary concludes that the greatest personal satisfaction is to be found only through private, individual, and productive creation—not through momentary victories in fashionable drawing rooms littered with the puppets of dust. And her lifelong series of "private" letters displaying her own superior artistry could be added to her list of "best" employments, even though such creations are also the source of her public humiliations.

She acknowledges this rejection of the public at the conclusion of this long letter: "I own I have lost all taste for worldly glory. This is partly your fault: I experienced last year how much happiness may be found with two amiable friends at a *legar repas,* and 'tis hard to return to political or galant conversations as it would be for a fat prelate to content himselfe with the small beer he drank at college. You have furnished me with a new set of notions; you ought to be punished for it, and I fancy you will (at least in your heart) be of opinion that I have very well revenged my selfe by this tedious unconnected letter" (3:221). In likening herself to a happy prelate made "fat" by the richness of the Steuarts' friendship, she can dismiss Murray and Co. as "small beer" and close on a quiet, emotional note: "[I] have only indulged the pleasure everbody naturally feels when they talk to those they love."

These two relationships—the one with her daughter and the other with the Steuarts—contain all the contradictions inherent in her later years and her exile: she grows old, separated from her homeland and her loved ones, but needing to express her affections. With her daughter, a woman living the life Lady Mary herself left behind—the court, politics, and the family—she works to develop a quiet, easy intimacy; with the Bute family generally and her granddaughters especially, she seeks to develop deeper emotional ties through attention to their future happiness. Thus she becomes the country squire, the educator, and the wise grandmother who celebrates her autonomy and productivity, her happiness in retreat, and the pleasures of reading and study. With the Steuarts, she is socially besieged but intellectually gratified, performing her part as a writer— not only sharing her fears, vulnerabilites, and anger but also generating the satiric energy of old to insist on their mutually superior judgment and intellectual compatibility.

Read exclusive of one another, these "biographical" accounts produce positively antithetical portraits. Together, however, rather than vex- ing the question of biography, they reveal accounts of Lady Mary's life equally "true." Her performances—fluid, contradictory, always chang- ing—display varying intentions, motives, desires, and affections. She is as adaptable in her correspondence as she needs to be, as human in her contradiction as anyone willing to unveil or costume a part of the self. Most of all, these late-in-life letters emphasize the power of the epistolary form to generate competing and complementary identi- ties, theatrical instances of the drama inherent in the negotiations for intimacy and the pleasures of epistolary performance.

Epilogue

"I Expect Immortality"

In January 1762, after Wortley's death, Lady Mary returned to England and settled in a house that her daughter had rented for her on Saint Georges Street, off Hanover Square. She spent her days renewing her affection for her family, entertaining visitors curious to see her, corresponding with distant friends, and working for the Steuarts' return.[1] By June of that year, however, she could no longer conceal her illness— a breast cancer so malignant that she would die two months later, on 16 August 1762.

Mr. Spectator's description of his life, as a "public sort of obscurity," in many ways accurately describes Lady Mary's own. As an aristocratic woman, she searched for a means by which she could resolve the tensions inherent in the divisions between public and private life. As a young woman, she tried to cultivate the private and contain the public aspects of her courtship with Wortley. From Turkey, she performed quite publicly, for she was empowered by the extraordinary character of her circumstances. Upon her return to the heart of the fashionable English social world, she celebrated and lamented the extravagancies of a beau monde that vex her notions of both class and gender. And later in life, she chose a retreat that she described to her daughter as empowering and productive but that the Steuarts knew was often painful and humiliating. All the while, she produced an astonishing textual record of her life in various performances that declared a series of identities, all fluidly shifting one to another: the resistant and passionate lover became the sophisticated world traveler and cultural relativist; the spectatress and social satirist metamorphosed into the literary critic and gentlewoman scholar; the wise grandmother was simultaneously Lady Bountiful and the exiled witch. A fifty-four-year correspondence, voluminous and substantial, remains her enduring achievement.

A final narrative, one drawn from her Continental correspondence, makes that monument "concrete." In it Lady Mary brings together her roles as a privileged member within a local community (the patroness) and as a writer in the culture at large (the witch) through the image of the saint—a figure that resonates with the otherworldly powers of rejuvenation and healing while it admits an equal claim to admiration and even reverence. The image of the saint takes shape in a letter she sends to Wortley in 1751 where she reveals that her fears of growing old could be temporarily allayed when she learns of the miraculous rejuvenation of "the old Woman of Louvere" (10 November 1751; 2:493–94). This account of the supernatural, quite out of character in their usually businesslike correspondence, concerns an old woman who lived to be one hundred years old. She remained in good health, with the exception of the decays common to old age: dimness of sight and a loss of her teeth and hair. In her hundredth year, however, her sight was restored, and she grew a new set of teeth and "a fresh Head of Brown Hair." Lady Mary herself viewed a portrait of the old woman painted after her rejuvenation and claimed it revealed "a vivacity in the Eyes and Complexion that would become five and twenty, tho' by the Falls in the Face one may discern it was drawn for a very old Person." The old woman's daughters (themselves "2 maids past 70") further intrigue her when they claim that "[their mother] had also another mark of youth that generally happens to Girls of 15." After living "in this renew'd vigour" for ten years, the woman died "meerly of an Accident" by falling down an old stone staircase. This story of late-in-life rebirth is so extraordinary that Lady Mary claims to be "surpriz'd [the old woman] is neither call'd Saint nor Witch." This incident of near-miraculous restoration has its analogue in an earlier letter, sent to the Countess of Oxford, in which

Lady Mary cites her *own* reputed powers as a healer: "[I] have had so much success that I am thought a great Physician and should be esteem'd a Saint if I went to Mass" (1 September 1747; 2:388).

The patron, the witch, and the healer—images that express thinly veiled hopes for her own future and pride in the improvements resulting from her local patronage—join the image of the writer in an ironic but poignant account of the community's desire to erect a statue of her. In June 1751 her Italian neighbors, thinking "themselves highly honnour'd and oblig'd by [her] residence," make plans to erect the statue. While she is pleased with the recognition, she absolutely forbids construction:

> The marble was bespoke and the Sculptor bargain'd with before I knew any thing of the matter, and it would have been erected without my knowledge if it had not been necessary for him to see me to take the Resemblance. I thank'd them very much for the Intention, but utterly re-fus'd complying with it, fearing it would be reported (at least in England) that I had set up my own Statue. They were so obstinate in the Design, I was forc'd to tell them my Religion would not permit it. I seriously beleive it would have been worshipp'd (when I was forgotten) under the name of some Saint or other, since I was to have been represented with a Book in my Hand, which would have pass'd for a proofe of canonization. (19 June 1751; 2:485)

While this projection of a future sainthood, albeit an anonymous one, touches her ironic sensibilities, her concern for her reputation in England—her fears that she will once again be misunderstood in the country she abandoned twelve years before—still takes precedence. So she turns her daughter's attention to the "honors" she claims to prefer, her domestic contributions to the community, improvements that form the source of her true "Immortality":

> This complement [of the statue] was certainly founded on reasons not unlike those that first fram'd Goddesses, I mean being usefull to them, in which I am second to Ceres. . . . I have introduc'd French rolls, custards, minc'd Pies, and Plumb pudding, which they are very fond of. . . . But I expect Immortality from the Science of Butter makeing, in which they are become so skillfull from my Instructions, I can assure you here is as good as in any part of Great Brittain. (2:485)

Thus, while she prohibits the "real-life" construction of the statue as a too public and too visible symbol violating the English decorums of her class and gender, she exploits the multiple meanings the experience generates by creating her own "textual" monument. Recorded with the same artistry, emotion, and amusement found in the whole of her correspondence, this narrative allows her once again to circumvent public censure while ensuring that her image remains. As Ceres, the ancient earth mother and source of life-giving sustenance, she will become a memory woven into the domestic fabric of daily life; as a scholar, woman of letters, and artist, she will be celebrated for her intellectual achievements. Thus this "statue" of Lady Mary—standing alone, with a book in hand, out in the Italian countryside—lives on as an epistolary tribute to the gifts of health and happiness she provides to her community and as a monument to a woman writer's contributions to the larger world of literary culture.

INTRODUCTION

1. Lady Mary Wortley Montagu, *The Complete Letters of Lady Mary Wortley Montagu,* ed. Robert Halsband, 3 vols. (Oxford: Clarendon Press, 1965–67), July 1725; 2:54. All subsequent references to this edition are placed parenthetically in the text. I have followed Halsband's editorial practice of using square brackets for editorial interpolations and angle brackets for doubtful readings.

2. Horace Walpole to Pinkerton, 26 June 1785; quoted by Robert Halsband, "Walpole versus Lady Mary," in *Horace Walpole: Writer, Politician, and Connoisseur,* ed. Warren Hunting Smith (New Haven: Yale University Press, 1967), 225.

3. See William Henry Irving, *The Providence of Wit in the English Letter Writers* (Durham: Duke University Press, 1955), 83.

4. Kathryn Shevelow, *Women and Print Culture: The Construction of Femininity in the Early Periodical* (London: Routledge, 1989), 90.

5. All references to the particulars of Lady Mary's life are drawn from Robert Halsband, *The Life of Lady Mary Wortley Montagu* (Oxford: Clarendon Press, 1956).

6. Her father, Evelyn Pierrepont, first Marquess of Dorchester, was a grandson of diarist Sir John Evelyn. Lord Dorchester was made Earl of Kingston in 1690, and upon inheriting the estate of his uncle Lord Pierrepont in 1715, he was elevated by the King to the Dukedom of Kingston-upon-Hull (ibid., 1, 47).

7. There were varying estimates of the value of Wortley's estate, although most cite his personal worth as £800,000 and the annual landed revenues as between £7,000 and £20,000. See Lady Mary, *Complete Letters* 3:254n.

8. Patricia Meyer Spacks, *Gossip* (New York: Alfred A. Knopf, 1985), 75.

9. Felicity Nussbaum, *The Autobiographical Subject: Gender and Ideology in*

Eighteenth-Century England (Baltimore: Johns Hopkins University Press, 1990), xiii, xii.

10. Ibid., xiv.

11. Shevelow, *Women and Print Culture,* 52, 5.

12. Ibid., 17.

CHAPTER ONE. Epistolary Performances

1. Wortley was such a conscientious correspondent that he endorsed every letter he received with the date and time and then cataloged it for his collection. Such collections were often preserved and handed down through the generations of a family. In Lady Mary's case, the letters remained in her daughter's hands until they were passed on to her grandson, Lord Bute, who in 1803 allowed them to be published in a bowdlerized version, but only after he burned a number of letters. (Lady Mary's daughter burned all of her mother's voluminous diary, fearful that publication of it would damage the family reputation.) It was left up to Lady Mary's great-grandson, Lord Wharncliffe, to produce a better but still incomplete edition in 1837. Lord Byron, always an admirer of Lady Mary—in *Don Juan* he called her "the charming Mary Montagu" (canto 5, stanza 3)—also participated in the recovery of some of her letters when he searched for information about her as he traveled in Venice. Acting on Byron's suggestion, publisher John Murray purchased a collection of Algarotti's letters on sale in England, stored them in his archives, and ultimately offered them to Lord Wharncliffe for the 1837 edition. Wharncliffe politely refused. The Bodleian Library later purchased some of these letters at Sotheby's, but the majority of Lady Mary's correspondence resides today in the Wortley Manuscripts Collection, owned by Lady Mary's descendant, Lord Harrowby. For more information about the history of the letters, see Halsband's *Life;* for a description of the part Byron played in the recovery of Algarotti's letters, see *Life,* 291.

2. Howard Robinson's *British Post Office,* a dated but still remarkable treatment of the history of the postal system, recounts its emergence and growth. Charles I's very limited system, designed for use by royalty and aristocrats, gave way to the seriously disorganized Cromwellian post. When Charles II returned and refused to recognize the "pretended" post office, he enacted the Post Office Charter: the new system made the king's brother, the Duke of York, receiver of the major portion of the significant revenues. In 1680, an ingenious private system was set up by William Dockwra for intra-London delivery: no matter the number of sheets, each letter was prepaid by the sender and deposited in one of a number of pick-up points around the city; after passing through Dockwra's clearinghouse, the mail was then delivered, sometimes as often as ten to twelve times a day for businesses and four to eight times a day for other urban areas. This practice, naturally enough, was seen

as a threat by the new government-controlled post, and when James II usurped Dockwra's fully functioning system, the first official penny post was born. See Robinson's *British Post Office* (Princeton: Princeton University Press, 1948), 48–76.

3. Complaints about the inefficiency of the system were loud, and slowly, with the excess revenue the post generated, crossroads were constructed. Other abuses of the post concerned complaints of slow delivery: sometimes the postboys' speed was only two or three miles per hour, and they were charged with loitering at inns and lounging in taverns along their routes. Bad roads were never well maintained by the neighborhood crews (large stones were thrown into the holes in the hope that the passing horses and carriages would crush them), and severe winter weather often slowed or even halted delivery. In 1711 the cost of delivery was also relatively expensive for its users. In England and Wales, one sheet could travel eighty miles for three pence, farther for four pence. Two sheets were doubly expensive, and "writs and deeds" were quadruple the rate for every ounce. Outside the borders, the rates ran even higher: six pence to Edinburgh, six pence to Dublin, and ten pence between any part of France and London (ibid., 96–127). R. W. Chapman reports that "the cost of letters was very high absolutely . . . and was almost always borne by the recipient." He adds that, because one sheet was cheaper, the universal use of the quarto began; because the letter writer also felt the need to fill the entire sheet, penmanship was fine, small, and even. On the fourth page, the writer left a blank space in the center so that when the letter was folded and sealed the space could carry the directions. See "The Course of the Post in the Eighteenth Century," *Notes and Queries* 183 (1 Aug. 1942): 67. Considering the expense of paper and postage, regular correspondence was clearly most easily accomplished by the leisured and moneyed class.

4. In 1688, the revenues totaled £90,000; by 1715, the total had grown to £150,000. In 1697–98 the number of letters delivered was 792,080, and by 1703 the number of pieces had grown significantly: 95,694 to the country; 951,090 penny letters total (Robinson, *British Post Office*, 85).

5. Marcus Billson, "The Memoir: New Perspectives on a Forgotten Genre," *Genre* 10 (1977): 265, 261.

6. H. Porter Abbott, "Letters to the Self: The Cloistered Writer in Nonretrospective Fiction," *PMLA* 95 (1980): 23, 29.

7. Walter J. Ong, S. J., "The Writer's Audience Is Always a Fiction," *PMLA* 90 (1975): 20.

8. James Winn, *A Window in the Bosom: The Letters of Alexander Pope* (Hamden, Conn.: Archon Books, 1977), 72–73.

9. Roy Roussel, "Reflections on the Letter: The Reconciliation of Distance and Presence in *Pamela*," *English Literary History* 41 (1974): 396.

10. Samuel Richardson, *The Correspondence of Samuel Richardson*, ed. Anna Laetitia Barbauld, 6 vols. (London, 1804), 3:246.

11. Roussel, "Reflections on the Letter," 387.

12. Bruce Redford, *The Converse of the Pen* (Chicago: University of Chicago Press, 1986), 2.

13. Janet Altman, *Epistolarity: Approaches to a Form* (Columbus: Ohio State University Press, 1982), 119.

14. Richard Steele, "The Spectator (No. 370)," in *Selected Essays from "The Tatler," "The Spectator," and "The Guardian,"* ed. Daniel McDonald (Indianapolis: Bobbs-Merrill, 1973), 439–40.

15. Erving Goffman, *The Presentation of Self in Everyday Life* (Edinburgh: University of Edinburgh Press, 1956), 132.

16. Michael G. Ketcham, *Transparent Designs: Reading, Performance, and Form in the "Spectator" Papers* (Athens: University of Georgia Press, 1985), 52.

17. For additional information about Lady Mary's remarks concerning Addison's *Cato,* see Robert Halsband, "Addison's *Cato* and Lady Mary Wortley Montagu," *PMLA* 65 (1950): 1122–29. For additional information concerning her play, *Simplicity,* see Halsband's "First English Version of Marivaux's *Le Jeu de l'amour et du hasard,*" *Modern Philology* (Aug. 1981): 16–23.

18. Bruce Wilshire, *Role Playing and Identity* (Bloomington: Indiana University Press, 1982), 171.

19. Ibid., 206.

20. Louise K. Horowitz, "The Correspondence of Madame de Sévigné: Letters or Belles-Lettres?" *French Forum* 6 (Jan. 1981): 13–27.

21. The interdependence of writer, reader, and text in the epistolary exchange points to the letter's status as a "fictive" rather than "natural" discourse, as Barbara Hernstein-Smith defines such "marginal" utterances (*On the Margins of Discourse* [Chicago: University of Chicago Press, 1978], 15–39). For a persuasive argument about the ways a letter both reflects and creates contexts and thus serves as an artifact that "straddles" the barrier between "natural" and "fictive" discourses, see Redford, *Converse of the Pen,* 8–9.

22. Gail Mensher, "Problems of Time and Existence in the Letters of Madame de Sévigné" (Ph.D. diss., University of Iowa, 1977), 57.

23. Altman, *Epistolarity,* 15.

24. Ibid., 120, 111.

25. Christina Gillis, *The Paradox of Privacy: Epistolary Form in "Clarissa"* (Gainesville: University of Florida Press, 1984), 7–8; ibid., 139.

26. François Jost, "L'Evolution d'un genre: Le Roman épistolaire dans les lettres occidentales," in *Essays de littérature comparée* (Fribourg, Switzerland: Editions universitaires, 1968), 2:89–179, 380–402; quoted in Altman, *Epistolarity,* 7–8.

27. Mensher, "Problems of Time and Existence," 23.

28. Lady Mary's Turkish Embassy Letters present a special problem in light of this dynamic. More outward looking still, these letters compose a collection she

edited and revised, and shortly before her death she made certain that the manuscript went into the hands of a clergyman who would see them into publication. In this publishable performance the emphasis rests on neither of the epistolary partners but on the external world, this time the wonders of an exotic locale. The "I" becomes a relatively impersonal recording consciousness, and she acts as a journalist or tour guide, describing local events and customs, detailing the history of the region, exploring ancient ruins and modern cities. The atmosphere is very much like that in a lecture hall—her tone is informative rather than comfortably chatty or intensely conflicted. To the Abbé Conti, for instance, she writes, on her return jouney, "Not many leagues sail from hence I saw the point of land where poor old Hecuba was bury'd, and abou a league from that place is Cape Janizary, the famous promontory of Sigaeum, where we anchor'd; and my Curiosity supply'd me with strength to climb to the top of it to see the place where Achilles was bury'd and where Alexander ran naked round his Tomb in his honnour, which, no doubt, was a great comfort to his Ghost" (31 July 1718; 1:417).

29. Bruce Redford and Michael G. Ketcham provide useful vocabularies for describing the rhetorical strategies writers use as substitutes for gesture, vocal inflection, and physical context: see *Converse of the Pen* and *Transparent Designs*.

30. Ong, "Writer's Audience," 17, 11.

31. Cicero is quoted by Keith Stewart in "Towards Defining an Aesthetic for the Familiar Letter in Eighteenth-Century England," *Prose Studies* 5 (Sept. 1982): 180. Alexander Pope, *Correspondence*, ed. George Sherburn, 5 vols. (Oxford: Clarendon Press, 1956), 18 Aug. 1716; 1:353. All subsequent references to this edition of Pope's letters are placed parenthetically in the text.

32. James Boswell, *Life of Johnson*, ed. G. B. Hill rev. L. F. Powell, 6 vols. (Oxford: Clarendon Press, 1934–50): 4:166 (quoted by Stewart, "An Aesthetic for the Familiar Letter," 180; Redford, *Converse of the Pen*, 3.)

33. Modern theorists have challenged the notion that any relationship exists between a "conversational style" and actual speech. To illustrate the critical misunderstanding about the relation of spoken to written language, Louis Milic uses an example of modern British conversation, transcribed verbatim and spoken by a person with a university education and much experience in speaking and writing: "You see um the the um the chief lecturer there is is er um—he is the main lecturer though really he has one or two subordinates but he is the—he gives the lectures the main lectures—there are seminars as well and discussions following upon those but the main lectures are given by him. . . ." As the transcription illustrates, the structure of spoken language is often tentative and quickly revised, with speakers displaying a "lack of interest in sentence-boundaries." Milic's conclusion—that certain written elements have come, through convention, to be seen as "colloquial"—is easily demonstrated in Sterne's prose, which contains asides and apostrophes to the reader, interrupted syntax, unusual use of punctuation

(especially the dash), and incompleteness of predication, elements often cited as conversational. Yet Sterne's prose is actually more akin to writing than to speaking because the Shandean dash does not correspond to the pauses one finds in speech (the dash does not interrupt syntactic construction, as the pause normally would) but is placed in legitimate boundaries, sometimes simply in addition to the normal punctuation. See Milic's "Observations on Conversational Style," in *English Writers of the Eighteenth Century,* ed. John H. Middendorf (New York: Columbia University Press, 1971), 273–87.

34. Howard Anderson and Irvin Ehrenpreis, "The Familiar Letter in the Eighteenth Century: Some Generalizations," in *The Familiar Letter in the Eighteenth Century,* ed. Howard Anderson, Philip B. Daghlian, and Irvin Ehrenpreis (Lawrence: University of Kansas Press, 1966), 273.

35. William Cowper, *The Letters and Prose Writings of William Cowper,* ed. James King and Charles Ryskamp, 4 vols. (Oxford: Clarendon Press, 1979), 374.

36. Lady Mary quotes these lines from her own "Epistle from Mrs. Yonge to Her Husband" (1724). See Lady Mary Wortley Montagu, *Essays, Poems, and "Simplicity, a Comedy,"* ed. Robert Halsband and Isobel Grundy (Oxford: Clarendon Press, 1977), 230.

CHAPTER TWO. Intimate Negotiations

1. Richmond Bond reports that Wortley submitted his remarks and information to Steele as memoranda rather than fully developed essays; the arguments show up in *Tatler* Nos. 199 and 223. See *The Tatler: The Making of a Literary Journal* (Cambridge: Harvard University Press, 1971), 14.

2. For further discussion of the marriage arrangements, see Halsband's *Life,* chap. 2.

3. Lytton Strachey describes the tension in their courtship in this way: "They were not ordinary lovers; they were intellectual gladiators, and their letters are like the preliminary wary passes of two well-matched wrestlers before they come to grips. If they had been less well-matched, there would have been no difficulties; but neither could ever be certain that the other was not too strong" ("Lady Mary Wortley Montagu," in *Biographical Essays* [New York: Harcourt, Brace, and World, 1969], 37).

4. The courtship with Wortley has its genesis in Lady Mary's friendship with his sister, and it is through Anne that Lady Mary communicates tangentially with Wortley. In the first extant letter sent from Anne to Lady Mary, Wortley's sister writes, "I am now in the room with an humble Servant of yourn [Wortley] who is arguing so hotly about marriage that I cant goe on with my Letter" (c. 3 August 1709; 1:4). She then proceeds to detail that argument: everyone seeks happiness in marriage, but they fail because people too often pursue money and too slavishly

follow fashion. Yet of Lady Mary, Anne writes, "But you have dar'd to have wit joyn'd with beauty, a thing so much out of fashion that we fly after you with as much invitertness [*sic*] as you often see the birds do when one superior com's near them" (1:5). Considering the elaborate nature of the compliment, coupled as it is with the issues of wit, marriage, and money (many of the prominent themes of the Lady Mary–Wortley courtship), it is possible that Wortley himself had a hand in the compliment (Halsband writes that Wortley "probably dictated the arguments" [1:4n]). Subsequent letters from Wortley confirm that before Anne died (a year after she and Lady Mary began their correspondence) he read much of Lady Mary's correspondence with her.

5. Sherry B. Ortner, "Is Female to Male As Nature Is to Culture?" in *Women, Culture, and Society,* ed. Michelle Zimbalist Rosaldo and Louise Lamphere (Stanford: Stanford University Press, 1974), 73–79.

6. Anthony, First Earl of Shaftesbury, *Characteristics,* ed. John M. Robertson, 2 vols. (Gloucester, Mass.: Peter Smith, 1963), 1:309.

7. If they marry without her father's consent, Wortley loses £20,000 in dowry and incurs his own father's anger. Lady Mary's sacrifice, however, is greater. The marriage contract with Clotworthy Skeffington made liberal provisions for her: she would have an allowance of £500 a year in pin money and £1,200 a year upon his death. An elopement meant that she alo forfeited the £8,000 raised by her father on her brother's marriage. Even though Wortley had a greater income and better reversions than her Irish suitor, without a marriage contract Lady Mary had no legal access to such wealth and the resources were valueless to her (Halsband, *Life,* 21–24).

8. The Turkish Embassy Letters extant today are not the letters Lady Mary actually sent but a compilation she edited throughout her lifetime (see chap. 3 for a complete discussion of the history of the Turkish letters). While it is clear from Pope's responses that much of the content of individual letters remained the same, the letters themselves are a revised and polished performance.

9. Patricia Meyer Spacks, always an intelligent and insightful reader of Lady Mary's letters, is one of the first to treat the Lady Mary–Pope correspondence as a serious, artistic endeavor. See "Imaginations Warm and Tender: Pope and Lady Mary," *South Atlantic Quarterly* 83 (1984): 207–15.

10. Geoffrey Tillotson, "Lady Mary Wortley Montagu and Pope's *Elegy to the Memory of an Unfortunate Lady,*" *Review of English Studies* 12 (Oct. 1936): 412.

11. Peter Quennell, calling *Eloisa to Abelard* the "most poignantly personal poem that [Pope] had yet composed and published," also sees Lady Mary as the genesis of the poem, which reflects "a guilty love" and "the agonized confusion of an individual human heart"; see *Alexander Pope: The Education of Genius, 1688–1728* (New York: Stein and Day, 1968), 147–48.

12. Maynard Mack also argues that Pope's object was merely to flatter Lady

Mary in unusual and pleasing ways. He claims that the poet's delicate feats of exaggeration serve to preserve the carnival tone and the comic distance; otherwise, "the whole game might collapse into bouts of heavy breathing." See *Alexander Pope: A Life* (New Haven: Yale University Press, 1985), 306, 302.

13. Edith Sitwell, *Alexander Pope* (New York: Cosmopolitan Book, 1930), 185.

14. For a complete discussion of Lady Mary's relationship with Algarotti, see Halsband's *Life,* chaps. 1–12, 15.

15. All translations have been taken from Halsband, *Complete Letters,* Appendix: "French Correspondence."

16. Virgil, *Aeneid,* 4.522–32; translation from Halsband, *Complete Letters,* 2:104n.

17. Lady Mary had been interested in the *Heroides* from as early as her twelfth year. Isobel Grundy, recording the variety of Lady Mary's youthful verse, reports that "an aura of secrecy and even furtiveness hangs about her adolescent devotion to 'poetry my dear my darling choice' " (" 'The Entire Works of Clarinda': Unpublished Juvenile Verse by Lady Mary Wortley Montagu," *Yearbook of English Studies,* vol. 7, ed. G. K. Hunter and C. J. Rawson [1977], 92) and that her second folio album of juvenile verse is dominated by Ovid (a shift from her earlier Horation pieces). Lady Mary reportedly told Joseph Spence that Ovid's *Metamorphoses* stimulated her desire to learn Latin. She was most responsive, however, to the *Heroides,* and at the early age of twelve, by her own reckoning, she wrote "An Epistle to Ovid" in the same tone and subject matter (she had earlier recorded, in the first folio, all the names of the personages in Ovid's epistles). According to Grundy, she was attracted to the theme of the forsaken woman and creates a love in these poems that was "the classical god-inspired madness highly romanticized" as she seeks "with authentic Ovidian masochism to extract the maximum pathos from her state" ("Entire," 99). See also Grundy, "Entire," 91–107, and "Ovid and Eighteenth-Century Divorce: An Unpublished Poem by Lady Mary Wortley Montagu," *Review of English Studies,* n.s., 23 (1972): 417–28. For the poems themselves, see Lady Mary, *Essays.*

18. Gillian Beer, " 'Our Unnatural No-Voice': The Heroic Epistle, Pope, and Women's Gothic," *Yearbook of English Studies* 12 (1982): 132–33.

19. Daniel P. Gunn, "Visionary Theater: Pope's Eloisa as Tragic Heroine," *Colby Library Quarterly* 21, no. 3 (Sept. 1985): 143. Gillian Beer argues that the performative nature of the epistle was recognized during the seventeenth and eighteenth centuries: by 1750, most readers of it knew *Eloisa to Abelard* by heart and could recite it; in his dedication Saltonstall imagines the readers of his translation reading Ovid aloud: "The dead letters form'd into words by your divided lips, may receive new life by your passionate expression." The adjective *operatic* is also more than a metaphorical description of the *Heroides,* for the emotions of the heroines caught the imaginations of composers: Monteverdi wrote two settings for Ariadne's epistle

(1614, 1621); Nicholas Lanier (1588–1666) used Hero's epistle to Leander; and later Haydn composed his *cantata a voce sola* "Arianna a Naxos" (1789). See Beer, "Our Unnatural No-Voice," 143.

20. Robert Halsband, "Algarotti as Apollo: His Influence on Lady Mary Wortley Montagu," in *Friendship's Garland: Essays Presented to Mario Praz on His Seventieth Birthday,* ed. Vittorio Gabrieli, 2 vols. (Rome: Edizioni di Storia E Letteratura, 1966), 1:230.

21. Beer, " 'Our Unnatural No-Voice,' " 134.

22. Because Bruce Redford perceives stoicism to be Lady Mary's most important and even her defining characteristic, he argues that her infatuation runs counter to a resistance and even an asceticism that are natural to her, a battle between head and heart reminiscent of Racine's tragic heroines (*Converse of the Pen,* 19–48). While in this instance she does describe the conflict in terms of her reason and her emotions, as evidenced above, she also celebrates the pains—and pleasures—of the relationship by drawing on varied sources and multiple forms of discourse for their expression.

23. Howard Jacobson, *Ovid's Heroides* (Princeton: Princeton University Press, 1974), 372; quoted in Karen Alkalay-Gut's "Woman in a Trap: Pope and Ovid in 'Eloisa to Abelard,' " *College Literature* 13, no. 3 (Fall 1986): 273.

24. Alkalay-Gut, "Woman in a Trap," 273.

25. Bruce Redford also writes that the *Heroides* informs Lady Mary's discourse, and he argues that her letters to Algarotti are pointedly "mediated by the Ovidian rhetoric of 'Eloisa to Abelard' " especially as it was present in Pope's love letters (*Converse of the Pen,* 45).

26. For a complete discussion of the openness of Lady Mary's confessions to Lord Hervey about her affection for Algarotti and for more information about the nature of their game of poetry, see Isobel Grundy's " 'New' Verse by Lady Mary Wortley Montagu," *Bodleian Library Record* 10 (Feb. 1981): 237–49.

27. The conclusion of this improbable "love triangle" comes after Lady Mary's disappointment in her "affair" and after Lord Hervey consoles her, with some seemingly genuine sympathy, for the loss of her young scholar.

28. Even though Halsband cautions that the paper, pen, and ink of this letter are similar to those of letters written before Lady Mary left England, he places this undated letter in the May 1741 collection. I have followed his choice in seeing the text as an expression of her final disillusionment with Algarotti.

29. Precisely because he was so impervious to her desire, Algarotti remained for her the one man to whom she presented her deepest emotions. Years later, long after the passion had cooled and she was able to call him "hors d'oeuvre" rather than Apollo, she remained vulnerable to him in ways she never revealed to others. In 1757, she expresses her sadness about being separated from her daughter and laments once again the lost pleasures of her exile: "Un certain Chevalier Sagromoso

(qui je hairai toute ma vie) me dit tout bas, par une maudite Politesse, qu'il avoit entendu chanter ma Fille a Londres. Mille images a la fois se presentent a mon esprit, l'Impression devint trop fort et, moi miserable, je fonds en larmes, et suis obligée de sortir pour ne pas troubler le concert par mes sanglots. Je retourne chez moi, outrée de m'avoir attirée le mepris public, a juste titre: une vieille tendre, quel Monstre!" ["A certain Chevalier Sagramoso (whom I shall hate all my life) whispers to me, out of an accursed Politeness, that he had heard my Daughter sing in London. A thousand pictures present themselves at the same time to my mind, the Impression becomes too strong and, fool that I am, I burst into tears, and am obliged to leave in order not to disturb the concert by my sobs. I return home, exasperated at having drawn public scorn on myself deservedly: a sentimental old woman, what a Monster!"] (12 Mar. 1757; 3:124, 302). This tale of tears and scorn is reserved for the man who produced and then crushed her desire through his absence and silence but who also provided her with a new access to unexplored regions of her powerful imagination and to the artistic pleasures of an extravagant rhetoric of passion.

CHAPTER THREE. The Veil of Romance: The Turkish Embassy Letters

1. Unlike most nineteenth-century travelers, Lady Mary's acquisitive impulses are surprisingly weak. She purchases her own Turkish habit, tries to buy gemstones (when they were inexpensive), and secures the Turkish love letter. Beyond these domestic items, on only one occasion does she try to take part in the nineteenth-century habit of "looting" Eastern treasures: on the voyage home, she and Wortley remove a marble inscription from the Temple of Minerva on the Acropolis of Sigeum. After Wortley's death and according to his direction, the stone was presented to Trinity College, Cambridge (Lady Mary, *Complete Letters* 1:418n).

2. For further discussion of the history of the letters, see ibid. 1:xiv–xvii, and Halsband, *Life*, 278–79, 287–89.

3. Tobias Smollett, *Critical Review* 15 (1763): 426; Voltaire, *The Complete Works of Voltaire* 110 (Oxfordshire: Voltaire Foundation, 1975), 410; Hester Lynch Piozzi, *Anecdotes of Samuel Johnson*, ed. S. C. Roberts (New York: Arno, 1980), 166; and Edward Gibbon, *The Private Letters of Edward Gibbon*, ed. Rowland E. Prothero, 2 vols. (London: John Murray, 1896), 1:53.

4. Edward Said, *Orientalism* (New York: Pantheon Books, 1978), 162.

5. Michael McKeon, *The Origins of the English Novel, 1600–1740* (Baltimore: Johns Hopkins University Press, 1987), 111.

6. H. F. M. Prescott cites travelers' reports (from the fifteenth and sixteenth centuries) about the substance that was said, beyond its use as a beauty treatment, to have great medicinal value. It was used by Muslims to cure nasal trouble, lumbago, and pains in the knees and by Christians to cure toothache, poisoning,

and snakebite. Lady Mary may not have used an authentic variety, for the balm of highest quality, conrolled by the sultan, was not readily available to foreign visitors. Even when Westerners paid fantastic sums, they usually acquired a faked balm or one adulterated with other sweet-smelling oils. See *Once to Sinai* (New York: Macmillan, 1958), 119–23.

7. Lady Mary goes on to make claims for the safety of the procedure: "There is no example of any one that has dy'd in it" (1:339). Perhaps at this early juncture of her interest in inoculation, she may actually have believed that the procedure was entirely harmless; however, people subsequently did succumb to the disease induced by the technique itself, for, unlike the dead vaccines that we use today, vaccines that are indeed relatively safe, in the eighteenth century live vaccines were introduced into the body of an otherwise healthy patient. Lady Mary herself was so convinced of the efficacy and safety of the procedure that she had the operation performed on her son in March 1718. It was eighty years, of course, before the techniques of vaccination (using cowpox, not smallpox) were refined by Edward Jenner, but Lady Mary is generally credited with introducing the technique to England and with some part of the success of the procedure.

8. And war with them she did. In 1721, three years after her return to England, when an outbreak of smallpox seemed imminent, Lady Mary supported Princess Caroline's interest in the procedure, and Lady Mary herself joined the pamphlet war concerning inoculation. See her essay "A Plain Account of the Innoculating of the Small Pox by a Turkey Merchant," *Essays,* 95–96; and Robert Halsband, "New Light on Lady Mary Wortley Montagu's Contribution to Inoculation," *Journal of the History of Medicine* 8 (Oct. 1953): 390–405.

9. Said, *Orientalism,* 20.

10. Anne-Marie Moulin and Pierre Chuvin comment on the difficulty of identifying Lady Mary's friend Achmet Beg: "Vocable énigmatique, comme la personnalité d'Ahmet bey, que nous voyons vivre cependant: il habite á Belgrade, en retrait de l'orthodoxie morose; il fait partie de la haute société, puisqu'il accueille les ambassadeurs sous son toit, et qu'il est qualifié d'efendi, c'est-à-dire de lettré. Il reste difficile de l'identifier. La banalité du prénom, l'absence de fonction officielle sont décourageantes" (*Lady Mary Wortley Montagu: L'Islam au péril des femmes* [Paris: François Maspero, 1981], 50–51).

11. Mary Louise Pratt, "Scratches on the Face of the Country; or, What Mr. Barrow Saw in the Land of the Bushmen," *Critical Inquiry* 12 (Autumn 1985): 119–43.

12. Paul Rycaut, *The Present State of the Ottoman Empire* (London, 1668), 165.

13. Said, *Orientalism,* 150.

14. Rycaut, *Ottoman Empire,* 129–30.

15. George Sandys, *Description of the Turkish Empire* (London, 1615), 60.

16. Cited by James Sutherland in *English Literature of the Late Seventeenth Century* (Oxford: Oxford University Press, 1969), 295.

17. The sentences written in French and quoted above are drawn from one of the few genuine letters and survives only in its printed form. In a MS copy of another letter addressed to the abbé but written in English, Lady Mary provides some of the same information but without the witty, cavalier style. She records her observation about Turkish women's desire to increase and multiply, but then she ends by saying, "This is a piece of Theology very different from that which teaches nothing to be more acceptable to God than a vow of perpetual Virginity. Which Divinity is most rational I leave you to determine" (1:364).

18. Ruth Perry calls Astell "a particular admirer of Lady Mary's" and claims she saw the younger woman "as a sort of spiritual daughter, an inheritor." When Lady Mary returned from her travels, Astell asked to read the manuscript and immediately urged Lady Mary to publish. Lady Mary demurred, but she carefully kept a copy of Astell's enthusiastic preface, which applauds not only Lady Mary's literary skills but her character: "If these *Letters* appear hereafter, when I am in my Grave, let this attend them in testimony to Posterity, that among her contemporarys *one Woman*, at least, was just to her Merit" (Ruth Perry, "Two Forgotten Wits," *Antioch Review* 39 [Fall 1981]: 436, 435).

19. Bernard Lewis writes that because "Islamic law prohibits the enslavement of any free Muslim or of any free non-Muslim who is a lawful, tax-paying subject of the Islamic empire, the slave population of the Islamic lands could be recruited only in two ways: by birth (children of a slave parent irrespective of religion were slaves) or from outside. . . . New slaves, therefore, had to come from beyond the Islamic frontiers and could be acquired as tribute, by capture, or simply by purchase" (*Muslim Discovery of Europe* [New York: W. W. Norton, 1982], 187). He adds that the white slaves in the Muslim west were known as *Saqāliba,* the Arabic plural of *Saqlabī* or *Slav:* "As in the languages of Europe, the term *Slav,* slave, seems to have combined an ethnic with a social content" (188). For additional discussion of the history of slavery in Turkey, see also 185–94.

20. Lady Mary's calling the sultana (born in about 1683 and a resident of Mustapha II's harem) a "favourite" is not as accurate as it could be, for a woman who bore a daughter of the sultan was called *Haseki Kadin,* or "Lady Favourite," and one who bore a son was called *Haseki Sultan,* or "Princess Favourite." As a "favourite," the Sultana Hafise would have been outranked in the harem hierarchy only by the *Valide Sultan,* or "Princess Mother," a woman whose son ascended the throne. For further details of harem life, see A. D. Alderson, *The Structure of the Ottoman Dynasty* (Oxford: Clarendon Press, 1956; rep. Westport, Conn.: Greenwood Press, 1982), 77–84.

21. Bernard Lewis cites historical instances of women taken captive because of their beauty: some were retained as concubines, but others were sent, by sale or as gifts, to the harems of the Middle East. He goes on to speculate that the mother of Sultan Mahmud II was actually Aimée du Buc de Rivery, a Frenchwoman from

Martinique. A more substantiated story concerns Cecilia Venier-Baffo (later Nur Banu), daughter of the Venetian governor of Corfu. Captured at the age of twelve by a Turkish raider, she was sent as a gift to Sultan Süleyman the Magnificent, who passed her on to his son Selim II, who fathered her son, Murad III. Later in her life, she is said to have begun a correspondence with friends in Venice and England (*Muslim Discovery of Europe,* 192).

22. N. M. Penzer, however, disputes Lady Mary's remarks about the handkerchief custom and the woman's crawling into the sultan's bed. He claims that Lady Mary's data refer only to the eighteenth century, and he cites Lady Mary's limited sources (the lack of such customs, Penzer speculates, could have been "the whim of a solitary Sultan"). He does, however, provide a fascinating piece of information not mentioned by Lady Mary: "Now this 'creeping up the bed' was obligatory in Constantinople on a man who had been married to one of the Sultanas. In these marriages the unfortunate husband is entirely ruled by his royal wife, and waits outside until he is summoned. He then timidly enters, kisses the coverlet, and creeps towards his wife by the same 'sliding scale' " (*The Harem* [London: Spring Books, 1936], 179–80). Fanny Davis also cites this story about the sultanas; however, she cautions that such "palace gossip necessarily passed through many people before it reached the Western observer and may have undergone many alterations in the process" (*Ottoman Lady* [Westport, Conn.: Greenwood Press, 1986], 19, 29n30).

23. Fanny Davis reports that the Sultan Ahmet III fathered fifty-two children, thirty of them daughters (*Ottoman Lady,* 5, 17).

24. Katharine Rogers, Introduction, *Before Their Time: Six Women Writers of the Eighteenth Century* (New York: Frederick Unger, 1979), x.

25. Aphra Behn, *Emperor of the Moon* (1687), act 3, scene 1; cited by Halsband, *Complete Letters* 1:327n.

26. Islamic scholar Joseph Schacht confirms Lady Mary's claim about Turkish women's separate property. The Muslim marriage contract, which developed out of the purchase of a bride, required the groom to present a nuptial gift (a *mahr*) to the bride herself. The *mahr* was not the Western equivalent of a dowry (or the English "portion"), nor was it akin to English "pin money," the annual sum paid to a woman from a fund administered by trustees. Instead, it was exclusively a nuptial gift intended for the bride's personal use (since she, like an English bride, was not obliged to bear any of the expenses of the matrimonial establishment). It was customary for the groom to pay part of the *mahr* immediately and to postpone payment of the rest. The husband was obligated, however, to pay the *mahr* in full if he repudiated (divorced) his wife after consummation; if the marriage was unconsummated, the groom was still obligated to pay half of the *mahr*. Muslim divorce was easily accomplished, for it required only a triple repudiation (*talāk*), an act that could be "revocable" (withdrawn during a waiting period) or "definite"

(with immediate effect). In some cases, the husband and wife could agree to a mutual waiving of any financial obligations or, in the case of *khul'*, the wife could redeem herself from the marriage for a consideration. Schacht admits that under a system of polygamy, concubinage, and repudiation, the legal position of the wife is "obviously less favourable than that of the husband," but a woman retains the possibility of divorce, and her situation is financially improved by the effects of the *mahr*. For further discussion of both the nuptial gift and Muslim divorce practices, see Schacht's *Introduction to Islamic Law* (Oxford: Clarendon Press, 1964), 161–68.

Susan Staves, arguing that the English concept of "pin money" was being legally codified from 1690 to 1834, claims that courts hoped to maximize the protective and maintenance functions of pin money (to ensure that a woman and her children would not be left destitute if the husband proved a scoundrel or a miser) while minimizing the possibility that a woman might use such funds as capital (and thus to ensure traditional control over women). As a result, the idiosyncratic rule of no arrears beyond a year was formed (a woman could sue her husband for pin money for a given year, but she could not collect for his failure to provide in years past). Ultimately, the courts ruled that pin money was to be used to dress and adorn the wife in keeping with the dignity and rank of the husband but was not to be used for the accumulation of a fund. Thus Englishwomen of rank lived with restrictions on their use of this form of married women's separate property. For additional discussion, see Staves, "Pin Money," in *Studies in Eighteenth-Century Culture*, ed. O. M. Brack, vol. 14 (Madison: University of Wisconsin Press, 1984), 47–77.

Lady Mary's concern about the inequitable English divorce laws and the punitive treatment a woman might endure can be seen in her "Epistle from Mrs. Y[onge] to her Husband" (1724). The poem concerns the scandal of the divorce of Mary Yonge (daughter and heiress of Samuel Heathcote) from the notorious William Yonge, from whom she had been separated. While Mr. Yonge was not opposed to extramarital affairs for himself, he would not tolerate his wife's relationship with another man. He successfully sued his wife's lover (and recovered damages) and, after winning a parliamentary divorce, gained control of his wife's considerable fortune as well; she was awarded an allowance. Lady Mary's complaint, in the form of a monologue in the voice of Mrs. Yonge, cites the sexual double standard ("Are we not form'd with Passions like your own? / Nature with equal Fire our Souls endu'd" [26–28]) and the lack of legal remedies ("For Wives ill us'd no remedy remains, / To daily Racks condemn'd and to eternal Chains" [22–24]).

27. Lewis (*Muslim Discovery of Europe*, 289) paraphrases *Masīr-i Tālibī ya Sefarnāma-i Mīrzā Abū Tālib Khan*, ed. H. Khadīv-Jam (Tehran, 1974), 225–26, and cites C. Stewart's English translation, *Travels of Mirza Abu Talib Khan* (London, 1814), 2:27–31.

28. "Letters of the Right Hon. Lady M——y W——y M——e: Written, during her Travels in Europe, Asia, and Africa," *Monthly Review* 28 (1763): 385, 392.

29. Jervas was not present, but later Ingres was so moved by Lady Mary's description that he copied into his notebook several passages from this letter (using his copy of a French translation of the 1805 edition), and it is generally agreed that her influence shows up in his painting *Le Bain Turc* (1862). See Norman Schlenoff, *Ingres: Ses Sources littéraires* (1956), 281–82 (cited by Halsband, *Complete Letters* 1:313n). Marilyn Brown provides a revealing and ironic aside: Ingres did *not* copy Lady Mary's remark about fellow painter Jervas in the notebooks ("The Harem Dehistoricized: Ingres' *Turkish Bath*," *Arts Magazine* [Summer 1987]: 67n).

30. Pratt, "Scratches," 121.

31. Wendy Steiner, *Pictures of Romance: Form against Context in Painting and Literature* (Chicago: University of Chicago Press, 1988), 23, 2–3.

32. Ibid., 3. See chap. 2 for an extended discussion of the tension in romance narrative as defined by Hayden White, Mikhail Bakhtin, Eugene Vinaver, and Paul Ricoeur, who all agree "on the connection between the self-sameness of the subject and the 'artificial' narrative cohesion found in the romance" (52).

33. *The Idylls of Theocritus,* trans. James Henry Hallar (London: Longmans, Green, 1894), 91.

34. Lady Mary is not altogether correct in citing the husband as the instrument of revenge. Traditionally, a Muslim woman's adultery was considered a blot on the honor of *her* family, not her husband's. As Sandra Mackey, studying the modern Saudis, puts it, "[The husband] escapes the burden of shame because society considers it demeaning for him to admit that a wife's frailty could move him to any emotion warmer than contempt"; accordingly, punishment generally came from the woman's family (*The Saudis: Inside the Desert Kingdom* [Boston: Houghton Mifflin, 1987], 139).

35. Lady Mary is correct in citing "blood-money," a system instituted by Muhammad as a means of limiting the scope of blood feuds. Islamic law limits retaliation to the offender himself (excluding other members of the family and tribe) and only if the offender is fully responsible and has acted with clear intent. Islamic law also recommends waiving retaliation "either gratuitously or by settlement, and [the next of kin] receives the blood-money or may waive his claim to it" (Schacht, *Islamic Law,* 184). Lady Mary's description of the dead woman, however, is problematic in the context she sets up. For anyone found guilty of adultery, there were severe punishments. One category of criminal act in Islamic penal laws, the *Hudud* (or crimes against God, punishments for which are specified in the Koran and *Sunna*), includes both adultery and fornication. The charge of adultery requires four witnesses or a confession, and the punishment for a married person is stoning to death: the convict is taken to a barren site, and stones are thrown first by the witnesses, then by the *qadi,* and finally by the community. If the convict is a woman, a grave is dug for the body. An unmarried woman is sentenced to one hundred lashes. That the young woman Lady Mary describes died from stab wounds seems

to indicate that she was not judged guilty of adultery in any formal proceeding. For more information on the *Hudud,* see Matthew Lippman, Sean McConville, and Mordechai Yerushalmi, *Islamic Criminal Law and Procedure: An Introduction* (New York: Praeger, 1988), 37–58.

36. See Stephanie H. Jed's *Chaste Thinking: The Rape of Lucretia and the Birth of Humanism* (Bloomington: Indiana University Press, 1989) for additional discussion of the Lucretia narrative as a literary topos.

37. Mark Bannister, *Privileged Mortals: The French Heroic Novel, 1630–1660* (Oxford: Oxford University Press, 1983), 79.

38. Gillian Beer, *The Romance* (London: Methuen, 1970), 12–13.

39. The conclusion to the Spanish woman's story, however, is anything but typical of women taken hostage in the eighteenth century: most such women remained lifelong captives, not seemingly contented and wealthy wives. Bernard Lewis writes that during the fifteenth and sixteenth centuries, the Ottoman jihad brought a steady stream of Albanian, Slavonic, Wallachian, Hungarian, and other Christian slaves. By the eighteenth century, the Tatar khans of the Crimea, an autonomous Muslim dynasty, captured slaves from Russia, Poland, and the Ukraine who were then sold and shipped to Turkey. He further cites historical instances of women taken captive because of their beauty, some of whom were retained as concubines and some sent, by sale or as gifts, to the harems of the Middle East. Lewis says that the "choicest often found their final destinations in the Imperial Seraglio in Istanbul as concubines of the sultans or other dignitaries. . . . Most [of the mothers of the Ottoman sultans] were slaves of the harem whose identities, origins, and even names are hidden from history by the discreet reticence of the Muslim household" (*Muslim Discovery of Europe,* 185–94).

CHAPTER FOUR. The "Spectatress": Satire and the Aristocrats

1. Norbert Elias, *Power and Civility: The Civilizing Process,* trans. Edmund Jephcott, 2 vols. (New York: Pantheon Books, 1939): 2:304–5.

2. Dorinda Outram, *The Body and the French Revolution* (New Haven: Yale University Press, 1989), 85.

3. Peter Stallybras and Allon White, *Trangressions* (Ithaca: Cornell University Press, 1986), 4–5.

4. John Cannon, *Aristocratic Century: The Peerage of Eighteenth-Century England* (Cambridge: Cambridge University Press, 1984), 31–33. Cannon estimates that, in the 1720s, there was a total of 1,384 members in the category he calls "the social elite"; for his list he includes the English peers, Irish peers, Scottish peers, baronets, and knights. He also argues that, during the whole of the eighteenth century, only 1,003 persons held peerages. His omission of "country gentlemen,

landed aristocracy, merchants or the middling ranks of society" (10–11) as well as the second sons and the daughters of nobility (such as Lady Mary herself) make his figures seem particularly small, a fact he acknowledges by granting that the sample taken "both underestimates and exaggerates the size of the political elite," and that "no more than a fragment of the governing class"—and one might add the "social" class—is represented in his underestimate (10).

5. Halsband reports that Finch did not actually die after the violence that arose over Finch's having given an opera ticket to Salisbury's sister in an attempt to seduce the girl. Salisbury, the alias of Sarah Pridden, became the subject of at least three published "biographies" in 1723. "Effigies, Parentage, Education, Life, Merry-Pranks, and Conversations of the Celebrated Mrs. Sally Salisbury" is a relatively mild defense of Pridden as an intelligent, accomplished young woman betrayed by "those rash, giddy, hair-brain'd hot spur fiery Gallants." Anthony Boles's "Genuine History of Mrs. Sarah Prydden, Usually Called Sally Salisbury, and Her Gallants" also takes a moral tone by insisting that the blame be placed on those who seduced and betrayed her. The most unpleasant of the trio, Captain Charles Walker's "Authentick Memoirs of the Life, Intrigues, and Adventures of the Celebrated Sally Salisbury," recounts in near obscene form her "polite Deviations from Virtue" and her "graceful Wantonness." Walker's particularly graphic story, illustrating a link between sex and money intended to titillate his readers, opens with an image of Salisbury standing on her head while two peers hold her legs; "thus every Admirer pleas'd with the sight, pull'd out his Gold," and took his part in the "sport": "With eye intent, each Sportsman took his Aim; / The merry Chuck-Hole border'd on the Rump, / And from this Play Sally deriv'd a Name. / Within her tifted Chink, the Guineas Shone, / And each she receiv'd, was all her own." Walker also includes in his narrative an account of her trial, which resulted in a guilty verdict for the assault charge but acquittal for attempted murder. Pridden was fined one hundred pounds and sentenced to a year's imprisonment.

6. Spacks, *Gossip,* 22. Jan B. Gordon, examining Anne Brontë's *Tenant of Wildfell Hall,* suspects the nature of gossip: "Gossip devalues because it has nothing standing behind it. Lacking the authenticity of a definable source, it is simultaneously financially, theologically, and narratively unredeemable." As a speech act, gossip in its rumormongering, unanchored form may indeed be "unredeemable"; however, Lady Mary's "gossip" does have the "authenticity of a definable source," and it "devalues" as a means of "revaluing" ("Gossip, Diary, Letter, Text: Anne Brontë's Narrative *Tenant* and the Problematic of the Gothic Sequel," *English Literary History* 51 [Winter 1984]: 725, 719–45).

7. Redford, *Converse of the Pen,* 8–9.

8. Spacks, *Gossip,* 5.

9. Horace Walpole, *Correspondence,* ed. W. S. Lewis, et al. (New Haven: Yale University Press, 1937); 34:258; quoted by Halsband, *Complete Letters* 2:78n.

10. The story concludes, however, on a less joyous note. When Miss Titchburne's sister, Lady Sunderland, "could not avoid hearing this Galant History," she invited all the participants, including Miss Leigh, to dinner. After apologizing to the unwanted intruder in front of all the guests and servants, Lady Sunderland claimed it was "high time" Mr. Edgcombe explained himself, and she issued an ultimatum: he had four months to decide whether "to marry or lose her [sister] for ever." Even though Lady Mary expected a wedding, Edgcombe (a widower) remained unmarried (2:80n).

11. Outram, *The Body,* 148.

12. Stallybras and White, *Transgressions,* 21.

13. Mrs. Delany [Mrs. Pendarves], *The Autobiography and Correspondence of Mary Granville* [also Mrs. Pendarves], 2 vols. (London: Richard Bentley, 1861), 2:44–45.

14. A. S. Turberville recounts almost the whole of Lady Mary's narrative of this episode, retaining her "Amazonian" metaphors: "The doors were kept locked despite the angry protests of the ladies, who thereupon adopted Amazonian methods anticipatory of the suffragette tactics of the twentieth century"; and "By the adoption of Amazonian tactics [the women] succeeded in forcing an entry into the Chamber" (*The House of Lords in the Eighteenth Century* [Westport, Conn.: Greenwood Press, 1970], 15, 238).

15. Outram, *The Body,* 150, 126–33.

16. Harriet Guest, "A Double Lustre: Femininity and Sociable Commerce, 1730–1760," *Eighteenth-Century Studies* 23, no. 4 (Summer 1990): 482. Guest cites John Brown's *Estimate of the Manners and Principles of the Times* (1757), 44–45, 51.

17. Homer Obed Brown, "The Errant Letter and the Whispering Gallery," *Genre* (Winter 1977): 581.

18. J. V. Beckett, *The Aristocracy in England, 1660–1914* (Oxford: Basil Blackwell, 1986), 103–4.

19. Halsband reports that the marriage did actually take place on 8 Jan. 1739 and that Lady Harriet brought with her a jointure of eight hundred pounds a year.

20. John Locke, *Second Treatise of Government,* ed. C. B. Macpherson (Indianapolis: Hackett, 1980), 7. See also Ruth Perry's "Mary Astell and the Feminist Critique of Possessive Individualism," *Eighteenth-Century Studies* 23, no. 4 (Summer 1990): 444–57, for an extended discussion of the way Locke's revolutionary discourse stripped women of power by defining the individual as a "property-owning being independent of all other property-owning beings," a definition that in seventeenth-century England excluded women (452).

21. The relationship is even more striking when one remembers that the Duchess of Cleveland had married a bastard son of Charles II (by Barbara Villiers) and so was a relation by marriage of Charles II's exquisite grandson.

22. Guest, "Double Lustre," 483.

23. Ketcham, *Transparent Designs,* 5.

24. Halsband reports that indeed she did not renounce her children; the court decided to leave them in her care until "riper of years" (*Complete Letters* 2:34n).

25. *Dictionary of National Biography* 13:1.

26. Lady Mary's interest both in Ovid and in the fairy-tale form has been discussed by her editors, Isobel Grundy and Robert Halsband: see Grundy's "'Entire'" and "Ovid" and Halsband's "Lady Mary Wortley Montagu and Eighteenth-Century Fiction," *Philological Quarterly* 45 (Jan. 1966): 145–56.

27. Terry Castle, *Masquerade and Civilization* (Stanford: Stanford University Press, 1986), 58–60, 77.

28. Halsband reports that Lady Mary may have met both Voltaire and Montesquieu when each visited England. She claims that during Voltaire's 1726–27 visit he showed her his analysis of *Paradise Lost,* and she probably met Montesquieu sometime during 1729–30, for he sent her a letter asking her to attend a benefit performance by the dancer Marie Sallé. See Halsband's "Lady Mary Wortley Montagu as a Friend of Continental Writers," *John Rylands Library Bulletin* 39 (1956): 63. For a more complete discussion of the philosophes' responses to England, see Peter Gay, *The Enlightenment: The Science of Freedom* (New York: Norton, 1969).

29. Horace Walpole to Thomas Mann, 14 Oct. 1751, as quoted in Robert Halsband, "Walpole versus Lady Mary," 226.

CHAPTER FIVE. Reading, Writing, and the Novel

1. In 1736 Lady Mary and her daughter had a falling out when the young woman fell in love with John Stuart, the Earl of Bute. Both Lady Mary and Wortley tried vigorously to persuade her against the match (Wortley went so far as to threaten to withhold the dowry), but the young couple was eventually married, with only grudging blessings from the Wortley-Montagus. The first extant letter that Lady Mary writes to the countess from the Continent was sent almost seven years after her sojourn began, and it opens with a statement of concern about her daughter's "uneasy Situation," that is, her poverty, and is accompanied by the unpleasant reminder that Lady Mary had warned her daughter that just such difficulties would arise (3 Mar. 1746; 2:366). Through the course of the twenty-year correspondence, however, these moments of concern gradually dwindle away as Lord Bute proves to be an able politician and is ultimately rewarded with the position of prime minister and as Lady Mary and her daughter begin to share the experiences of their lives.

2. Between 1738 and 1750, the countess had borne eight children. This prompts Lady Mary to lament to her husband, "[I] am sorry she breeds so fast, fearing it will impair her condition" (2:455). Altogether the countess had twelve children: six daughters (Mary, Jane, Anne, Augusta, Caroline, and Louisa) and six sons (Edward [who died in infancy], John [later the fourth Earl of Bute], James Archibald [heir to Wortley's estate], Charles, Frederick, and William).

3. "Ladies of Letters in the Eighteenth Century," Papers Read at a Clark Library

Seminar, 18 Jan. 1969 (Los Angeles: William Andrews Clark Memorial Library), 34–35.

4. Nussbaum, *Autobiographical Subject,* xiii–xvi.

5. *The World* was an eighteenth-century periodical edited by Robert Dodsley.

6. Sarah Pennington, *An Unfortunate Mother's Advice to Her Absent Daughters, in a Letter to Miss Pennington* (London, 1761), 39.

7. John Bender, *Imagining the Penitentiary* (Chicago: University of Chicago Press, 1987), 108.

8. The sale catalog of her library contains such titles as *The Adventures of Dick Hazard,* Jane Barker's *Patch-Work Screen for the Ladies,* John Cleland's *Memoirs of a Coxcomb,* Coventry's *Pompey the Little,* Defoe's *Roxanna,* Elizabeth Griffith's *Series of Genuine Letters between Henry and Frances,* Haywood's *Betsy Thoughtless,* Manley's *Rivella,* and Lennox's *Female Quixote.* For the complete list, see Hugh Amory's *Poets and Men* [sic] *of Letters,* vol. 7, *The Sale Catalogue of Libraries of Eminent Persons* (London: Mansell with Sotheby Parke-Burnet, 1973).

9. Miss Smythies, *The Stage-Coach: containing the character of Mr. Manly and the History of his Fellow-Travellers,* 2 vols. (London: 1753), 10.

10. Francis Coventry, *The History of Pompey the Little; or, the Life and Adventures of a Lap-Dog* (London, 1751), 8.

11. Charlotte Lennox, *The Life of Harriot Stuart, Written by Herself,* 2 vols. (London, 1751), 2:15.

12. She applauds both *The History of Sir Harry Herald and Sir Edward Haunch* (Dublin, 1755) and Edward Kimber's *Life and Adventures of Jo Thompson* (1750) because they contain kind portraits of the Duke of Montagu, a bit of family history Lady Mary wants to preserve. Of *Sir Harry Herald,* Lady Mary writes, "I am pleas'd with Sir Herald for recording a generous action of the Duke of Montagu (which I know to be true, with some variation of Circumstances)" (22 Sept. 1755; 3:89). In the novel, Captain Worthy, who has fallen on hard circumstances, meets a "tall, thin gentleman, wrapped up in a great coat," who offers to mitigate the captain's grief. The gentleman, instinctively recognizing Captain Worthy's inherent goodness and civility, later presents him with a commission and says, "Well, sir, when you wet your commission in Ireland, among other friends, remember the D—— of M——nt——g——u." The captain, later discovering that he was also given two bank notes for one hundred pounds each, concludes by confirming that "a *nobility* of *mind,* which distinguished this truly great man, more than that of his high birth," had forced him to leave town before the captain could express his gratitude (192–93). Lady Mary appreciates this portrait certainly for personal reasons but equally for its "proper" representation of her aristocratic class.

13. Quennell, *Pope,* 120–21.

14. At his death, Lady Mary laments not only the loss of his artistry but his huge capacity for happiness: "I am sorry for H[enry] Fielding's Death, not only as

I shall read no more of his writeings, but I beleive he lost more than others, as no Man enjoy'd life more than he did. . . . His happy Constitution (even when he had, with great pains, halfe demolish'd it) made him forget every thing when he was before a venison Pastry or over a Flask of champaign, and I am perswaded he has known more happy moments than any Prince upon Earth. His natural Spirits gave him Rapture with his Cookmaid, and chearfullness when he was Fluxing in a Garret" (22 Sept. 1755; 3:87). Ending with a lament for both Fielding and Richard Steele, Lady Mary writes, "Each of them [was] so form'd for Happiness, it is pity they were not Immortal" (3:88).

15. Lady Mary's antipathy to Pope finds its best expression when she meets him on her own epistolary terms. She retrieves a medieval image of the corrupted moralist and preaching fox out to dupe his unsuspecting public to describe the picture Pope paints of himself in his letters: "His general preaching against money was meant to induce people to throw it away that he might pick it up. There cannot be a stronger proofe of his being capable of any Action for the sake of Gain than publishing his Literary Correspondence, which lays open such a mixture of Dullness and iniquity that one would imagine it visible even to his most passionate admirers" (23 June 1754; 3:58).

16. Nussbaum, *Autobiographical Subject,* xx, 188, 29.

17. See Halsband's "Lady Mary and Eighteenth-Century Fiction" for a detailed discussion of the various fictional genres in which Lady Mary herself wrote; included are romances, fairy tales, a romantic pastoral allegory, an English *histoire amoureuse,* essays, and literary criticism.

18. Robert Halsband, "Virtue in Danger: The Case of Griselda Murray," *History Today,* Oct. 1967, 694. Unless otherwise noted, all subsequent references to the events of this incident are taken from this essay.

19. Lady Mary was surely aware that a gentlewoman had the status of a genuine commodity in the marriage market, of real public property in an aristocratic and landed economy, and that her letters themselves form a "pattern of public declaration of identity" existing as an alternative species of "consumable interiority." Yet she implies that her writing—epistolary (private) and historical (factual)—is a more reliable source of "truth."

20. Bender, *Imagining the Penitentiary,* 8.

21. Lady Mary's comments about novels she deems aesthetic failures reveal her sensitivity to narrative structure. Because many eighteenth-century novels were published anonymously, Lady Mary often speculates—usually incorrectly—about authorship, which she generally assigns to the Fieldings: "There is something Humourous in R. Random that makes me beleive the Author is H. Fielding. I am horridly afraid I guess too well the writer of those abominable insipidities of Cornelia, Leonora, and the Ladie's Drawing Room" (3:9). Her guess was Sarah Fielding, a writer who almost always earns her displeasure. While none of the

"novels" listed above was actually written by Sarah Fielding, they, along with Jane Collier's *Art of Tormenting* (which Lady Mary claims "tormented" her [3:88]), form a paradigm for her dismissal of the works that fail to meet her aesthetic standards for coherent plotting. First, she has no patience for incoherent, collective "talk"; of *Leonora* (1745), she challenges, "I defy the greatest chymist in morals to extract any Instruction: the style most affectedly Florid and naturally insipid, with such a confus'd heap of admirable characters that never were, or can be, in Human Nature" (16 Feb. 1752; 3:5). The novel does indeed introduce, by page 73, a total of twenty-eight different characters whose relationships are only barely established, and Lady Mary's final judgment is definite: "I flung it aside after 50 pages" (3:5). *The Lady's Drawing Room* (1744), also a mixture of stories and commentary exchanged among a lady, three gentlemen, and various visitors, promises in the preface to be a mirror and a likeness for all who look in it. The narrator claims that while "the groundwork is satire" it is not without panegyric, love, a "few sprinklings of Morality, and a small, very small Dash of Philosophy, all blended together" (iii). As an example for Lady Mary of an "abominable insipidity" it is matched only by Jane Collier's *Art of Tormenting* (1753). Couched in the form of an "anticourtesy" manual, the narrator's primary imperative to readers is that they "do unto others what you would *least* wish to have done unto yourself" (232), and therefore various chapters—directed to parents, husbands, wives, lovers, and friends—offer typical advice urging readers to abuse servants, show too great a fondness for small animals, and berate one's companions. While the text is intended as satire, behind the flippant tone exists a painful lament about the lack of civility in the polite world and even outright abuse. That Lady Mary is impatient with a satire that fails to hit the mark is not surprising.

22. Nor does Lady Mary distinguish between the romance and the novel: she equates a story about a woman of quality who endangers her status through an alliance with a commoner (a plot common in the romance) with stories of low-born women who acquire status through marriage to men of privilege or through the revelation of aristocratic birth (the stuff of the novel). She certainly knew, as Michael McKeon has argued, that gender precedes class: a man raises a woman's status, no matter the circumstances of her birth, whereas a woman's status can rise with an "advantageous" match or fall with a mean marriage (*Origins of the English Novel,* 156). Yet according to Lady Mary, the emotional response provoked by the unreality of both fictional forms encourages fairy-tale expectations and poor judgment.

23. *The History of Charlotte Summers, the Fortunate Parish Girl,* 2 vols. (London, 1749), 2:36.

24. Bender, *Imagining the Penitentiary,* 212.

25. Robert Markley, "Sentimentality as Performance," in *The New Eighteenth*

Century, ed. Felicity Nussbaum and Laura Brown (New York: Methuen, 1987), 219.

26. *History of Charlotte Summers,* 1:3; 2:313.

27. Markley, "Sentimentality," 217.

28. J. Paul Hunter, "The World as Stage and Closet," in *British Theater and the Other Arts, 1660–1800,* ed. Shirley Strum Kenny (Washington, D.C.: Folger Books, 1984), 277–79.

29. Halsband, *Complete Letters,* 3:75n.

30. John Richetti, "Richardson's Dramatic Art in *Clarissa,*" in *British Theater and the Other Arts, 1660–1800,* ed. Shirley Strum Kenny, 289–306.

31. Ibid., 290–91.

32. Ronald Paulson, *Satire and the Novel in the Eighteenth Century* (New Haven: Yale University Press, 1967), 106.

33. In Delariviere Manley's "Husband's Resentment: Example II," the same excuses are uttered by the guilty adulterer Pavure Peter Poussin when he is caught with the wife of the president: "[Poussin] threw himself at [the President's] Feet upon his Knees in his Shirt, implored his Pardon, and begged him to save his Life; with the naughty Children, he cry'd, *pray, pray, he would never do so no more.* Madam *la President,* fell a weeping, and vow'd, amidst her Tears, that this was her first Offence; the Plea of the oldest Sinner, *One is never guilty 'till one be caught.*" See Manley's *Power of Love* (London, 1702), 281.

34. Outram, *The Body,* 151.

CHAPTER SIX. Retirement

1. Bute's sisters lived in the country, out of the social spotlight (Halsband, *Complete Letters* 3:25n.).

2. Ketcham, *Transparent Designs,* 29, 62.

3. Bathsua Makin, *An Essay to Revive the Antient Education of Gentlewomen, in Religion, Manners, Arts, and Tongues. With an Answer to the Objections against This Way of Education* (London, 1673), 26.

4. This comment takes on particularly powerful connotations when one remembers the continuing problems Lady Mary had with her own wayward son. Edward Wortley Montagu, Jr. (b. 16 May 1713), was, from the time he reached adolescence to the time of Lady Mary's death, a constant source of disappointment for her. The precocious "mistakes" of his youth—running away to Oxford or stowing away aboard ship—became serious and limiting constraints on his adult behavior. His impulsiveness landed him in constant debt, and his father would not supply the money to get him out of it. Young Wortley's pride in the family name, which he abused in his schemes, became a badge of shame for the family. And while he

behaved well enough during his time in the army, his sexual energies later in life resulted in a bigamous marriage. Lady Mary effectively disowned him, although she did agree to meet with him in Italy if he arrived incognito and avoided using the family name (promises he broke). At his death, the elder Wortley took care that his son would not want, but he left the bulk of his estate to his daughter, Lady Bute. Lady Mary herself left her son a single guinea, acknowledging that his father had seen to his welfare.

Edward Wortley Montagu, Jr., has been the object of at least three biographies, the earliest published in 1779, shortly after his death. Called *The Memoirs of the Late Mr. W———ly M———tagu, with Remarks on the Manners and Customs of the Oriental World* (Dublin) and claiming to be collected and published from original papers, the text is little more than an excuse for scandal and titillation. Beyond the enumeration of Wortley's amours, the narrative that would have scandalized (or amused) Lady Mary the most had she been alive and that surely must have scandalized the Butes concerned his reputed "parentage." The narrator writes that, during Lady Mary's visit to Turkey, she was "introduced into the *seraglio* of his sublime highness, that *sanctum santorum* of voluptuous gratification, and grand respository of terrestrial beauties" (16–18); claiming that no woman was permitted to enter without being subservient to the "inclinations of his sublime highness," the narrator says that Lady Mary made a virtue of necessity and "suffice it to say, that in the spring of the year 1718, our hero came into the world" (19). Later, when Wortley visits Turkey, the grand signor is described as welcoming him with "fraternal" pleasure (167).

Later biographers agree that Wortley did indeed return to the Middle East, including a visit to Turkey and a lengthy stay in Egypt. Upon his return to Venice late in his life, he had his rooms furnished in a Turkish style that delighted visitors. He died in Venice at the age of eighty-three. See Jonathon Curling's *Edward Wortley Montagu, 1713–1776: The Man in the Iron Wig* (London: Andrew Melrose, 1954) for a more recent account.

5. Jacqueline Pearson writes that "the University of Bologna had an extraordinary record, going back as far as the fourteenth century, for employing female academics, including in the eighteenth century two mathematicians, a professor of Greek and a professor of anatomy (Bologna also had a distinguished tradition of women painters)" (*Prostituted Muse: Images of Women and Women Dramatists, 1642–1737* [New York: Harvester, 1988], 15). Pearson cites Susan Raven and Alison Weir's *Women in History* (1981) and Laura M. Ragg's *Women Artists of Bologna* (1907).

6. Mary, Lady Chudleigh, *Essays upon Several Subjects* (London, 1710), 1.

7. Some readers mistake these deliberate rhetorical strategies for lack of emotional involvement. Bruce Redford contrasts the "judicial detachment" he sees in the Bute correspondence with the "emotional involvement" of the Lady Mar correspondence (*Converse of the Pen,* 31–43). Patricia Meyer Spacks perhaps comes closer

to describing the competing desires that inform Lady Mary's discourse with her daughter: in providing "intellectual nurturance," Lady Mary "sustains her precarious tie with her daughter only by her extreme tact—and the degree of that tact is the measure of her neediness." And I would add that it is also a measure of the degree of her affection. See Spacks's *Imagining a Self* (Cambridge: Harvard University Press, 1976), 74.

8. Makin, *Education of Gentlewomen*, 41.

9. Ibid., 22.

10. Jacqueline Pearson reports that in the late seventeenth century there were thirteen women for every ten men in London. In the eighteenth century almost a quarter of the population of both sexes in their early forties were still not married and by the end of the century "a staggering *quarter* of upper-class girls would never marry." See Pearson's *Prostituted Muse*, 85.

11. Lord Chesterfield, *Letters to His Son* (New York: G. P. Putnam's Sons, 1901), 2 vols. 22 Feb. 1748, 1:208.

12. Katharine M. Rogers, *Feminism in Eighteenth-Century England* (Urbana: University of Illinois Press, 1982), 93; Spacks, *Imagining a Self*, 82, 88.

13. Lady Mary did not actually purchase the house and its land, even though she thought she had. The confusion arises as a result of her acquaintance with Count Ugolino Palazzi, a thirty-year-old heir to an impoverished Brescian family who systematically bilked her out of an estimated twenty-five hundred pounds during their ten-year acquaintance. They met in Avignon in 1746, when the count offered his assistance in escorting Lady Mary to Brescia, a journey that required getting past warring Spanish and Austrian troops. Fallen ill after the journey and nursed back to health by the count's mother, Lady Mary was invited to use the family's country house in Gottolengo. Thinking that she had subsequently purchased the house and a nearby garden (in signing a deed in the presence of witnesses), she worked to improve both properties.

The count's underhanded dealings soon came to light. When Lady Mary entrusted him with her jewelry or the delivery of expensive furnishings, the goods disappeared, much to the count's vocal (and disingenuous) laments for the loss of his "honor." When she attempted permanent moves, the count again insisted that she wait until his "honor" has been restored, even as he devised scheme after scheme for separating her from more of her money. There were even reports that the count was holding her prisoner, accounts Lady Mary herself had to deny to the local magistrate. In the fall of 1755, she determined to move to Venice, and on the journey discovered that all her notes and deeds had been turned into blank paper, another of the count's swindles that was resolved as successfully as it could be: all the deeds were restored to her, except the one for the house in Gottolengo, which was entailed. Her embarrassment about the way her "friendship" with such a scoundrel had progressed remained acute, and she never wrote of the problems to any family member. For complete information concerning the events, see Halsband's *Life* and Lady Mary's "Italian Memoir."

14. Gamaliel Bradford, *Portraits of Women* (Boston: Houghton Mifflin, 1916), 15.

15. Spacks, *Imagining a Self,* 73.

16. No original copies of the Steuart manuscripts have survived (or have yet been found). Halsband reports that a collection of the Steuart letters was privately printed in 1818; when Lady Mary's granddaughter, Lady Louisa Steuart, helped to prepare the 1837 edition of Lady Mary's own letters, she borrowed the original manuscripts from Sir James's son and transcribed them. Halsband used Lady Louisa's transcript, collated with the 1818 edition, as the copy text.

17. For a more detailed discussion of the Steuarts and their friendship with Lady Mary, see Halsband's *Life,* 268–85.

18. Steuart's 1842 biographer, Dr. Kippis, celebrates the friendship between Sir James and Lady Mary. He applauds her "humanity and benevolence" and the fact that she possessed "a fine genius, an uncommon knowledge, a retentive memory, and a happy facility of expression." Kippis claims that Sir James was charmed by her company because "her judgment was accompanied by a refined taste, and her opinions of things were pronounced with a decision which rendered them lively and forcible, if not absolutely convincing." Steuart's highest praise was reserved for her liveliness: "Sir James used to say that when Lady Mary Wortley Montagu was in spirits, he derived more enjoyment from some hours of her conversation than he could have done from the most interesting and entertaining book that was ever written." See Dr. Kippis, "The Life of Sir James Steuart Denham," in *The Coltness Collection,* printed for the Maitland Club (Edinburgh, 1842), 309–11.

19. Isobel Grundy, "The Politics of Female Authorship," *Book Collector* 3 (Spring 1988): 19–20, 25.

20. See ibid., 19–37, for a complete discussion not only of the incident of misattribution discussed above but also of Lady Mary's having annotated in 1758 four volumes of the six-volume Dodsley collection owned by Consul Joseph Smith (another of Lady Mary's "enemies"). The annotations are fascinating because they reveal Lady Mary's initial reaction—ten years after the fact—to the publication of a significant number of her poems. Some she owns, some she renounces, and many she "corrects," but the fact of their publication makes her that much more vulnerable to Murray's attempts to humiliate her.

EPILOGUE. "I Expect Immortality"

1. Walpole, who visited her shortly after her return, writes in his characteristically severe way of her appearance: "Lady Mary Wortley is arrived; I have seen her; I think her avarice, her dirt, and her vivacity are all increased. Her dress, like her languages, is a galimatias of several countries; the groundwork, rags; the

embroidery, nastiness. She wears no cap, no handkerchief, no gown, no petticoat, no shoes" (Walpole to George Montagu, 2 Feb. 1762). This account from Walpole, who was never an admirer of Lady Mary, is contradicted by Elizabeth Montagu, who spoke of being highly entertained by Lady Mary, a woman who "neither thinks, speaks, acts nor dresses like anybody else." Mrs. Montagu also remarked that Lady Mary looked no older than when she had left England and that she possessed both a vivacity and a unique memory (Halsband, *Life,* 281).

Index